Grand Finales

A MODERNIST VIEW OF PLATED DESSERTS

Grand Finales

TISH BOYLE and **TIMOTHY MORIARTY**
Editors of Chocolatier *and* Pastry Art & Design

Introduction by
MICHAEL SCHNEIDER
Editor-in-Chief, Chocolatier *and* Pastry Art & Design

Photography by
JOHN UHER

A MODERNIST VIEW OF PLATED DESSERTS

JOHN WILEY & SONS, INC.

New York • Chichester • Weinheim • Brisbane • Singapore • Toronto

Plate credits:
page xvi, Cyclamen Studio
page 21, Rosenthal
page 32, Oggetti
page 40, Jena Glass
page 46, Rosenthal
page 56, Annie Glass
page 66, Annie Glass
page 77, Cyclamen Studio
page 82, Bernardaud
page 91, Studio D'Or
page 100, Mexican Gift House
page 142, Villeroy & Boch
page 145, Bernardaud
page 149, Villeroy & Boch
page 178, Rosenthal
page 204, Dan Levy
page 218, Annie Glass
page 240, Sasaki.

This publication is designed to provide accurate and authoritative information in regard to the subject matter covered. It is sold with the understanding that the publisher is not engaged in rendering professional services. If professional advice or other expert assistance is required, the services of a competent professional person should be sought.

Library of Congress Cataloging-in-Publication Data:

A modernist view of plated desserts: grand finales / [compiled by] Tish Boyle and Timothy Moriarty; created by Michael Schneider; photography by John Uher.
     p. cm.
     Includes index.
     ISBN 0-471-29251-6
     1. Desserts. 2. Pastry. I. Boyle, Tish. II. Moriarty, Timothy.
TX773.G682   1997
97–24171   97–24171
641.8'6—dc21
Printed in the United States of America

1 2 3 4 5 6 7 8 9

ACKNOWLEDGMENTS

First and foremost, my thanks to the richly talented and extremely good-tempered pastry chefs who made this book possible. I count many of them as my good friends. To Carole Harlam and Faith Robyn Fernbach, the troubleshooters who tested many of these difficult recipes with good humor, patience, and precision. To Mark Kammerer and Stephanie Banyas, for their impeccable attention to detail. To Judy Prince and Fran Shinagel of J.B. Prince for the great book party and for their continued support. To John Uher, the Czar of Dessert Photography. To Michael Schneider for having so much faith in me. And finally, to my husband Dick Eggleston, for his encouragement, love, and sense of humor.

TB

My sincere thanks to each of the chefs whose work is represented here; all were supremely generous with their time and expertise. Thanks also to the public relations staffs, management, and chefs of the Four Seasons Hotels in Palm Beach and Beverly Hills, the Las Vegas Hilton, the Ritz-Carlton Chicago, and the Phoenecian in Scottsdale. Special thanks to Melissa Rosati, for listening and advising, and to Faith Robyn Fernbach, who compiled the source table and lent vital assistance in the preparation of the manuscript. Thanks also to Judy Prince and Rennis Garner of J.B. Prince in New York, Karen Deutsh of LaMalle Cookware in New York, Daphna Epstein, Matthew Stevens, Stephanie Banyas, Mary Goodbody, and Janice Wald Henderson. And as always, thanks and love to Ryan, Evan and, especially, Geri.

TM

CONTENTS

RECIPE CONTENTS

MODERNIZING THE CLASSICS

EQUIPMENT, MOLDS, AND MODERNISM

MODERNIZING GARNISHES

PREFACE

A Modernist View of Plated Desserts is the second book in our Grand Finales series and, unless I miss my guess, will draw considerable criticism from the dessert community. While the overwhelming majority of pastry chefs is eager to push the limit on dessert creativity, there is that undertone from the outspoken minority which decries such outlandish creations. More than once have I heard food critics state, "they've sacrificed flavor for altitude" or "you just want to look at it, not eat it." There is some validity to these comments but only when the talent of the pastry chef is less than of the highest quality. But, when the talent is there, the desserts take on a life of their own. It's a beautiful thing to see these desserts and then to sample how delicious they are. Can everyone make them? No. Can everyone aspire to reach that level? Certainly. And that is the essence of the Grand Finales series. To present each and every school so that pastry chefs can have a frame of reference in the pursuit of their artistic expression.

Why choose Modernism for our first school specific work? Attitude. It takes a strong sense of self to break from tradition. I believe the Modernist school, more than any others, allows the pastry chef that freedom of expression. As Tim so eloquently put it in *Grand Finales: The Art of The Plated Dessert*, "*in a Modernist plated dessert, the components are carefully crafted forms arranged in such a way that they do not represent anything outside themselves. The forms are often completely abstracted, neither geometric nor organic.*" Modernist desserts, like modernist artworks, are created by chefs who feel that need to express themselves as individuals. And it's that kind of attitude, that willingness to buck the system that we feel should lead the way for our series.

As I did in *Grand Finales: The Art of The Plated Dessert*, I wish to give my sincerest thanks to the professionals who were involved with this book. To the pastry chefs who gave of their time, energy and enormous talent. To Tim, Tish, Mark, and John, my family from 9 to 5, you make the work fun. To Marianne, Michael, Louise, Michelle, Pam, John(s), and the rest of the staff at VNR, your attitude and desire make it so important to us to never let you down.

Also, my thanks to the people at the Four Seasons in Palm Beach and Beverly Hills, The Ritz-Carlton in Chicago, The Las Vegas Hilton and, The Phoenician in Scottsdale. Your hospitality is greatly appreciated.

On a personal note, thank you Libby, Danny, Matthew, Jeff, Charlie, Anne, Stephanie, and Melissa. To Richard, I can never repay your kindness and generosity, and to Andrea, who makes it all worthwhile.

We should never forget that dessert is a form of entertainment. Our dessert schools provide a way in which to appreciate them for the art form they have become. As with all creative endeavors, self expression will always find a way to rise up. The chefs in this book have done just that. Enjoy.

Michael Schneider
Editor-in-Chief
Chocolatier *and* Pastry Art & Design *Magazines*

INTRODUCTION

This book is the second in a series, following the publication of *Grand Finales: The Art of The Plated Dessert* in 1996. In these books we celebrate the achievements of American pastry chefs. These men and women—some working in kitchens about the size of your thumb—are creating desserts that are both delicious and visually sophisticated. Their works of palatal/visual art are called *plated desserts*.

A plated dessert is one that is prepared at the last minute, upon the individual order of the customer. The pastry chef assembles several components, most of which were prepared that very day, and artfully arranges them on the plate. A plated dessert usually consists of the main item, a garnish, and a sauce, but the chef has complete freedom within the boundaries of economics, flavor, and common sense; there can be one garnish or several; there should be contrasts in texture and flavor—most chefs believe there should be several textures, a tangy element to contrast with sweetness, and if there can be a warm item to contrast with cold, so much the better. A plated dessert can be as complex or as simple as the chef's sensibility allows. The trend toward plated desserts—and away from the dessert cart, simple slice of cake, scoop of ice cream, and other single item desserts—was first seen in Europe and in culinary competitions in the late 1980s; American chefs in the appropriate settings and with the necessary budgets have been presenting these desserts since approximately 1990.

Because plated desserts are compositions, they lend themselves to many different visual approaches. In *Grand Finales: The Art of The Plated Dessert*, we classified the visual presentations of American plated desserts into nine categories, using schools of the visual arts as a frame of reference. Impressionist desserts use abstract and literal forms to convey an image or feeling; Architectural desserts are strongly vertical; Performance Art desserts move or involve action by the diner in some way. In this book we concentrate on the most abstract, perhaps the most difficult, of the schools, Modernism. We challenged 25 of the most talented pastry chefs in the country to create desserts within the confines of the definition of Modernist desserts as outlined in *Grand Finales: The Art of The Plated Dessert.*

The techniques used to "modernize" desserts include the employment of unfamiliar or unusual molds (Chapter 3), sheer creativity in garnishing (Chapter 4), and stylish sauce painting (Chapter 5). In this book we will examine some of the new equipment that makes presentation desserts possible, and we will discuss some principles by which a pastry chef can run a profitable kitchen, and prove it to management.

Pastry chefs in this country are undergoing a renaissance of sorts. New technologies in freezing and packaging combined with electro-fast air shipping, make exotic ingredients a phone call and a few hours away. New equipment makes it possible to combine spectacular, intricate forms, and do it in production for large restaurants and hotel banquets. And the unquenchable American thirst for experimentation provides an environment in which the novel, the innovative, is what is expected.

For that reason, we do not regard this book as simply an academic exercise—assigning a theme to chefs and seeing what they come up with. Pastry chefs in hotels often must accept an assignment from a banquet manager, to create a dessert that coordinates with a theme of a client. And occasionally, a lucky chef will open a restaurant, creating an entire menu to coordinate with a pre-established theme. This chef is asked to use his or her knowledge of food and composition toward a specific task. Often, these chefs find that to be forced to produce within the confines of rules, to limit compositions and tools, can compel creativity.

One of the chefs in this book, Krista Kern, experienced this first-hand when she was named to be the opening pastry chef at Sullivan's, the restaurant adjoining the theater in New York City where David Letterman's show is taped, and where Ed Sullivan's historic variety show of the 50s and 60s was presented. "Two months prior to the opening [the owners] decided they wanted to go with a theme," Kern recalls. "I was terrified. We knew ahead of time that we would be reviewed by *The New York Times,* so there was pressure. [Executive chef] Neil Murphy and I didn't want a theme. We felt that it could be really silly. And at first, the owners' ideas and my ideas were completely different." For example, the owners wanted one dessert to be A Really Big Shoe (based on an Ed Sullivan catchphrase). "I told them I didn't want to do a big shoe on a plate," says Kern. "It's not my style, it's not who I am. I like things more abstract. Eventually, I won out and we took a more sophisticated approach." Images she did adopt included a coffee cup and a 1930s-style microphone, but the images were spare, subtle. "It was a good experience," says Kern, "but hard on my brain, to pull all these references from the last forty years and try to combine them to meet certain requirements."

Why all the fuss about presentation? Because it is shrewd business. Not every restaurant or hotel can afford the labor to create such plates, but in high-end, competitive settings, it makes business sense. It attracts media attention. And it sells. "Americans have a major sweet tooth," observes Norman Love, corporate pastry chef of the Ritz-Carlton Hotel Company. "We love sugar, we consume a ton of chocolate. Today's diner will sacrifice another part of the meal in order to eat dessert." Dessert sales have increased in Ritz-Carlton property restaurants in general. And this trend is parallelled in restaurants across the country. "Americans are beginning to recognize quality and expect quality," says Love. "The best restaurants in the country are packed, and desserts are playing a more important role than ever."

And, says Love, "there's a very large profit margin in desserts. The prices that restaurants feel justified in charging for desserts is rising. And they are getting it." To justify the higher prices, perceived value, as in more elaborate presentations, is called for. Most chefs in upscale venues will tell you that when diners see a beautiful dessert carried by a waiter through the dining room, it seduces diners into buying dessert.

Martin Howard, pastry chef at Rainbow! in New York, observes that the first dessert served during dinner service is invariably the dessert that sells the most that evening. Each time it is carried through the room, it lures diners into buying another. "The trick is, if you want to sell something," he adds, "just send it out. Ask a waiter to walk it through the room. I've done that with a special I needed to move."

"I've heard the criticisms that pastry chefs focus too much on decor, and you don't know what you're eating," says Norman Love. "I believe that flavor is first, it has to be the most important thing, no question. But desserts have to wow. When you sit in the dining room and the description is of chocolate mousse on the menu, and you wait, and then out comes this incredible, edible sculpture, and you hear, how do you eat this or how did they put this together?, it's all part of the excitement of eating dessert. And it's necessary. The element of surprise is the most important part of dessert."

Modernism is all about dashing expectations, creating new forms of expression, turning our notions of beauty and artistry upside down. So it is ever-so-Modern of us, isn't it, that the greater the beauty of the dessert, the more craft that went into its construction, the greater is our pleasure when we destroy it. When she is asked by a customer how to eat one of her desserts, Krista Kern says, "I tell them, take the fork, pop the top off, knock it over and smoosh it around. It's meant to be destroyed, mutilated, and enjoyed."

Amen.

Grand Finales

CHAPTER **ONE**

PURE MODERNISM

MARTIN HOWARD

Pastry Chef
Rainbow!,
New York.

BORN: August 1962,
Gouverneur, New York.
TRAINING/EXPERIENCE: The
Culinary Institute of America;
home cake decoration business;
La Crémailliere, Bedford, New
York; Pier House, Key West,
Florida.

*"What I want my plates to evoke,
besides hunger, is this: 'Forget your
troubles, come on, get happy.'
Dessert is entertainment, the plate is
a stage. Some of what I do is camp.
For lunch we have to tone down
because we have a business clientele.
But at night we can let loose a little. People who are into dessert are
usually fun people. They want a
childish thing, or something that
evokes memories of childhood. In
The Village Voice [newspaper],
they called my desserts 'kiddie city,'
but they didn't mean it as a compli-
ment. And at the time I hadn't gone
as far as I do now."*

JACQUY PFEIFFER

Co-owner, *Ecole de Patisserie
Francaise, Chicago.*

BORN: February 1961,
Molsheim, Alsace, France.
TRAINING/EXPERIENCE:
apprenticeship, Jean Clauss's;
various pastry shops and hotels
in France, Saudi Arabia, and
California; pastry chef for the
Sultan of Brunei, Borneo; Hyatt
Regency Hotel, Hong Kong;
Fairmont Hotel and Sheraton
Hotel and Towers, Chicago.

*"Some of the culinary schools are
guilty of telling their students, 'Once
you come out of the school you will be
the best,' and they are nothing. They
just learned something for two years
or maybe six months. They know
how to make one of this, one of that,
but they don't know production or
how to behave in a kitchen. In a
kitchen, that's where you prove yourself. It's an apprenticeship that continues until you die. Work hard and
always stay humble no matter what.
You think you are the best and you
turn around and see someone else's
work. There is always something
and someone better."*

Norman Brosterman, a New York City architect, man-
aged to annoy a number of people with his 1997
book, *Inventing Kindergarten.* In it, he proposed that the
forms, shapes, and symbols commonly found in the works
of modern artists (The Modernists—Mondrían, Picasso,
O'Keeffe, et al.), were probably inspired by the construc-
tions formed with blocks and Tinkertoy-style components
that were standard issue to kindergartners of the nineteenth
century.

That theory outraged a number of art critics and historians,
but it is bound to have appeal to pastry chefs, who work in
a field where a serious attitude toward a frivolous product
is de rigueur.

In this chapter we present pure examples of what we call
Modernist desserts—pure in the sense that the main component, the garnishes, and the sauces are in balance, and all
contribute to the Modernist presentation.

A Modernist dessert is one which is composed of forms that
do not represent anything outside themselves—that is,
they do not compose an architectural construction or con-
jure a poetic image or mimic a known object unless there
is a deliberate effort to undermine or subtly satirize the
object or image. The forms are, in most cases, completely
abstract, either geometric or inorganic in inspiration.
Classic recipes can be, and frequently are, the heart of
Modernist desserts, but the presentation is emphatically
nontraditional, as you will see in Chapter 3. Surfaces are
generally sleek. The forms are clean and finished, but some
loose platings are seen. If literal images are included, they
are not reinforced elsewhere to create a theme. If a recog-
nizable object is employed, it is generally for the purpose
of satire, camp, or to undermine itself or to call attention
to the fact that this is dessert, this is food. What Modernist
desserts give diners is the anticipation, a moment to
admire something that they have never seen before.
Desserts that look like dessert, and even desserts that look
like sombreros or musical instruments, do not delight in
quite this way.

Although we use the term "Modernism" only as a frame of
reference when describing the works of contemporary pas-
try chefs, it might be useful to review Modernism to see if any valid analogies can be made.

The history of painting in the last 120 years is a tale of rebellion toppling rebellion. The
Impressionists and Post-Impressionists rebelled against the tyranny of color, materials, and
subject matter imposed by the Salon establishment in France. They succeeded in time, but
subject matter continued to be a matter of doctrine—only certain subjects were fit to be
painted, and any distortion of the outward appearance of an object was still considered to
be a violation of Truth.

The turn-of-the-century Modernists were continuing the rebellion of color and materials begun by the Impressionists and continued by the Post-Impressionists; but subject matter continued to be a matter of tyranny, and Modernists strived against it. Cezanne was among the first to dethrone the representational nature of Impressionist works. Then came a flood of artists and splintering labels. In America, the Modernist movement in painting began to establish itself roughly around 1910; among those identified with the movement are Arthur G. Dove, Max Weber, and Georgia O'Keeffe.

The Modernist sensibility, in general, called into question two of the assumptions of the hundreds of years of realistic painting, and even the works of the Impressionists—that one should look to nature as the model for a subject and technique in painting, and that art should be "finished," refined, a display of technical virtuosity. Modernists strived to do away with what people traditionally looked for in a painting—technical polish, sentiment, resemblance, charm. They aspired to reach to the very soul of art—it should not serve a moralistic point of view; it should not pique memories or intimate desires.

To that end, Modernists replaced literal colors with colors that reveal states of feeling; fragmented objects, arranged objects, or parts of objects in overlapping or kaleidoscopic form to convey, in a nonrepresentational way, a sense of motion; presented shapes and colors that bore no resemblance to anything in the world the eye recognized; presented illogical groupings of objects; maintained that much of the pleasure of a work of art is found in the materials themselves and the way the artist handles the materials. Modernists believed that art should not be concerned with surface aspects of life, but rather states of feeling, with expression rather than representation. It sprang from the intensity of modern, industrial life rather than the perceived leisurely existence of the agricultural life of yore.

In the next chapter, we will deal with criticisms of Modernism; they have resonance for the chef who is determined to break all the rules, create something all new, smash the classics.

The chefs who contributed recipes to this book have created some most unusual and highly edible forms—Thaddeus Dubois's Vanilla Salad, a crazy jumble of a pastalike cookie; the cones presented by Norman Love and Donald Wressell, both defying physics and diner expectation—Wressell's crowned with a gracefully warped cookie ring, Love's by an Art Deco complex of chocolate lines. Jacquy Pfeiffer's wheel surrounding his Chocolate Ice Cream Dome has the harsh teeth of an industrial gearpiece and the most luxuriant, swanlike spokes imaginable, in one form.

EN-MING HSU

Assistant Pastry Chef
Ritz-Carlton Hotel, Chicago.

BORN: Richmond, Virginia. TRAINING/EXPERIENCE: Baking and Pastry Program, The Culinary Institute of America (first graduate); catering company, Connecticut; Cafe Didier, Washington D.C.; L'Espinasse, New York.

"I've been fortunate to meet people in this career who pushed me in the right direction—not to go so much for financial gain, but for what the work is, and for what you get from the work. It is something you have to enjoy—spending the long hours and working hard. People say to me, 'You spend so much time to make a dessert and in five minutes the customer eats it and it's gone!' But that's the pleasure of it too: if you didn't enjoy the work, or if you minded that it is gone in five minutes, then you wouldn't be doing this. It would be too much of a letdown."

THADDEUS DUBOIS

Pastry Chef
Duquesne Club, Pittsburgh, Pennsylvania.

BORN: November 1966, Los Angeles, California. TRAINING/EXPERIENCE: restaurants and bakeries in Montana and California; The Culinary Institute of America, Baking and Pastry Program; confectionery assistant, International School of Confectionery Arts, Gaithersburg, Maryland; ANA Hotel, Washington D.C.

"To me, 'Modern' is getting away from traditional flavors and things that are very centralized on the plate; for example, sauces that are piped around the plate. Chefs are experimenting more and combining more. They're working hard. This field requires hard work and determination. Talent is second to that. If you can work hard, have faith in yourself, and get proper training under the right people, you can really develop into a talented pastry chef. [CIA instructor and Certified Master Pastry Chef] Joe McKenna really had a big impact on me, mainly because of his dedication to his craft and his willingness to learn as much as he can from any person and any book. He showed me that dedication is every day."

NORMAN LOVE

Corporate Pastry Chef
*Ritz-Carlton Hotel Company,
Naples, Florida.*

BORN: December 1959,
Philadelphia, Pennsylvania.
TRAINING/EXPERIENCE: various
restaurants, bakeries, and country
clubs; Sheraton, InterContinental
and Mayfair hotels; Caribbean
Cruise Lines; pastry shop,
Mougins, France; Beverly Hills
Hotel; Ritz-Carlton Hotel, St.
Louis, Missouri.

*"From my heart I believe that you
can be as great as you want to be. I
think about pastry all the time. I
have a passion about what I do and
an incredible desire to chase a level
of accomplishment that, perhaps, I
will never reach. There is always
someone who knows so much more
and is so much more talented, it
keeps driving me harder and harder.
Our C.E.O. will ask us, if a base-
ball player hits three home runs in
a game, is he successful? Yes. But
does he get a new contract after that
game? No. If he hits three home
runs a game for a season, will he
get a new contract? Probably yes.
People believe that success is in the
future, where really success is now.
Reward is the future for being successful now. If you're successful every
day in what you do, you will be
rewarded."*

There is beauty in these compositions—Thaddeus Dubois's riotous Salad, anarchic but drawing the eye firmly to the sphere; Martin Howard's Hot Lips, pouting prettily amid the flames of chocolate and sauce; the lithe spiral surrounding Jacquy Pfeiffer's Ice Cream Dome; the cones of Wressell and Love; Krista Kern's circuslike, delirious Fool.

Our Modernist chefs have attitude in abundance. Martin Howard's Hot Lips is an image so bizarre it makes you smile, while Top of the World seems to call attention to its own blissful dessert experience. Also calling attention to the dessert medium is Eric Perez's Soda, which is like a self-conscious comment on the dessert experience, especially that old soda fountain kind. Richard Ruskell's MOMA is an unabashed celebration of Modernism and is the only unironic entry in the book. Pastillage is uncharacteristic of contemporary American chefs and Ruskell's work in particular; in that sense, it is such a rule-breaker that it has to be included here.

Ruskell, in particular, is known for the rich, complex flavors of the desserts he serves at the Phoenician. He has won many a competition partially on the basis of his flavors. "I did some outrageous things for this book," he admits, "but I did them because I don't normally do them. My sense of Modernism, or at least my hope, is that it represents a return to desserts that taste good."

ON TOP OF THE WORLD

MARTIN HOWARD

Pastry Chef, *Rainbow!,*
New York.

Inside a milk chocolate globe are layers of fruit compote, mango sorbet, milk chocolate mousse, and whipped cream, with chocolate cake forming the base. When the customer applies a fork, the contents should spill forth. White chocolate spears, strawberry slices, raspberry sauce, more chocolate sauce, and whipped cream top off this world. The name of the dessert, says Chef Howard, was inspired by a song by the ever-modern Carpenters.

YIELD: 10 SERVINGS

Special Equipment:
Ten 8" (20.3 cm) balloons
Ten 3" (7.6 cm) ring molds

CHOCOLATE ALMOND CAKE			
5.5 oz	*156 g*	*unsalted butter, softened*
4 oz	*113 g*	*granulated sugar*
3.9 oz	*111 g*	*egg yolks*
4 oz	*113 g*	*almond flour*
8 oz	*227 g*	*semisweet chocolate, melted*
1 tsp	*5 ml*	*vanilla extract*
6.3 oz	*179 g*	*egg whites*

1. Preheat the oven to 350°F (177°C). Line two 13 x 9" (33 x 22.9 cm) baking pans with parchment paper. Butter and flour the pans.

2. In a mixer fitted with a paddle attachment, cream together the butter and sugar. Beat in the egg yolks until well combined. Blend in the almond flour, chocolate, and vanilla.

3. In a mixer fitted with a whisk attachment, beat the egg whites to soft peaks. Fold into the creamed mixture.

4. Scrape the batter into the prepared pans and bake for 15 minutes or until set. Let cool completely.

CHOCOLATE SAUCE			
8 oz	*227 g*	*bittersweet chocolate, chopped*
8 liq oz	*237 ml*	*heavy cream*
4 liq oz	*118 ml*	*corn syrup*

1. Place the chopped chocolate in a bowl.

2. In a saucepan bring the heavy cream and corn syrup to a boil.

Dessert shown on page xx

3. Pour the hot cream mixture over the chocolate and stir until the chocolate is melted and the sauce is smooth.

MILK CHOCOLATE MOUSSE			
	1.95 oz	*55 g*	*egg yolks*
	1.25 oz	*35 g*	*granulated sugar*
	2 liq oz	*59 ml*	*dry white wine*
	7 oz	*198 g*	*milk chocolate, melted*
	16 liq oz	*473 ml*	*heavy cream*
	1 tsp	*5 ml*	*vanilla extract*
	1 Tbs	*15 ml*	*dark rum*

1. In a large bowl over simmering water, whisk togethe r the egg yolks, granulated sugar, and white wine until light and thick. Whisk in the melted chocolate. Let cool.

2. In a mixer fitted with a whisk attachment, combine the heavy cream, vanilla extract, and rum. Whip to soft peaks. Fold into the yolk-chocolate mixture. Chill the mousse until firm.

MIXED FRUIT SALAD			
	12 oz	*340 g*	*mixed diced fruit, such as raspberries, kiwi, mango, and pineapple*
	2 oz	*57 g*	*granulated sugar*
	1 liq oz	*30 ml*	*dark rum*

Place the diced fruit, granulated sugar, and rum in a large bowl and toss to combine.

RASPBERRY SAUCE			
	22.5 oz	*638 g*	*fresh raspberries*
	8 oz	*227 g*	*granulated sugar*
	1/2	*1/2*	*whole lemon*

1. In a medium saucepan, combine the raspberries, granulated sugar, and lemon. Bring to a boil, reduce the heat, and simmer until thickened, about 10 minutes.

2. Remove the lemon half. Strain through a chinois to extract the seeds. Chill.

MANGO SORBET			
	36 oz	*1020 g*	*mango purée*
	8 liq oz	*237 ml*	*simple syrup*
	2 liq oz	*59 ml*	*lemon juice*

1. Combine the mango purée, simple syrup, and lemon juice.

2. Process in an ice cream machine.

MILK CHOCOLATE GLOBES			
	26 oz	*737 g*	*milk chocolate, melted and tempered*
			dark chocolate, melted and tempered, for decoration

1. Line a sheet pan with parchment and place ten 3" (7.6 cm) ring molds on it (this is done to secure the chocolate-dipped balloons). Blow up ten balloons to 4" (10.2 cm) diameter.

2. Place the tempered milk chocolate in a bowl slightly larger than the portion of balloon to be dipped. Dip the top half of the balloon into the milk chocolate. Lift up the balloon and allow the excess chocolate to drip back into the bowl. Place the dipped balloon, chocolate-side-up, onto a ring mold. Repeat to make ten chocolate-dipped balloons. Refrigerate until set.

Note. More milk chocolate than is actually needed is tempered, so that there is sufficient amount for dipping.

3. Remove the balloons from the refrigerator; pop and discard balloons. Fill a parchment cone with the tempered dark chocolate and pipe thin vertical and horizontal lines on the outside of the chocolate domes to represent the longitude and latitude lines, respectively, of a globe. Let set.

ASSEMBLY

Whipped cream
Strawberries
Mango purée
White chocolate spears

1. Cut chocolate cake into ten 4" (10.2 cm) circles with a cutter. (This may be done ahead of time.)

2. Place a small amount of whipped cream in the bottom of a chocolate globe. Spoon some of the fruit salad over the whipped cream to come halfway up the globe. Spread a 1/3" (.85 cm) thick layer of softened mango sorbet over the fruit. Finish filling the globe with milk chocolate mousse and top with a round of chocolate cake. Press firmly in place.

3. Invert the filled globe onto a dessert plate. Pipe a border of whipped cream around the base. Arrange a circle of sliced strawberries on top of the globe and place a trimmed strawberry half on top of the slices.

4. Decorate the plate with chocolate-sauce stars and dots of raspberry sauce and mango purée. Garnish with the white chocolate spears. Serve immediately.

MANGO BERRY FOOL

KRISTA KERN

Pastry Chef, *Three Fish, Westerly, Rhode Island.*

The madness of Modernism comes to life in this colorful, calamitous plate. A mango fool is served with raspberry sorbet in its center and berries affixed to its side, with a brown sugar shortbread as its base and shaped, dried mangoes as witnesses. Raspberry, mango, and blackberry coulis also call the tune. "A fool? Okay. I like doing it with a wink, a little nod," says Krista Kern. "I'm not above that."

YIELD: 8 SERVINGS

Special Equipment:
Eight 3" high (7.6 cm) timbale molds
One silicone baking mat

MANGO FOOL

2	2	ripe mangoes, peeled and pitted
1 liq oz	30 ml	cold water
3 sheets	7.5 g	gelatin, soaked in water
1 Tbs	15 ml	lime juice
1 pt	473 ml	crème fraîche
1.8 oz	50 g	granulated sugar
8 liq oz	237 ml	heavy cream

1. In a food processor, purée mangoes and transfer to a large bowl.

2. In a small saucepan, heat water until warm. Drain gelatin, add to water, and stir until dissolved. Stir in lime juice. Whisk gelatin mixture into mango purée. Whisk in crème fraîche and sugar.

3. In a mixer with a whisk attachment, whip heavy cream to soft peaks. Whisk one-half of the whipped cream into the mango mixture; fold in the remaining whipped cream. Cover and refrigerate until ready to assemble the timbales.

RASPBERRY SORBET

4 pts	1.9 lt	raspberries
3 Tbs	45 ml	simple syrup (50%)
1 Tbs	15 ml	lemon juice
4 liq oz	118 ml	water

1. In a food processor, purée raspberries. Add the remaining ingredients and process until just combined. Transfer to a bowl, cover, and refrigerate until cold, about 2 hours.

2. Process the mixture in an ice cream machine according to manufacturer's instructions. Transfer the sorbet to a container, cover, and place in freezer.

ASSEMBLY

1. Place timbale molds in the freezer until thoroughly chilled.

2. Remove the sorbet from the freezer. Fill the timbale molds one-quarter of the way with mango-fool mixture. Scoop 2 to 3 tablespoons of sorbet into each mold and smooth out. Fill the molds with mango-fool mixture. Tap the molds gently to settle the fool and sorbet and to remove bubbles. Place the timbales on a sheet pan, cover with plastic wrap, and freeze 8 hours or overnight.

BROWN SUGAR
SHORTBREAD

10.5 oz	298 g	sifted cake flour
.25 tsp	1.25 g	ground cloves
8.8 oz	250 g	unsalted butter
5.6 oz	160 g	light brown sugar
1/2	1/2	vanilla bean, split and scraped

1. In large bowl, gently whisk together cake flour and cloves; set aside.

2. In mixer with a paddle attachment, cream butter with brown sugar and vanilla bean scrapings. At low speed, mix in dry ingredients. Transfer dough to work surface, roll into ball, and wrap in plastic wrap. Chill dough for at least 1 hour.

3. Preheat oven to 350°F (175°C). Roll dough out to a scant 1/4" (.63 cm) thickness. Using a 2" (5 cm) round cutter, cut out at least 8 circles of dough. Place the circles on a sheet pan and bake until golden, 15 to 20 minutes.

RASPBERRY COULIS

2 pts	946 ml	raspberries
2 Tbs	25 g	granulated sugar
1 Tbs	15 ml	lemon juice

1. In food processor, purée raspberries, sugar, and lemon juice.

2. Pass mixture through a chinois, pour into a squeeze bottle, and refrigerate.

MANGO COULIS

1	1	ripe mango, peeled and pitted
1 Tbs	15 ml	lime juice
2 Tbs	25g	granulated sugar

1. In a food processor, purée mango, lime juice, and sugar.

2. Pass this mixture through a chinois, pour into a squeeze bottle, and refrigerate.

BLACKBERRY COULIS

2 pts	946 ml	blackberries
1 Tbs	15 ml	lemon juice
2 Tbs	25 g	granulated sugar

1. In a food processor, purée blackberries, lemon juice, and sugar.

2. Pass the mixture through a chinois, pour into squeeze bottle, and refrigerate.

VANILLA ANGLAISE

12 liq oz	355 ml	heavy cream
4 liq oz	118 ml	milk
1	1	vanilla bean, split and scraped

| 3.9 oz | 111 g | *egg yolks* |
| 3.5 oz | 99 g | *granulated sugar* |

1. In a medium saucepan, combine cream, milk, and vanilla bean; scald. Remove from heat and allow to infuse for 20 minutes.

2. In a mixer fitted with a whisk attachment, beat yolks and sugar at high speed until light. At low speed, mix in half of the cream mixture. Return the entire mixture to a saucepan and cook over low heat until the sauce coats the back of the spoon.

3. Strain the sauce into a bowl set in an ice bath and stir until chilled. Pour the sauce into a squeeze bottle and refrigerate.

DRIED MANGO TRIANGLES

| 2 | 2 | *ripe mangoes, peeled and pitted* |

1. Preheat oven to 200°F (95°C).

2. In a food processor, purée the mangoes until smooth. Using a metal spatula, spread the purée onto a silicone baking mat-lined baking sheet. Dry the purée in the oven for at least 4 hours, or until it is no longer tacky.

3. Remove the rectangles from the baking mat and cut into 24 triangles, each with a 1" (2.5 cm) base and 3" (7.6 cm) sides. Return the triangles to the silpat and reheat until softened. Remove each triangle from the silpat and place over a rolling pin to create a curved shape. Store the triangles in an airtight container until ready to serve.

SUGAR SPIRALS

| 6 oz | 170 g | *isomalt* |
| 2 liq oz | 59 ml | *water* |

1. Line a sheet pan with parchment paper. Place the isomalt and water in a heavy saucepan and stir to combine. Cook over low heat until the isomalt is dissolved.

2. Increase the heat to medium and cook the syrup to 340°F (171°C); immediately plunge the bottom of the pan into cold water to stop the cooking process. Allow the sugar to cool until slightly thickened, about 5 minutes.

3. Using a teaspoon, drizzle the sugar into a spiral question mark pattern, about 2" (5 cm) in diameter. Repeat to form a total of 16 spirals. Allow the sugar to harden completely.

PLATE ASSEMBLY

Fresh assorted berries
Fresh mint

1. Place a brown sugar shortbread round on a dessert plate. Invert one of the fools onto the round. Arrange 3 of the dried mango triangles evenly around the fools, inserting the tips of the triangles into 3 berries.

2. Lay a sugar spiral flat on top of the fool, and insert the tail of another spiral into the top of the fool so that it is perpendicular to the other spiral. Place a scoop of raspberry sorbet on top of the fool and garnish with fresh mint. Drizzle each of the 3 sauces onto the plate and serve immediately.

MOMA

RICHARD RUSKELL

Pastry Chef, *The Phoenician, Phoenix, Arizona.*

Lemon chibouste with cubes of lemon chiffon cake is served in a pastillage sculpture. The form was inspired by a stroll through the Museum of Modern Art (MOMA) in New York. "For the book I've done some outrageous things," says Richard Ruskell, "but I did them because I don't normally do them."

YIELD: 8 SERVINGS

Special Equipment: Eight 3" (7.6 cm) diameter x 1" (2.5 cm) high metal ring molds

LEMON CHIFFON CAKE

8 oz	227 g	cake flour
10.5 oz	300 g	granulated sugar, divided
.5 tsp	2.5 g	baking soda
.5 tsp	3.35 g	salt
4 liq oz	119 ml	peanut oil
4.5 oz	128 g	egg yolks
6 liq oz	177 ml	water
3 Tbs	45 ml	lemon juice
2 Tbs	12 g	grated lemon zest
1.5 tsp	3 g	vanilla extract
10.5 oz	298 g	egg whites
1 tsp	3 g	cream of tartar

1. Preheat the oven to 325°F (165°C). Line the bottom of a half-sheet pan with parchment paper. In a mixer fitted with the paddle attachment, combine the flour, 8 oz (227 g) of the sugar, the baking soda, and salt. Add the oil, yolks, water, lemon juice, zest, and vanilla; beat until smooth.

2. In a clean bowl, using a whisk attachment, beat the whites to soft peaks. Beat in the cream of tartar. Add the remaining sugar and beat until stiff peaks form. Carefully fold the beaten whites into the remaining batter. Scrape the batter into the prepared pan and bake until the cake springs back when touched in the center, about 20 minutes. Cool the cake completely, then cut into 1/2" (1.27 cm) cubes.

LEMON CHIBOUSTE

3.25 oz	92 g	egg yolks
5.25 oz	149 g	granulated sugar, divided
2 tsp	5 g	cornstarch
4 liq oz	118 ml	lemon juice
4 liq oz	118 ml	heavy cream
2 sheets	5 g	gelatin leaves, bloomed and drained
2 Tbs	20 g	light corn syrup
1 Tbs	15 ml	water
5.25 oz	149 g	egg whites, at room temperature

1. In a mixer fitted with the whisk attachment, whip the yolks and 2 Tbs (.875 oz/25 g) of the sugar until pale. Beat in the cornstarch.

2. In a nonreactive saucepan, combine the lemon juice and heavy cream and bring to a boil. Whisk some of the hot cream mixture into the yolk mixture. Return the entire mixture to the saucepan and whisk to combine. Whisking constantly, bring the mixture to a boil. Remove the mixture from the heat and strain into a medium bowl. Whisk in the gelatin.

3. In a small saucepan combine 3.5 oz (99 g) of the sugar, the corn syrup, and the water. Bring to a boil and cook to 248°F (120°C), washing down the side of the pan to prevent crystals from forming. When the temperature of the syrup reaches 240°F (115°C), begin whipping the whites.

4. In a mixer fitted with a whisk attachment, beat the whites until frothy. Gradually add the remaining 2 Tbs (.875 oz/25 g) of sugar and beat to soft peaks. When the sugar syrup reaches 248°F (120°C), slowly add it to the meringue and beat until the mixture forms stiff peaks and is completely cool.

5. Fold the Italian meringue into the lemon cream. Fold in the cubed lemon chiffon cake.

6. Arrange the eight 3" (7.6 cm) ring molds on a parchment-lined sheet pan. Fill the molds with the chibouste mixture, smoothing the tops with a metal spatula. Freeze the molds for several hours.

PASTILLAGE

.5 oz	15 g	unflavored powdered gelatin
5 liq oz	150 ml	cold water
2 lbs, 1.5 oz	95 k	confectioners' sugar
5 oz	142 g	cornstarch
1/2 tsp	1.5 g	cream of tartar

1. Sprinkle the gelatin over the cold water and set aside.

2. Sift together the sugar, cornstarch, and cream of tartar. Place the sugar mixture in a mixer fitted with a paddle attachment.

3. Melt the softened gelatin in a bain-marie. While mixing at low speed, gradually add the melted gelatin. Continue mixing, scraping down the side of the bowl occasionally, until the mixture forms a smooth, elastic paste. Cover the pastillage with a wet towel immediately.

PASTILLAGE SCULPTURES

1. Take a piece of the pastillage and roll out to 1/4" (.6 cm) thickness. Using a corn-starch-dusted knife or pizza cutter, cut out a 3 1/2 x 5" (8.9 x 12.7 cm) rectangle. (Cover the remaining pastillage with a wet towel.) Using a 3" ring mold as a guide, cut a U-shape out of one of the long sides of the rectangle. Cut a 4 1/2 x 1 1/2" (11.4 x 3.8 cm) strip out of the pastillage. Lay this strip around the inside of the ring mold to form a curved shape (this is the piece on which the dessert will lie).

2. Cut out a 1 x 2 1/2" (2.54 x 6.3 cm) rectangle. Cut a diagonal through the rectangle to form two triangles. These will be the legs to hold up the sculpture.

3. Repeat this process to make enough pieces for eight pastillage sculptures. Allow all the pieces to dry completely, at least 48 hours, turning them over every few hours so that they dry evenly.

ASSEMBLY

Royal icing

1. Score all the surfaces that will be "glued" so that they are not smooth (see photograph). Place the royal icing in a parchment cone. Using the royal icing, glue the long straight sides of the triangles onto the front and back of the rectangles to act as supports (see photo). Stand the piece up and glue on the pastillage arc, where the dessert will be nestled. Allow the sculpture to dry for several hours, until it is stable.

2. Place a sculpture on a serving plate. Unmold one of the frozen lemon desserts and lay it on its side into the sculpture. Repeat with the remaining desserts. Serve the desserts when the chibouste has thawed.

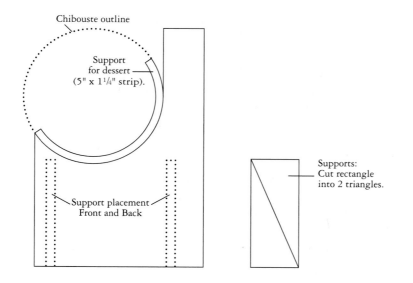

CHOCOLATE ICE CREAM DOME

JACQUY PFEIFFER

Co-owner, *Ecole de Patisserie Francaise, Chicago.*

This dessert is adapted from a piece offered in competition at the 1997 World Pastry Cup in Lyons. Within a dome of chocolate ice cream is a thin layer of raspberry coulis, vanilla parfait, and vanilla shortdough. The velvety appearance is achieved by spraying a cocoa butter and chocolate mixture on the frozen surface. What is the significance of the numeral three? "Any decorations should come in odd numbers," says Chef Pfeiffer, "and three is the best. The three is to call attention to the three elements on the plate." The cookie atop the dome is the famous soft clock from a painting by Salvador Dali.

YIELD: 24 SERVINGS

Special Equipment:
Twenty-four 3" (7.6 cm) diameter demi-sphere molds
Wagner airless paint sprayer
Clock-face silkscreen
Clock stencil

VANILLA SHORTDOUGH			
5.3 oz	150 g	*unsalted butter (82%)*
2.3 oz	65 g	*confectioners' sugar, sifted*
2.5	2.5	*Tahitian vanilla beans, scraped*
1.9 oz	53 g	*hard-boiled egg yolks*
6.6 oz	188 g	*cake flour*
.5 tsp	2 g	*baking powder*

1. In a mixer fitted with the paddle attachment, cream together the butter, sugar, and vanilla bean seeds. Pass through a sieve to remove the strings from the vanilla bean.

2. Strain the egg yolks through a tamis and add them to the butter mixture. Sift together the flour and baking powder. Add to the mixture and blend just until combined. Form the dough into a disc, wrap it in plastic, and chill for at least 30 minutes.

3. Preheat oven to 325°F (165°C). On a floured surface, roll out the dough to 1/8" (.3 cm) thickness. Cut the dough into circles using a 2 1/2" (6.2 cm) diameter cutter. Place the circles on a parchment-lined half sheet pan and bake for 12 to 15 minutes or just until the edges are golden.

VANILLA TUILES			
3.5 oz	100 g	*unsalted butter (82%)*
3.5 oz	100 g	*confectioners' sugar*
1	1	*Tahitian vanilla bean, scraped*
3.2 oz	90 g	*egg whites*
2.6 oz	75 g	*cake flour*
8 oz	227 g	*cocoa paste, melted*

1. Preheat oven to 350°F (180°C). In a mixer using the paddle attachment, cream together the butter, sugar, and vanilla bean seeds until light. Add half the egg whites, then half the flour and repeat with the remaining egg whites and flour. Mix just until combined.

2. Pass the cocoa paste through a clock-face silkscreen onto a sheet pan lined with a silicone baking mat. Let set.

3. Spread the tuile batter thinly through a clock-shape stencil on top of each clock face. Bake for 8 to 10 minutes or just until golden.

CHOCOLATE ICE CREAM			
	34 *liq oz*	1 *lt*	*whole milk (3.6%)*
	.7 *liq oz*	20 *ml*	*heavy cream (35%)*
	4.3 *oz*	121 *g*	*granulated sugar*
	2.3 *oz*	64 *oz*	*inverted sugar*
	2 *oz*	58 *g*	*nonfat milk powder*
	7.8 *oz*	220 *g*	*DGF 64% bittersweet chocolate*
	1.8 *oz*	50 *g*	*DGF cocoa paste*
	1.7 *oz*	48 *g*	*egg yolks*
	1 *tsp*	4 *g*	*Sevarome ice cream stabilizer*
	1 *tsp*	5 *g*	*Sevarome monostearate*

1. In a saucepan combine milk, cream, sugar, inverted sugar, and milk powder; place over high heat. At the same time, melt the chocolate and cocoa paste separately. When the milk mixture reaches 140°F (60°C) add the melted chocolate and cocoa paste, egg yolks, stabilizer, and monostearate. Cook gently, stirring, until the mixture reaches 185°F (85°C).

2. Strain the mixture over an ice bath and cool to 40°F (4°C), stirring occasionally. Refrigerate for at least 4 hours.

3. Process in an ice cream machine according to the manufacturer's instructions.

RASPBERRY COULIS			
	5.3 *oz*	150 *g*	*raspberry purée (10% sugar)*
	1.8 *oz*	50 *g*	*inverted sugar*
	.1 *oz*	4 *g*	*gelatin sheets*
	1.8 *oz*	50 *g*	*dextrose*
	.8 *liq oz*	24 *ml*	*framboise d'Alsace*

1. Combine the purée and inverted sugar and blend until smooth. Bloom the gelatin in cold water. Slightly warm 3.5 oz (100 g) of the purée and melt the gelatin in it. Temper into the remaining purée. Add the dextrose and liqueur. Cover tightly and chill until set.

2. When ready to line the bombes, warm the coulis very slightly.

VANILLA PARFAIT			
	6.4 *oz*	181 *g*	*granulated sugar*
	1.7 *liq oz*	50 *ml*	*water*
	7	7	*Tahitian vanilla beans*
	4.7 *oz*	132 *g*	*egg yolks*
	.4 *oz*	12.5 *g*	*egg whites*
	1 *pt*	473 *ml*	*heavy cream (35%), whipped to soft peaks*

1. Combine the sugar, water, and vanilla bean pods and seeds; let rest overnight.

2. Strain the vanilla pods out of the sugar mixture. Place the sugar mixture in a saucepan with the egg yolks and whites; cook gently, stirring, until the mixture reaches 185°F (85°C). Transfer to a mixer and whip until cool.

3. Fold in the whipped cream.

SPRAYING CHOCOLATE

17.6 oz	500 g	*cocoa butter*
17.6 oz	500 g	*Valrhona Manjari couverture*
17.6 oz	500 g	*Valrhona cocoa paste*

1. Melt the cocoa butter, couverture, and cocoa paste separately.

2. Combine and keep in a warm, dry area until needed for spraying.

ASSEMBLY

White chocolate gears sprayed with green cocoa butter
Pulled sugar rods

1. Line the demi-sphere molds with the chocolate ice cream, packing it in well to ensure that there are no air bubbles. Cover the ice cream with a thin coat of raspberry coulis. Freeze until set.

2. Pipe in the vanilla parfait almost to the top of the mold. Top with a shortdough circle and freeze to set.

3. Unmold the bombes by running them under warm water. Return to the freezer until ready to spray.

4. Spray the bombes with the warm spraying mixture using a Wagner airless paint sprayer. Keep them in the freezer until ready to serve.

5. Place each bombe on a chocolate gear. Garnish with a clock tuile and a pulled sugar rod.

The wheel is white chocolate with a light spray of green cocoa butter. You can color cocoa butter with any kind of coloring agent, but Pfeiffer uses an oil-based powder. Pfeiffer always adds a touch of yellow to any chocolate or sugar that he is coloring, except when his object color is blue or white. "The yellow makes the finished color warmer, less harsh," he says, "and it also gives the sensation of light going through the piece."

To make the numeral "3": make a syrup by boiling three parts sugar to one part water. Pour into a pan, cover with plastic and cool overnight. Then pipe the numeral in Sweetex Copper (or another high-ratio shortening) onto a Silpat; sprinkle it with sugar, remove the excess, and freeze it. Take the cooled syrup, carefully skim off any sugar crystals on the surface, and place the number on the surface, face side down.

Refrigerate for 24 to 36 hours, until you have a thin coat of sugar. Much of the aesthetic lies in the thin nature of the form. Put the number in a warm spot (not an oven)—100 degrees—and the Sweetex will melt out.

CONE OF SILENCE

DONALD WRESSELL

Executive Pastry Chef, *Four Seasons Hotel, Beverly Hills, California.*

This presentation has been much admired ever since Donald Wressell entered a version of it in competition years ago. Professionals and home chefs alike wondered, How does he get the cone to stand up like that? The secret lies in a bottom-heavy chocolate cone anchored with a drop of chocolate that is concealed in sauce. The flavor lives up to the spectacle: gianduja Bavarian flavored with Frangelico and praline paste is nestled inside the cone, and accompanied by Manjari ice cream, burnt orange sauce (camouflage), and a honey wafer. "People say to me, does it kill you to see customers break it and eat it? It doesn't, because I had my fun making it," says Wressell. "That is where my interest in the plate lies. I then pass it off to the diner and hope that he or she will take a moment to admire it."

YIELD: 14 SERVINGS

Special Equipment:
Fourteen plastic cone molds, 3.5 oz (103 ml) capacity with a 2.5" (6.3 cm) diameter opening
Silicone baking mat

CHOCOLATE CONES | *24 oz* | *680 g* | *bittersweet chocolate, melted and tempered*

1. Ladle chocolate into one of the cones to fill completely. Turn the cone upside down on a rack and allow excess to drip out. Let the cone set at room temperature for one hour. Refrigerate for at least 15 minutes.

2. Remove the cone from the refrigerator and dislodge it from the mold. Anchor the cone to the center of a dessert plate with a small amount of chocolate (see photos below). Lean the cone against 2 pieces of Plexiglas glued together at right angles until set. Repeat with the remaining cones.

Positioning the chocolate cone.

> "Chocolate is a lot more structurally sound than most people realize," says Donald Wressell. "When you mold the cone, you have to physically throw the chocolate out of the mold so that it becomes as thin as paper toward the top. This is not just for stability, though. When the diner applies a fork and just touches the top of the cone, it breaks away in pieces instead of toppling over into the sauce and ruining her evening gown."
>
> To unmold chocolate more easily, advises Chef Wressell, let it cool to room temperature, about an hour. Then put it in the refrigerator for ten minutes. It should pop out easily.

GIANDUJA BAVARIAN

16 liq oz	473 ml	milk
8 oz	227 g	gianduja chocolate, finely chopped
.24 oz	6.7 g	gelatin sheets, softened in cold water
2 oz	57 g	praline paste
2 liq oz	59 ml	hazelnut-flavored liqueur, such as Frangelico
16 liq oz	473 ml	heavy cream, whipped to soft peaks

1. In a large saucepan, bring the milk to a boil. Reduce the heat and add the chocolate, drained gelatin, and praline paste. Stir until the chocolate and gelatin are melted and the mixture is smooth. Remove the pan from the heat and stir in the liqueur. Let cool to room temperature.

2. Fold the whipped cream into the chocolate mixture and pour into the prepared cones. Chill for at least 1 hour.

MANJARI ICE CREAM

9.75 oz	276 g	egg yolks
16 liq oz	473 ml	milk
16 liq oz	47 ml	heavy cream
9 oz	255 g	granulated sugar
.5 tsp	3.4 g	salt
1	1	vanilla bean, split and scraped
13 oz	369 g	Valrhona Manjari chocolate, finely chopped

1. In a medium bowl, whisk the yolks until smooth.

2. In a saucepan, bring the milk, cream, sugar, and salt to a boil. Temper the yolks with the cream mixture. Return to the saucepan and cook to the custard stage.

3. Place the chopped chocolate in a large bowl and strain the custard over the chocolate, discarding the vanilla bean. Stir until the chocolate is completely melted and the mixture is smooth.

4. Cool and chill.

5. Process in an ice cream machine according to the manufacturer's instructions.

BURNT ORANGE SAUCE

24 liq oz	710 ml	fresh orange juice
1.5 Tbs	18 g	tapioca starch
3 oz	85 g	granulated sugar
1.5	1.5	vanilla beans, split and scraped

1. In a saucepan, whisk together the orange juice and tapioca starch. Bring to a boil; lower the heat and keep the mixture warm.

2. In a heavy-bottom saucepan, cook the sugar and vanilla bean seeds to a dark caramel color.

3. Slowly add the warmed orange juice mixture to the caramel, stirring constantly, until the caramel is completely dissolved. Bring to a boil and boil for 2 minutes. Remove from heat.

4. Strain and chill.

HONEY "ECLIPSE" WAFER			
7.5 oz	213 g	*unsalted butter, softened*
12 oz	340 g	*confectioners' sugar*
1/4 tsp	1.7 g	*salt*
1.5 oz	43 g	*honey*
10.5 oz	298 g	*all-purpose flour, divided*
7.5 oz	213 g	*egg whites*

1. In a mixer fitted with a paddle attachment, cream the butter with confectioners' sugar, salt, and honey.

2. On low speed, add half the flour and all the egg whites and mix until smooth. Add the remaining flour and continue mixing until the batter is well-blended. Chill for at least 2 hours.

3. Preheat the oven to 350°F (177°C). Line a sheet pan with parchment paper or a silicone baking mat. Cut an oval stencil whose major axis is 6" (15.2 cm) and whose minor axis is 3.75" (9.5 cm).

4. Place the stencil on the prepared sheet pan and spread a thin layer of batter over it. Repeat to make 14 wafers.

5. When the tuiles are half-baked (the dough will be pale but set), about 5 to 6 minutes, remove the sheet from the oven. Cut out the inside of each wafer with an oval cutter, leaving a 5/8" (1.6 cm) border. Return the "eclipse" rings to the oven and continue to bake until golden, about 5 to 6 minutes longer.

6. Remove wafers from the pan and bend each over a bowl to give it a slight curve. Let cool.

SESAME SEED WAFERS			
4.5 oz	128 g	*unsalted butter*
4.5 oz	128 g	*granulated sugar*
1.5 oz	43 g	*glucose*
1.5 liq oz	44 ml	*milk*
8 oz	227 g	*sesame seeds*
2 oz	57 g	*poppy seeds*

1. In a medium saucepan, melt together the butter, sugar, and glucose.

2. Remove the pan from the heat and stir in the sesame and poppy seeds.

3. Chill for at least one hour.

4. Preheat the oven to 325°F (163°C). Line a sheet pan with a silicone baking mat.

5. Remove the sesame mixture from the refrigerator. Take 1/4 tsp of the mixture, form it into a ball with the palms of your hands, and place on the prepared pan. Continue forming the balls of mixture, placing them about 2" (5 cm) apart on the pan. (As these wafers are *extremely* fragile when baked, make more than needed.) Bake for 8 to 10 minutes, until toasted. Let cool completely.

6. With a small spatula, carefully transfer the wafers to a parchment-lined pan and reserve.

ASSEMBLY   *Strawberry slices*

1. Remove a dessert plate with the attached Bavarian-filled cones from the refrigerator.

2. Spoon 2 to 3 Tbs (30 to 45 ml) of the burnt-orange sauce around the tip of the cone to create a "pool" of sauce about 4 to 5" (10.2 to 12.7 cm) in diameter.

3. Place a small scoop (#60) of Manjari ice cream, three slices of strawberry, and two sesame-seed wafers on the Bavarian cream. Arrange an "eclipse" wafer on top of the cone. Repeat with the remaining plates.

MILK CHOCOLATE-GINGER MOUSSE
WITH LIQUID CHOCOLATE CENTER

NORMAN LOVE

Corporate Pastry Chef, *Ritz-Carlton Hotel Company, Naples, Florida.*

Part of the inspiration for this dessert was the image of the cone and the sphere, but, says Norman Love, a further inspiration was the almond biscuit. "I attended a school at Valrhona in France, and one of the biscuits they taught was this one," he says. "It is primarily used with frozen desserts because it is moist and always stays very soft in the freezer. You're able to put crushed nuts or candied fruits or chocolate on the surface that will help accent the flavor of the dessert. Here, to accent the ginger and chocolate, I used pistachios and pine nuts."

YIELD: 20 SERVINGS

Special Equipment:
Twenty 2" (5 cm) PVC molds (2 1/2" (6.3 cm) high)
Forty Cocoa Barry 1" (2.5 cm) polycarbonate demi-sphere molds
Plastic cone molds, 2 3/4" base and 4 1/4" high (6.9 cm x 10.8 cm)

BISCUIT ALMANDE MOELLEUX			
2.1 oz	60 g	pine nuts, roasted
2.1 oz	60 g	pistachio nuts, roasted
3.9 oz	110 g	confectioners' sugar
3.9 oz	110 g	almond powder
1.8 oz	50 g	all-purpose flour
.9 oz	25 g	heavy cream
10.6 oz	302 g	egg whites, divided
4.4 oz	125 g	granulated sugar
1 oz	30 g	bittersweet chocolate, finely chopped

1. Preheat the oven to 400°F (205°C) and line a sheet pan with a silicone baking mat.

2. In a food processor, coarsely grind the pine nuts and pistachio nuts and set aside.

3. Sift the confectioners' sugar and the almond powder into a bowl. Gently whisk in the flour until combined. Whisk in the cream and 2.6 oz (75 g) of the egg whites.

4. In a mixer fitted with a whisk attachment, begin whipping the remaining 8 oz (227 g) of egg whites. Gradually add the granulated sugar, beating until stiff peaks form. Fold in the almond mixture in two batches. Spread the batter evenly over the prepared baking mat. Sprinkle the nuts and chocolate over evenly and bake until set, about 7 minutes. Cool completely.

5. Cut out 1" (2.5 cm) wide strips of the biscuit to fit the interior of the PVC molds. Line the molds with the strips, nut-studded side against the mold.

PUR CARAIBE CHOCOLATE SPONGE			
6.3 oz	180 g	Valrhona Pur Caraibe chocolate, chopped
3 oz	85 g	unsalted butter, melted
6.3 oz	180 g	egg whites
1.8 oz	50 g	granulated sugar
2.5 oz	70 g	egg yolks

1. Preheat the oven to 350°F (175°C) and line a half-sheet pan with a silicone baking mat.

2. Melt the chocolate with the butter to approximately 110°F (43°C)

3. In a mixer fitted with the whisk attachment, beat the egg whites with the sugar to stiff peaks. Gently whisk in the egg yolks, then fold in the chocolate mixture. Scrape the batter into a pastry bag fitted with a medium plain tip. Pipe the batter into 1 1/2" (3.8 cm) discs, and bake until set, about 10 minutes. Cool.

4. Place the chocolate sponge discs in the bottom of each of the lined PVC molds.

CHOCOLATE SAUCE			
1 qt	946 ml	water
9 oz	255 g	corn syrup
17 oz	482 g	granulated sugar
6 oz	170 g	cocoa powder
1 lb	454 g	Valrhona Pur Caraibe chocolate, chopped

1. In a saucepan, combine the water, corn syrup, and sugar. Bring the mixture to a boil. Whisk in the cocoa powder and return the mixture to a boil, whisking until smooth.

2. Remove the pan from the heat and add the chocolate, stirring until smooth.

3. Line a half hotel pan with plastic wrap. Scrape the sauce into the pan. Freeze the sauce for several hours, until set.

4. Using a 3/4" (1.9 cm) round cutter, cut out 20 rounds of the frozen sauce. Return the rounds to the freezer until ready to assemble the dessert.

MILK CHOCOLATE-GINGER MOUSSE			
4.4 oz	125 g	granulated sugar
2 liq oz	59 ml	water
1.8 oz	50 g	fresh ginger, finely chopped
5.3 oz	150 g	egg yolks
17.6 oz	500 g	Valrhona Javara milk chocolate
3 sheets	7.5 g	gelatin leaves, bloomed
33.8 liq oz	1 lt	heavy cream, whipped to soft peaks

1. In a saucepan, bring the sugar and water to a boil. Remove the pan from the heat and add the ginger. Allow the ginger to infuse in the syrup for at least 30 minutes.

2. Strain the syrup and return to the saucepan. Cook the syrup to 250°F (121°C).

3. Meanwhile, in a mixer fitted with a whisk attachment, begin beating the egg yolks. Gradually add the hot syrup in a thin stream to the beating yolks. Beat the mixture at medium speed until completely cool.

4. Melt the milk chocolate to 104°F (40°C); set aside.

5. Drain the gelatin and, in a small saucepan, heat on low until dissolved.

6. Fold half of the cream into the chocolate. Fold in the egg yolk mixture and gelatin. Fold in the remaining cream. Transfer the mousse to a pastry bag fitted with a medium plain tip.

7. Pipe the mousse into the prepared molds, filling them halfway. Place one of the frozen chocolate sauce discs in the center of each mold. Pipe more mousse on top, filling the molds completely and smoothing the top with a spatula. Freeze the molds for a few hours, until set.

SPHERICAL BASES		
8 oz	*227 g*	*cocoa butter*
as needed	*as needed*	*fat-soluble food coloring (red, blue, and violet)**
8 oz	*227 g*	*white chocolate, tempered*

*Note. Fat-soluble food coloring is available from Gourmand, Herndon, VA, (800) 627-7272.

1. Melt the cocoa butter and add a small amount of each color of the food coloring, until the mixture turns burgundy red. Using your finger, spread some of the mixture into the demi-sphere molds, coating them so that some areas are darker than others. Let the molds set for 5 minutes (see photos below).

2. Pour the tempered white chocolate into the prepared molds, filling them. Tap the molds sharply on a table to remove the air bubbles. Turn the molds upside down over a rack-covered bowl and tap to allow the excess chocolate to drip into the bowl. Using a dough scraper, remove the excess chocolate from the top of the molds and place the molds upside down on a parchment-lined sheet pan. Allow the molds to set completely.

3. Remove the demi-spheres from the molds. Heat a half-sheet pan in the oven until hot. Remove the pan and place it on a flat surface. Touch one of the chocolate demi-spheres to the hot sheet pan for less than 1 second. Immediately attach another chocolate demi-sphere to the first demi-sphere, creating a sealed sphere.

Making the spherical bases.

| CHOCOLATE CONES | 1.5 lbs | 680 g | bittersweet chocolate, tempered |

1. Ladle about 3 oz (85 g) of the melted chocolate into each cone. Turn the cones upside down and allow the excess chocolate to drip out. Allow to set.

2. Repeat with another layer of chocolate. Allow the cones to set completely.

| CHOCOLATE DISCS | 1 lb | 454 g | bittersweet chocolate, tempered |

1. Place a silicone baking mat on a flat work surface, with the textured side up. Pour the tempered chocolate onto the mat and, using a palette knife, spread it into a very thin and even layer. Allow the chocolate to set for a few minutes.

2. Using a 3" (7.6 cm) round cutter, cut out 20 discs from the chocolate; allow them to set completely.

CHOCOLATE GLAZE			
	1 qt	1 lt	milk
	15.8 oz	450 g	unsalted butter, cubed
	15.8 oz	450 g	granulated sugar
	8.8 oz	250 g	alkalized cocoa powder, sifted
	26.4 oz	750 g	bittersweet chocolate couverture, chopped
	8.8 oz	250 g	pâte à glacé, chopped

1. In a saucepan, whisk together the milk, butter, sugar, and cocoa powder over medium heat; bring this to a boil.

2. Add the couverture and pâte à glacé and whisk until smooth. Cool the glaze to about 85°F (29°C).

3. Remove the mousse molds from the freezer and, without unmolding them, spread a thin layer of the glaze over each dessert. Place the molds in the refrigerator until ready to serve.

CHOCOLATE TRIANGLES			
	1 lb	454 g	milk chocolate couverture, tempered
	1 lb	454 g	bittersweet chocolate couverture, tempered

1. Make two triangular stencils out of cardboard using the drawing on the following page as a guide, making one 5 x 2 1/2 x 4 1/2" (12.7 x 6.3 x 11.4 cm) and the other 3 1/2 x 1 1/2 x 3" (8.8 x 3.8 x 7.6 cm). Place 2 silicone baking mats on a flat work surface, with the textured sides up. Pour some of the tempered milk chocolate onto one of the mats and, using a palette knife, spread it into a thin, even layer. Allow the chocolate to set for a few minutes.

2. Repeat the procedure with the bittersweet couverture.

3. Using the stencils as a guide, cut out several triangles from each of the chocolates using an X-acto knife. Set the triangles aside until ready to garnish the dessert.

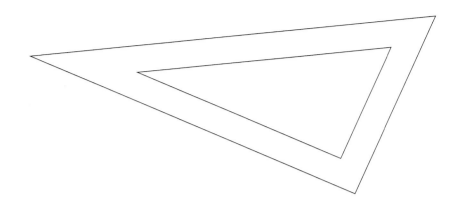

ASSEMBLY   *Tempered bittersweet chocolate couverture*
Chocolate sauce

1. Place a dot of tempered couverture in the center of a dessert plate. Glue one of the spheres to the plate. Allow to set.

2. Heat a small plain writing tip and poke a small hole in the top of the sphere. Dip the tip of one of the chocolate cones in the tempered couverture and place in the hole. Allow it to set.

3. Place one of the chocolate discs on top of the cone. Unmold one of the glazed desserts and place it on top of the disc.

4. Dip the tip of two of the larger triangles into the chocolate and attach them to the disc, as in the photograph. Stick two of the smaller triangles into the top of the dessert. Place a few graduated drops of chocolate sauce on the plate. Repeat with the remaining plates.

HOT LIPS

MARTIN HOWARD

Pastry Chef, *Rainbow!, New York.*

White chocolate mousse covered in raspberry sauce is placed on a chocolate chip cookie that has been glazed with chocolate. More white chocolate mousse and a mixed berry compote are placed underneath. To complete this provocative image are raspberry sauce, apricot sauce, and white chocolate flames submerged in chocolate cups filled with Grand Marnier ganache. The cookie should ideally be crunchy on the outside, slightly soft on the inside.

YIELD: 15 SERVINGS

CHOCOLATE CHIP COOKIES

7.5 oz	*213 g*	*cake flour*
1 tsp	*5 g*	*baking soda*
8 oz	*227 g*	*unsalted butter, softened*
4 oz	*113 g*	*light brown sugar*
3.5 oz	*99 g*	*granulated sugar*
1.75 oz	*50 g*	*eggs*
.5 tsp	*2 g*	*salt*
1 tsp	*5 ml*	*vanilla extract*
8 oz	*227 g*	*large-size chocolate chips*

1. Preheat the oven to 325°F (163°C). Line a sheet pan with parchment paper.

2. In a bowl, sift together the cake flour and baking soda.

3. In a mixer fitted with a paddle attachment, beat the butter until creamy. Gradually add the light brown and granulated sugars and continue to beat until smooth. Add the eggs, salt, and vanilla extract; beat until blended. On low speed add the dry ingredients. Mix in the chocolate chips.

4. Using a #24 scoop, which is a scant 2 oz (57 g) of dough, drop the dough onto the prepared pan and bake for 15 to 18 minutes, until golden. (The edges of the cookies will be set, but the centers will still be soft.) Let the cookies rest on the pan for 5 minutes, then transfer to a rack to cool completely.

CHOCOLATE GLAZE

8 oz	*227 g*	*bittersweet chocolate, chopped*
8 liq oz	*237 ml*	*heavy cream*
4 liq oz	*118 ml*	*corn syrup*

1. Place the chopped chocolate in a bowl.

2. In a saucepan bring the heavy cream and corn syrup to a boil.

3. Pour the hot cream mixture over the chocolate and stir until the chocolate is melted and the sauce is smooth.

WHITE CHOCOLATE MOUSSE			
3.75 oz	106 g	egg yolks
2.5 oz	71 g	granulated sugar
4 liq oz	118 ml	dry white wine
14 oz	397 g	white chocolate, melted
32 liq oz	946 ml	heavy cream
2 tsp	10 ml	vanilla extract
2 Tbs	30 ml	kirsch liqueur

1. Line a sheet pan with parchment paper.

2. In a large bowl over simmering water, whisk together the egg yolks, granulated sugar, and white wine until light and thick. Whisk in the melted chocolate.

3. In a mixer fitted with the whisk attachment, combine the heavy cream, vanilla extract, and kirsch. Whip to soft peaks. Fold into the yolk-chocolate mixture. Chill the mousse until firm.

4. Fill a pastry bag fitted with a plain tip (Ateco #6) with the mousse and pipe out 15 pairs of lips (about 3 1/2"/8.8 cm wide) onto the prepared pan. With the remaining mousse, pipe out 15 mounds of mousse 1" (2.5 cm) diameter x 1 3/4" (4.4 cm) high and pipe out 15 mounds of mousse 1 1/4" (3.1 cm) diameter x 1 1/2" (3.8 cm) high. Freeze the mousse lips and mounds.

MIXED BERRY SALAD			
44 oz	1.2 kg	mixed berries, such as strawberries, raspberries, and cherries
2 oz	57 g	granulated sugar
1 liq oz	30 ml	Grand Marnier

1. Roughly chop the berries.

2. Place the berries, granulated sugar, and Grand Marnier in a large bowl and toss to combine.

RASPBERRY SAUCE			
36 oz	1 kg	fresh raspberries
12 oz	340 g	granulated sugar
1/2	1/2	whole lemon

1. In a medium saucepan, combine the raspberries, granulated sugar, and lemon half. Bring the mixture to a boil; reduce the heat and simmer until thickened, about 10 minutes.

2. Remove the lemon. Strain through a chinois to extract the seeds and chill.

APRICOT SAUCE			
18 oz	510 g	apricot purée
4 oz	113 g	granulated sugar

In a medium saucepan, combine the apricot purée and sugar; bring to a boil. Reduce the heat and simmer for 10 minutes. Chill.

GANACHE CUPS	16 oz	454 g	bittersweet chocolate, finely chopped
	12 liq oz	355 ml	heavy cream
	2 oz	57 g	granulated sugar
	2 oz	57 g	unsalted butter
	1 liq oz	30 ml	Grand Marnier liqueur
	75	75	small chocolate cups*

*Note. Small chocolate cups are available from Patisfrance, (800) PASTRY-1.

1. Place the chopped chocolate in a bowl.

2. In a saucepan, bring the heavy cream, granulated sugar, and butter to a boil.

3. Pour the hot cream mixture over the chocolate. Stir until the chocolate is melted and the mixture is smooth. Add the Grand Marnier.

4. Spoon about 2 teaspoons of the ganache into each chocolate cup.

WHITE CHOCOLATE FLAMES	12 oz	340 g	white chocolate, tempered

Spread a thin layer of the chocolate onto the parchment. When set, cut into 75 curved triangular shapes, about 3/4 x 5 1/2" (1.9 x 14 cm).

ASSEMBLY

1. Place the chocolate chip cookies on a rack set over a sheet pan so that the bottom of each cookie is facing up. Pour the chocolate glaze over the cookies and drain on the rack until set.

2. Remove 1 pair of lips, 2 large mounds of mousse, and 2 small mounds of mousse from the freezer. Paint the lips with raspberry sauce and place on the center of a glazed cookie.

3. Place four mounds of mousse near the center of the dessert plate, so that the larger ones are behind the smaller ones. These are arranged so that the cookie will be propped up at an angle. Spoon about 1/3 cup of the berry salad in the center of the mousse. Place the cookie on top of the berries.

4. Arrange 5 white chocolate flames around the cookie. Garnish the plate with apricot and raspberry sauces in a flame motif.

CHOCOLATE RASPBERRY CAKE

EN-MING HSU

Assistant Pastry Chef, *Ritz-Carlton Hotel, Chicago.*

"I was trying to do something classic—chocolate and raspberry, which we know go well together—with some crunch and smooth elements," says En-Ming Hsu. The chocolate cream that encases the sablée and raspberries is not quite a mousse and not quite a ganache—based on an anglaise, it has a very silky, custard-like texture. Chocolate apricot glaze covers all, and the raspberries used as garnish are filled with mascarpone.

YIELD: 12 SERVINGS

Special Equipment:
Twelve ring molds, 2.3" (6 cm) diameter x 1.6" (4 cm) high
Two 9" (22.8 cm) cake rings

VANILLA SABLÉE			
2.2 oz	65 g	*unsalted butter*
1.1 oz	30 g	*confectioners' sugar*
2	2	*large egg yolks, hard boiled*
1	1	*vanilla bean, split and scraped*
3 oz	85 g	*cake flour*
1/8 tsp	.5 g	*baking powder*

1. Preheat oven to 325°F (165°C). In a mixer fitted with a paddle attachment, beat the butter and sugar untl light and fluffy. Pass the egg yolks through a tamis and add it to the butter along with the vanilla bean seeds. Sift together the flour and baking powder and add it to the mixture. Mix just until incorporated. Form the dough into a disc, wrap it in plastic, and refrigerate overnight.

2. On a lightly floured surface roll the dough to a 1/8" (3 mm) thickness. Dock and cut the dough into 2" (5 cm) rounds. Place on a parchment-lined sheet pan and bake for 15 to 20 minutes or until pale golden in color. Cool completely.

CHOCOLATE CREAM			
14 liq oz	400 ml	*heavy cream*
14 liq oz	400 ml	*whole milk*
5.3 oz	150 g	*granulated sugar, divided*
4.6 oz	130 g	*egg yolks*
19.8 oz	560 g	*Valrhona Pur Caraibe chocolate, chopped*

1. In a saucepan combine the cream, milk, and 2.7 oz (75 g) of the sugar and bring to a boil. Whisk together the egg yolks with the remaining 2.7 oz (75 g) of the sugar. Temper the yolks into the milk mixture and cook gently, stirring, until the mixture coats the back of a wooden spoon.

2. Strain the cream into a bowl containing the chopped chocolate. Whisk until the chocolate is completely melted and incorporated with the cream. Cover the surface with plastic wrap and chill until it is firm enough to pipe.

CHOCOLATE SOUFFLÉ BISCUIT			
3.5 oz	100 g	Valrhona Pur Caraibe chocolate
.9 oz	25 g	cocoa paste
6.3 oz	180 g	egg yolks
5.5 oz	155 g	granulated sugar, divided
8 oz	225 g	egg whites

1. Preheat oven to 350°F (175°C). Melt the chocolate and cocoa paste together over a double boiler. Keep the melted chocolate in a warm spot to hold it at about 110°F (43°C).

2. In a mixer, whip the egg yolks with 2 oz (55 g) of the sugar until very light and pale. Whip the egg whites with the remaining 3.5 oz (100 g) of sugar to a stiff meringue. Fold the melted chocolate into the yolks, then fold in the meringue. Evenly divide the batter into two 9" (22.8 cm) cake rings on a parchment-lined sheet pan. Bake for 15 to 20 minutes or until a cake tester comes out clean. Cool completely and freeze until firm enough to cut.

MIRROR GLAZE			
13.5 liq oz	400 ml	heavy cream
16.2 oz	460 g	Valrhona Pur Caraibe chocolate, chopped
1.6 oz	45 g	unsalted butter, softened
3.2 oz	90 g	corn syrup

1. In a saucepan bring the cream to a boil and pour it into a bowl containing the chocolate. Whisk until the chocolate is thoroughly dissolved and let it cool to room temperature.

2. Whisk in the butter and corn syrup until fully incorporated.

RASPBERRY FILLING			
1 pt	1 pt	fresh raspberries
1 liq oz	30 ml	raspberry purée, 10% sugar
1 liq oz	30 ml	simple syrup
		Lemon juice to taste

Combine all the ingredients, tossing gently, so as not to damage the raspberries. Add a few drops of lemon juice if desired.

RASPBERRY COULIS			
8 oz	227 g	fresh ripe raspberries
1 oz	28 g	granulated sugar
2 oz	57 g	dextrose

Combine all ingredients in a food processor and purée. Pass the mixture through a chinois.

ASSEMBLY

Fresh raspberries
Mascarpone
Bubble sugar
Pulled-sugar rods

1. Place the ring molds on a plastic- or parchment-lined sheet pan. Pipe in a layer of chocolate cream until the molds are half full. Place a small amount of the raspberry filling (about 6 raspberries) in the center and press gently into the cream. Cut the biscuit into 1.75" (4.5 cm) rounds and place a circle on top of the berries. Pipe chocolate cream around the biscuit to fill in the sides. Press a sablée round on top. Clean the edges of the mold and freeze until firm, at least 45 minutes.

2. Unmold the cakes by warming the sides with your hands or a warm damp towel and pushing on the sablée. Place the cakes with the sablée on the bottom on a dipping screen on top of a sheet pan. Refrigerate.

3. Heat the mirror glaze over a double boiler until it reaches a pourable consistency. Pour the glaze over the cakes. Refrigerate until set.

4. Place each cake on a dessert plate and garnish the plate with a mascarpone-filled raspberry, bubble sugar, and a pulled-sugar rod. Serve with raspberry coulis on the side.

VANILLA SALAD

THADDEUS DUBOIS

Pastry Chef, *Duquesne Club,*
Pittsburgh, Pennsylvania.

A modern presentation—this is what Thaddeus Dubois was targeting with his dessert salad. "I thought about tossing green salads—you toss it, it's composed. I like the looseness of it," he says, noting that so many desserts are "cold, contrived . . . with all that tight piping. I tend to lean the other way." In a citrus orange sauce are tangerine-lemongrass sorbet, chocolate ice cream, and raspberry-mascarpone ice cream, topped with a tuile, which has been tossed in the chef's hands, right out of the oven. "A refreshing, light experience," says the chef.

YIELD: 16 SERVINGS

RASPBERRY-MASCARPONE ICE CREAM			
1 pt, 8 liq oz	710 ml	milk, divided
8 liq oz	237 ml	heavy cream
1	1	Tahitian vanilla bean, split and scraped
2.6 oz	74 g	egg yolks
4 oz	113 g	granulated sugar
1 lb	454 g	mascarpone cheese
8 oz	227 g	trimoline (invert sugar)
18 oz	510 g	Boiron raspberry purée
2 liq oz	59 ml	raspberry liqueur

1. In a saucepan, combine 8 liq oz (237 ml) of the milk with the heavy cream and vanilla bean seeds. Bring to a gentle boil. Remove from the heat.

2. In a bowl, whisk together the yolks and sugar until thick and light, 3 to 4 minutes, then stir in the hot milk.

3. Return the custard to the saucepan and heat gently. Stir constantly until the custard thickens slightly. Cool the mixture and chill for several hours.

4. In a bowl, whisk together the remaining 1 pt (473 ml) of milk and the mascarpone cheese until smooth. Whisk in the trimoline, raspberry purée, raspberry liqueur, and chilled crème anglaise. Chill for several hours.

5. Process the mixture in an ice cream maker according to the manufacturer's instructions.

CHOCOLATE ICE CREAM

54 liq oz	1.6 lt	milk
1 liq oz	30 ml	heavy cream
6.5 oz	184 g	granulated sugar, divided
3 oz	85 g	trimoline
3 oz	85 g	nonfat milk powder
12 oz	340 g	Valrhona Caraque bittersweet chocolate
3 oz	85 g	Valrhona cocoa paste
3 oz	85 g	egg yolks
1 tsp	5 g	Sevarome ice cream stabilizer

1. In a saucepan, combine the milk, heavy cream, 6 oz (170 g) of the sugar, trimoline, and milk powder; cook over medium heat, just until warm.

2. Meanwhile, melt the bittersweet chocolate and cocoa paste separately and then whisk together.

3. Add some of the warm milk mixture to the chocolate mixture and whisk until smooth. Add this mixture to the remaining milk mixture and whisk to combine.

4. In a bowl, whisk together the yolks, ice cream stabilizer, and the remaining .5 oz (14 g) of sugar; add this to the chocolate mixture. Stirring constantly with a rubber spatula, cook to 185°F (85°C). Strain the mixture and cool over an ice bath to 40°F (4°C). Cover the mixture and chill overnight, to allow the flavors to mature.

5. Process the mixture in an ice cream machine according to the manufacturer's instructions.

TANGERINE-LEMONGRASS
SORBET

1 pt	473 ml	simple syrup (60%)
2 stalks	2 stalks	lemongrass, chopped
48 liq oz	1.4 lt	tangerine juice
2 tsp	10 g	sorbet stabilizer
1 oz	28 g	granulated sugar

1. In a saucepan, combine the simple syrup and lemongrass. Bring the mixture to a boil, remove from the heat, cover, and allow to infuse for 2 hours. Strain and chill for several hours.

2. Combine the syrup and the tangerine juice. In a separate bowl, combine the sorbet stabilizer and the sugar. Add this to the syrup mixture and whisk until well combined. Process the mixture in an ice cream machine according to the manufacturer's instructions.

CITRUS SAUCE

32 liq oz	946 ml	fresh orange juice, strained
6 oz	170 g	orange blossom honey
6 oz	170 g	granulated sugar
2 Tbs	30 ml	cold water
2 tsp	10 g	arrowroot
2 liq oz	59 ml	Grand Marnier liqueur

1. In a saucepan, combine the orange juice, honey, and sugar; bring mixture to just under a boil. Remove from the heat.

2. In a small container, combine the water and arrowroot. Add the mixture to the saucepan; and cook until just slightly thickened. Stir in the liqueur. Strain the sauce and chill.

VANILLA SALAD

1 lb 3 oz	539 g	granulated sugar
1 lb 3 oz	539 g	bread flour
4	4	Tahitian vanilla beans, split and scraped
1 lb 3 oz	539 g	unsalted butter
12 oz	340 g	egg whites, warmed slightly

1. In a bowl, combine the sugar and the flour.

2. In a mixer fitted with the paddle attachment, combine the vanilla bean seeds and butter; mix until well blended. Pass the butter through a fine sieve and melt.

3. Whisk the egg whites into sugar-flour mixture. Whisk in the melted butter. Pour the mixture into plastic squeeze bottles and chill for several hours.

4. Line a sheet pan with a silicone baking mat and preheat the oven to 350°F (175°C). Pipe the batter onto the baking mat in four spiral patterns. Pipe the spirals from the center out, leaving about 1/2" (1.27 cm) between each line. Bake until golden brown, about 8 minutes. Remove the pan from the oven and quickly but gently pull each spiral off the mat and toss it in your hands until a round ball or "salad" has formed. Place in a tightly covered container that has a drying agent in it (such as limestone). Repeat with the remaining batter to form a total of 16 "salads."

ASSEMBLY

Confectioners' sugar
Assorted diced tropical fruit
Assorted berries
Edible flower petals
Chocolate spiral garnish

1. Place a scoop of the chocolate ice cream, raspberry-mascarpone ice cream, and tangerine-lemongrass sorbet in a triangular pattern in the center of a dessert plate. Thinly cover the rest of the plate with the citrus sauce.

2. Gently place a vanilla salad round on top of the scoops. Dust the salad with confectioners' sugar.

3. Garnish the sauce with a mixture of diced tropical fruits, berries, and edible flower petals. Finish the plate with a chocolate spiral.

BLACKBERRY—RASPBERRY "SODA"

ERIC PEREZ

Executive Pastry Chef, *Ritz-Carlton, Tyson's Corners, Virginia.*

Chef Perez has devised a sleek, attention-getting way to present sorbets: a blackberry tuile encloses lemon sherbet and raspberry sorbet. The cone is served with berries, blackberry pâte de fruit, a blown sugar ball, and bubble sugar. The base of the cone is chocolate. With the dominant flavors of blackberry, raspberry, and lemon, this is a very tart but palate-pleasing dessert.

YIELD: 20 SERVINGS

BLACKBERRY PÂTE DE FRUIT			
.5 oz	14 g	pectin
30 oz	851 g	granulated sugar, divided
26.5 oz	751 g	blackberry purée
6.5 oz	184 g	glucose
.5 oz	14 g	citric acid

1. In a saucepan combine the pectin with 2.5 oz (71 g) of the sugar. Stir in the purée and bring the mixture to a boil. Add the remaining 27.5 oz (780 g) of the sugar and the glucose and cook to 221°F (105°C).

2. Remove the pan from the heat, add the citric acid, and pour onto a half-sheet pan lined with aluminum foil. Let cool completely and cut into 1" (2.5 cm) squares. Coat each square with granulated sugar.

BLACKBERRY TUILE			
28 oz	794 g	granulated sugar
7 oz	198 g	all-purpose flour, sifted
4 liq oz	118 ml	orange juice
5 oz	142 g	blackberry purée
10 oz	284 g	unsalted butter, melted

1. Preheat oven to 375°F (190°C). Place a sheet pan in the oven to warm. Combine the sugar and flour. Add the orange juice and purée. Mix in the melted butter.

2. Drop the batter onto a silicone baking mat using a 1.5 oz (44 ml) scoop as a measure. Spread the batter into a thin circle with an offset spatula. Transfer the baking mat to the warm sheet pan and return it to the oven. Bake for 8 to 10 minutes or just until the edges turn golden. Immediately flip each tuile over and roll it around a cone. Let set.

LEMON SHERBET			
1 qt	946 ml	whole milk
12 oz	340 g	granulated sugar
5	5	lemons, zest and juice

1. In a saucepan combine the milk, sugar, and lemon zest and bring the mixture to a boil. Strain it through a chinois over an ice bath and cool completely.

2. Process the sherbet base in an ice cream machine. Add the lemon juice while the machine is running.

RASPBERRY SORBET	6 oz	170 g	granulated sugar
	.75 tsp	2.5 g	sorbet stabilizer
	4 liq oz	118 ml	water
	3 oz	85 g	glucose
	1 qt	946 ml	raspberry purée

1. In a saucepan combine the sugar and stabilizer. Add the water and glucose and bring the mixture to a boil. Cool completely and refrigerate overnight.

2. Combine the syrup with the raspberry purée. Process in an ice cream machine according to the manufacturer's instructions.

CHOCOLATE CYLINDERS AND BASES	8 oz	227 g	cocoa butter
	A few drops		Chefmaster oil-based purple coloring
	1 lb	454 g	white chocolate, tempered

1. Melt the cocoa butter and add purple coloring to desired color. When the cocoa butter has cooled and thickened a bit (it may be necessary to temper it for a few seconds on a marble slab), spread it thinly on acetate right triangles 7" (17.8 cm) long x 1" (2.5 cm) high and acetate circles 3.5" (8.9 cm) in diameter. Let set completely.

2. Spread the white chocolate over the cocoa butter.

3. To make the cylinders, twist the acetate around a 2" (5 cm) diameter PVC pipe. Let set completely. For the bases, let the chocolate set and remove the acetate.

CHOCOLATE STRAWS	1 lb	454 g	cocoa butter
	A few drops		Chefmaster oil-based purple coloring
	1 lb	454 g	white chocolate, tempered

1. Melt the cocoa butter and add purple coloring to desired color. When the cocoa butter has cooled and thickened a bit (it may be necessary to temper it for a few seconds on a marble slab), spread it thinly on marble and drag a fine-tooth comb through it. Let set.

2. Spread a thin coat of white chocolate over the cocoa butter. When the chocolate has just started to set, use the metal blade of a bench scraper to form tight cigarettes.

ASSEMBLY	Bubble sugar
	Pulled-sugar straws
	Mint sprigs
	Assorted fresh berries

1. Heat the narrow end of each tuile cone with a torch to melt it slightly. Attach it to a chocolate base and let set completely.

2. Place a scoop of lemon sherbet in each cone and top it with a scoop of raspberry sorbet. Place a piece of bubble sugar in the sorbet. Add a chocolate straw, pulled-sugar straw, and mint sprig to each cone.

3. Place a chocolate cylinder on the plate and fill it with fresh berries. Add two pâte de fruit squares and a blown-sugar ball to each plate.

Making the chocolate cylinders (see above).

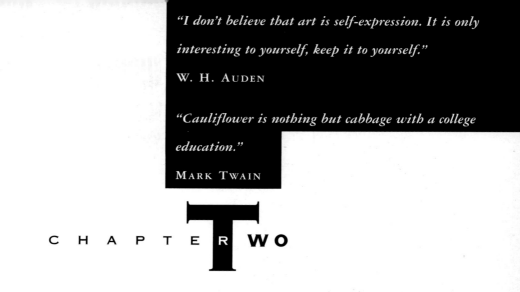

CHAPTER **T** WO

MODERNIZING THE CLASSICS

D. JEMAL EDWARDS

Pastry Chef
SoHo Sushi, New York.

BORN: September 1966,
Ankara, Turkey.
TRAINING/EXPERIENCE: Mirador
and the Cypress Club, Chicago;
Elka and Liberté, San Francisco;
Montrachet, Nobu, and
Maxim's, New York.

*"I'm really dedicated to what I'm
doing. It's basically 95 percent of
my life. That's a bad balance, I
know, to have that much of your life
be your job or your career. Perhaps
time spent doing other things could
be fulfilling as well. There are
other things I would like to do, but
can't. I'm doing what I need to be
doing right now. Maybe in five
years I'll rethink my priorities and
perspectives, but right now my prior-
ity is my career."*

KRISTA KERN

Pastry Chef, *Three Fish, Westerly,
Rhode Island.*

BORN: November 1966,
Toronto, Canada.
TRAINING/EXPERIENCE: The
Elms, Maine; Symphony Cafe,
New York; Bang, Greenwich,
Connecticut; Sullivan's, New
York.

*"I love intricate plates. I love play-
ing and making pastry fun. I'm
always thinking about it. Elizabeth
DeFranco, who was the chef at the
Elms, taught me to respect the ingredients I'm working with, and that
everything you work with and
everything you do is important. You
never take shortcuts. It's always better in the long run to do it correctly.
It's more of a feeling than a set of
rules she imparted to me, but wher-
ever I go, it's always with me."*

"In France they have a tendency to stick to the rules too
much," observes Jacquy Pfeiffer of Ecole de Patisserie
Francaise School in Chicago. "If you are overcreative, you'll
get hit over the head by the old-timers. In America it is the
opposite. You have maybe too many people creating too
many things and forgetting the basics. But it's good to be
creative. Even if there are nine bad ideas and one good, still
that's one good idea."

It's an age-old tension, often characterized as the familiar,
staid grandeur of classic works versus the passionate experimentation of the romantic. The Modernist movement in
the arts, as we have seen, was all about toppling rules, out-
raging conservative sensibilities, venturing into the new.

So how does that translate into the pastry kitchen? Are
there rules when it comes to creating quality pastry? If so,
what are they? Who can successfully break the rules—old
masters, confident in their abilities, or brash youngbloods,
disdainful of all rules?

There is one rule that is often cited by pastry chefs as a
viable, common-sense rule: the Three-Flavor Rule. "Some
chefs play so much that the flavors get muddled. It gets too
bizarre," says En-Ming Hsu of the Ritz-Carlton Chicago.
"Stick to three flavors. Classic combinations. You always
know what works from the basics. It's fairly foolproof."

"There are rules," admits Martin Howard, that perennial
rule-breaker from Rainbow! in New York. "There are some
that can be broken and some that can't. There are certain
leavening techniques, other elements of the science of baking, that you cannot fool with."

But many of the rules of classic French training, which
have solid historical footing, may not pertain anymore.
"Because there was no refrigeration, they were limited as to
what they could prepare and preserve," Richard Ruskell,
pastry chef at the Phoenician in Phoenix, points out. "Hence you had a lot of things with
marzipan because they were sitting out a long time. So there were rules."

That having been said, however, both Ruskell and Howard assert that there *are* no rules:
"A lot of people don't want you to mess with the classics," says Howard, "but I believe that
if you can make it better or more interesting, why not?" After further thought, Howard
admits that he has one unshakable dessert rule: "Bigger is better."

"The only rule is your taste," says Ruskell. "Taste in a five senses sort of way, and taste in
your sense of visual appeal."

Other chefs disagree, and with glee: "There are no rules, no boundaries," says Thomas
Worhach of the Ocean Grand in Palm Beach, "and I think it's exciting, it's fun. Everyone
has their own style. Some people will say that it should be this way or that way, but you
can't speak for all the guests who come into your restaurant. All these people have different tastes also."

"I can't think of any rules," says Wayne Brachman of Mesa Grill in New York. "There are preferences, styles. I don't like to place things very specifically. I like to place things in haphazard ways, but that's not a rule. There is practical advice. For example, I've worked with people who need to hear: don't put sauce on the center of the plate if you're going to put a piece of cake on it. If you're a putz, you need that rule."

"There are no rules," agrees Philippe Laurier of Patisfrance. "If the balance is right, and the basic dessert is good, why not? Anything goes."

A sentiment only a Modernist could love—anything goes. But in the fine arts, there was an inevitable backlash to Modernism's freewheeling destruction of centuries of classic aesthetics. One of the most thoughtful essays in reaction to Modernism was written in 1984 by Suzi Gablik. In "Has Modernism Failed?" she points out that the "steady violation of expected continuities . . . is radically at odds with systemic wisdom and equilibrium.

So many metamorphoses and revolutions ...so many different values presented simultaneously, have finally done away with the frame of things—and destroyed any conviction that there are any limits to art at all..." Gablik writes. "Having removed any standards...we no longer know what rules we ought to follow, much less why we ought to follow them.... Only with hindsight can we now see that tradition and authority may be necessary, even to make a genuine avant garde possible, in order to provide something to revolt against."

Gablik cites a law of history that Heraclitus called enantiodromia: when one principle reaches the height of its power, it collapses into its opposite. "Artists are finding that the only way to make something new is to borrow from the past," writes Gablik. Modernism's "renunciations of so much that is crucial to human well-being—in the name of freedom and self-sufficiency—are what will have failed us."

So it is interesting that so many chefs in this book express the hope, as delineated in Chapter 1, that "Modernism" may mean a return to pure flavors, to simplicity. Enantiodromia anyone?

"It's important for a pastry chef to have a solid grounding in the basics," says Donald Wressell of the Four Seasons Beverly Hills, echoing what many other chefs in this volume stated. "Once you have that, it's okay to venture off and break the rules. I tend to assign new people to make cookies, cakes, chocolate mousse, ice cream bases, syrup, lemon curd, pastry cream. Once they master that, they can become part of the group that generates ideas."

"When you work with a lot of people, have them under your tutelage," says Stanton Ho of the Las Vegas Hilton, "you find that some break away and experiment on their own, which is okay. I encourage them to do that. But most come full circle. They come around to my way of doing things."

Throughout this book, of course, classic recipes are being exploited, as they are everywhere, every day. But with the desserts in this chapter the chefs have deliberately taken the major components of classic recipes and, by tinkering with the presentation, arrived at something new. Or, in some cases, they have taken major liberties with the classic recipe itself. They vividly demonstrate how imagination, daring, and affection can combine to create something new from the tried (sometimes trite) and true.

For her Rhubarb Strawberry Strudel, Krista Kern takes the classic strudel and shapes it vertically, using phyllo, which is an acceptable, fairly common substitute for traditional strudel dough. She only tinkers with the classic formula by providing some four garnishes, rather than the classic dollop of ice cream. Michael Hu lightens the classic Mont Blanc,

MARSHALL ROSENTHAL

Executive Pastry Chef
Trump Taj Mahal Hotel and Casino, Atlantic City, New Jersey.

BORN: September 1959, Baltimore, Maryland.
TRAINING/EXPERIENCE: various patisseries and bakeries, Baltimore area; Hyatt Hotels; Royal Sonesta, Boston; Renaissance Harborplace Hotel, Baltimore.

"Constantly steer your boat into the wind. Go for the challenge. From year to year I don't know what's next, but I know there will always be new challenges. You have to run your daily operation, but you also have to keep up with the profession—read, go to seminars and competitions, and always, always remain hands-on. There are times when I wonder, why am I trying so hard? But if you collect a check, you're accountable. As one of my mentors used to say to us: 'Shut up and work.'"

PHILIPPE LAURIER

Executive Pastry Chef
Patisfrance USA,
East Rutherford, New Jersey.

BORN: August 1941, Paris,
France.
TRAINING/EXPERIENCE:
apprenticeship, St. Horer, Paris;
La Grenouille, Tavern on the
Green, New York; Fairfax
College, Virginia; Culinary Art
Institute, Washington, D.C.

*"I have dedicated all of my life to
teaching, and to bringing this profession to where it is today. In the
last ten years, it has grown in this
country, and it is now recognized. I
love this profession because everything is a challenge to the pastry
chef. You must constantly create and
come up with something no one has
seen before. I never follow a recipe;
I'm a very bad chef for that. I use a
recipe as a starting point, and
always add my own touch."*

PASCAL JANVIER

Pastry Chef, Instructor,
Technical Manager
Barry Callebaut Training Center,
Pennsauken, New Jersey.

BORN: November 1962,
Villaines la Juhel, France.
TRAINING/EXPERIENCE:
preapprenticeship, apprenticeship, master's degree; various
pastry shops, including Mellot
and Clamart, near Paris.

*"For me, happiness is in making
good products. We are better off taking our time, making good food
with good ingredients, than rushing
it with inferior ingredients. Use
quality ingredients and you will
have quality results. I'm happier
making five bucks on something
that looks good, than ten on something that does not. There are no
shortcuts in learning, no shortcuts
in product, no shortcuts in time. It's
a job, not a hobby."*

using mousse rather than chestnut purée. He then gives it a further Modernist spin with candied chestnuts, a spiral of white chocolate, and a vivid chocolate fence. With his Warm Raspberry Pudding with Sour Cream Terrine, Richard Leach takes us on a fanciful detour around a classic raspberry tart—using pâte sucrée rather than a tart shell, and crème frâiche rather than pastry cream or frangipane. Leach then takes the term "pudding" and runs with it, creating a hybrid of bread pudding and traditional, creamy pudding and submerging it in a deep pool of sauce with a spun-sugar silo containing fruit and a scoop of sorbet. With his Lemon Parallax, Jemal Edwards has fun with the frozen soufflé normally prepared in a ramekin. This soufflé is formed by Edwards into a cone with a pistachio and praline paste core buried in its cold, cold heart. Edwards also re-imagines the classic charlotte with his Banana Star-lotte: an individual serving, rather than a charlotte served in a large bowl, using joconde and mousse rather than sponge and Bavarian. Stanton Ho takes liberties with the opera, using mousse rather than buttercream, and serving an undersized slice so that he can accompany it with a chocolate tower filled with caramel mousse, a creamy, flavorful counterpoint to the coffee-tinged opera. Angel food cake is served in a big, raggedy slice—ask anyone who ever had a childhood. Krista Kern transforms that inelegant slice and creates a richer dessert experience, making an individual serving in a mini-angel-food cake pan and placing a white chocolate parfait in its center, topped with a truffle. Donald Wressell reconfigures tarte Tatin with his Caramelized Braeburn Apples. Normally a tarte Tatin employs puff pastry or pâte brisée, and fruit and pastry are baked together. Wressell uses date crisps and cooks this "pastry" separately from the apples and combines the two elements later. It is like a naked tarte; its beautiful fruity works exposed.

Classic visual compositions arise from this classic-smashing exercise. The dramatic chocolate Lace Wave seems as if it will engulf the apple cinnamon mousse and cake; the serene color scheme hints at peace before the storm. Marshall Rosenthal's bread pudding is framed in a wicker-like cookie form, as if it is sitting grandly in a chair, King of the Caribbean. Michael Hu's Mont Blanc is a pleasingly chaotic concoction of whipped cream, mousse, nuts, etc., but the chaos is well contained in a chocolate fence. If you examine Jemal Edwards's Banana Star-lotte, you will find many stars—in the joconde, in the chocolate—and then you discover that the entire plate is one large starburst. "Parallax" is a term from astronomy, and deals with the apparently different displacement or direction of an object when viewed from various points of view. There is much illusion involved in Edwards's celestial Lemon Parallax, with the chocolate rings at odd angles and the star cookie and its precarious perch, the blown sugar sphere; adding to the disorientation is the mad-as-a-hatter sauce display on a plate sprayed with dark chocolate, simulating a dark sky. Stanton Ho's classic slice of opera cake is all but invisible under the triangular tower with its dramatic white chocoolate shelves and the soaring, luxuriant sugar whorl; triangular forms abound on the plate.

Breaking the rules, but all in the spirit of good cooking; that's what our Modernists are up to. They do it because the buying public is in a mood to break rules, try something new. "Talk about breaking a rule," says Thaddeus Dubois of the Duquesne Club in Pittsburgh. "I made a dessert called Lemon Tower. It was a five-inch-high tower of lemon mousse, very tart, with tart lemon cake. It was served with a tart raspberry sauce. All of it was tart, but it was the consistent top seller for two months."

In this light, breaking the rules, or finding an individual stamp in the pastry kitchen, is the only way to remain vital, creative—and employed. "You have to be willing to try new things," insists Dubois. "I see people who are stagnant, who do the same things over and over. I don't care if you're 20 or you're 50, if you're doing the same things that you've done five years in a row, you need to change things. It doesn't have to be modern. You just need to show that you're thinking, that you're using the new technologies and techniques."

LEMON PARALLAX

D. JEMAL EDWARDS

Pastry Chef, *SoHo Sushi, New York.*

Jemal Edwards further modernizes a thoroughly modern dessert—the frozen soufflé—with this cone form. Inside this tangy frozen soufflé is a core of crunchy pistachio and praline paste. Green-colored white chocolate is then drizzled on the cone, and around the cone is a puddle of pistachio anglaise and raspberry coulis.

YIELD: 23 SERVINGS

Special Equipment: Wagner airless paint sprayer

CRUNCHY PISTACHIO CORE			
1 lb	454 g	hazelnut praline paste
6 oz	170 g	Delipaste ground pistachio paste
12 oz	340 g	chopped Sicilian pistachios
12 oz	340 g	paillete feuilletine

1. Using a rubber spatula, combine the praline and pistachio paste together until smooth. Fold in the chopped pistachios and the paillete feuilletine. Freeze the mixture for at least 1 hour.

2. Scoop 1" (2.5 cm) balls from the mixture and put the balls into the freezer.

FROZEN LEMON SOUFFLÉ			
.26 oz	7.5 g	gelatin leaves
16 liq oz	473 ml	lemon juice
18.75 oz	531 g	granulated sugar, divided
9.75 oz	276 g	egg yolks
12 liq oz	355 ml	heavy cream, whipped to firm peaks
12.6 oz	357 g	egg whites
6 oz	170 g	white chocolate, melted
as needed	as needed	green food-coloring paste

1. Soak the gelatin in cold water and squeeze dry.

2. In a bowl, combine the lemon juice and 15.75 oz (446 g) of the sugar and place the bowl over a pot of simmering water, stirring until the sugar is dissolved. Whisk in the egg yolks and continue to cook over the water bath, stirring constantly, until the mixture thickens and resembles lemon curd. Remove the bowl from the water bath and stir in the drained gelatin leaves.

3. Pass the mixture though a fine chinois and chill thoroughly.

Dessert shown on page 46.

4. Stir the lemon mixture with a rubber spatula until smooth. Fold in the whipped cream.

5. In a mixer fitted with a whisk attachment, beat the egg whites with the remaining 3 oz (85 g) of sugar until stiff peaks form. Fold into the lemon mixture.

6. Using parchment paper, form 10 cones, each 4 1/2" (11.4 cm) high and 2 1/2" (6.3 cm) in diameter.

7. Turn an empty milk crate upside down on a work surface. Place 10 metal cream horn molds into the holes in the milk crate. Place the parchment cones into the metal molds.

8. Place the melted white chocolate in a small bowl. Whisk in the food-coloring paste until it becomes a light mint-green color. Pour some of the chocolate into a small parchment cone. Pipe swirls of chocolate in a random pattern into the cones. Refrigerate the cones until the chocolate is set.

9. Scrape the soufflé mixture into a pastry bag fitted with a medium plain tip. Pipe the soufflé mixture into the parchment cones, filling them halfway. Place a pistachio core into each cone. Fill each cone with the remaining soufflé mixture. Freeze the soufflés overnight.

PISTACHIO ANGLAISE			
	16 liq oz	473 ml	milk
	16 liq oz	473 ml	heavy cream
	4 oz	113 g	granulated sugar
	5.2 oz	147 g	egg yolks
	5.4 oz	153 g	Delipaste ground pistachio paste

1. In a saucepan, combine the milk, cream, and sugar. Cook until simmering. Remove from the heat.

2. Whisk the yolks in a bowl and add some of the hot milk mixture to temper the yolks. Return the entire mixture to the saucepan. Cook over medium heat, stirring constantly with a wooden spoon, until the custard thickens slightly. Pass sauce through a fine chinois into a bowl. Whisk in the pistachio paste. Chill the sauce over an ice bath.

RASPBERRY COULIS			
	8 liq oz	237 ml	fresh raspberry purée
	3.5 oz	99 g	granulated sugar

In a saucepan, combine the purée and sugar and cook over medium heat, stirring constantly, until the sugar is dissolved. Pass the sauce through a fine chinois and chill thoroughly.

STAR TUILES			
	8 oz	227 g	unsalted butter
	5.8 oz	167 g	honey
	8 oz	227 g	confectioners' sugar
	8.4 oz	239 g	egg whites
	10 oz	283 g	all-purpose flour

1. In a saucepan, over medium heat, cook the butter and honey together until melted.

2. In a mixer fitted with the whisk attachment, blend the confectioners' sugar at low speed; gradually add the butter and honey mixture and mix until combined. Add the egg whites and mix until combined. Add the flour and mix just until combined.

3. Cut a star stencil (3"/7.6 cm wide) out of heavy plastic (see photo, page 46).

4. Line a sheet pan with a silicone baking mat and preheat oven to 325°F (165°C). Using a small offset metal spatula, spread the tuile batter over the stencil, onto the baking mat. Repeat until the sheet pan is full. Bake the tuiles until golden brown, about 8 minutes. Store the stars in an airtight container.

SPRAY COATING FOR PLATES			
1 lb	*454 g*	*Guayaquil chocolate, chopped*
1 lb	*454 g*	*cocoa butter, chopped*
as needed	*as needed*	*black food-coloring paste*

1. Place plain dessert plates in the freezer. Melt the chocolate and cocoa butter in a bowl over simmering water. Using a toothpick, add enough of the black food coloring to turn the mixture a charcoal color.

2. Transfer the mixture to a Wagner airless spray gun. Spray the plates with the mixture so that they are evenly coated. Allow the plates to dry completely.

> *Chef Edwards has sprayed this plate with melted Guayaquil (from Cocoa Barry), which was tinted with black food coloring. This ensures that the sauce will bead when drizzled on the plate.*

WHITE CHOCOLATE ORBITS

1 lb	*454 g*	*white chocolate, tempered*

1. Spread the white chocolate thinly and evenly over a large sheet of acetate. Allow it to set slightly.

2. Using 3" (7.6 cm), 2" (5 cm), and 1 1/2" (3.8 cm) oval cutters, cut at least 23 ovals of each size out of the chocolate. Use the 2" oval to cut out the centers of the 3" ovals, the 1 1/2" oval to cut out the centers of the 2" ovals, and a 1" oval to cut out the centers of the 1 1/2" ovals. Allow the chocolate to set completely, then peel the orbits off the acetate and set aside for garnish.

ASSEMBLY

Chopped Sicilian pistachio nuts, toasted
Blown-sugar ball

1. Unwrap the parchment cones from the frozen soufflés. Cut the bottom of the cones with a chef's knife, if necessary, so that the cones stand up straight. Place a cone onto one of the sprayed dessert plates. Place 3 orbit rings of each size over the cone, as in the photograph. Stick a tuile star into the cone.

2. Garnish the plate with the pistachio anglaise, raspberry coulis, chopped pistachio nuts, and a blown-sugar ball.

BANANA STAR-LOTTE

D. JEMAL EDWARDS

Pastry Chef, *SoHo Sushi, New York.*

Chocolate and banana is a favorite flavor combination of pastry chef D. Jemal Edwards, and he uses it to pay a faint hommage to the classic French charlotte. Here, a printed joconde dome (rather than the classic charlotte mold) is filled with white chocolate banana mousse, crunchy praline, and pecan cake. It is accompanied by praline rum sauce, chocolate sauce, and mango. The dome is crowned with dried banana chips.

YIELD: 24 SERVINGS

Special Equipment: Twenty-four Flexipan 4 oz (118 ml) dome molds

PÂTE CORNET			
14 oz	*397 g*	*unsalted butter, divided*
14 oz	*397 g*	*confectioners' sugar, divided*
14 oz	*397 g*	*egg whites, divided*
14 oz	*397 g*	*all-purpose flour, divided*
1.6 oz	*47 g*	*unsweetened cocoa powder, sifted*
as needed	*as needed*	*yellow food coloring as needed*

Cocoa Pâte

1. In a mixer fitted with the paddle attachment, cream together 7 oz (198 g) of the butter and 7 oz (198 g) of the confectioners' sugar. Blend in 7 oz (198 g) of the egg whites. Blend in the flour and the cocoa powder; set aside.

2. Line a baking sheet with a silicone baking mat. Cover the mat with a star stencil. Spread a thin, even layer of the cocoa pâte over the stencil. Remove the stencil and freeze the pâte-covered sheet for about 1 hour.

Yellow Pâte

1. In a mixer fitted with the paddle attachment, cream together the remaining 7 oz (198 g) of the butter and the remaining 7 oz (198 g) of the confectioners' sugar. Blend in the remaining 7 oz (198 g) of the egg whites. Blend in the remaining 7 oz (198 g) of flour and enough yellow food coloring to make it an egg yolk hue.

2. Line a baking sheet with a silicone baking mat. Cover the mat with a star stencil. Spread a thin, even layer of the yellow pâte over the stencil. Remove the stencil and freeze the pâte-covered sheet for about 1 hour.

JOCONDE

13.25 oz	*376 g*	*confectioners' sugar*
3.5 oz	*99 g*	*cake flour*
4 oz	*113 g*	*unsweetened cocoa powder*
13.25 oz	*376 g*	*almond flour*
17.5 oz	*496 g*	*whole eggs*
2.75 oz	*78 g*	*unsalted butter, melted*
11.5 oz	*326 g*	*egg whites*
1.75 oz	*50 g*	*granulated sugar*
as needed	*as needed*	*yellow food coloring as needed*

COCOA JOCONDE

1. Preheat oven to 375°F (130°C). In a bowl, sift together 6.6 oz (188 g) of the confectioners' sugar, 1.75 oz (50 g) of the cake flour, and the cocoa powder. Whisk in 6.6 oz (188 g) of the almond flour.

2. In a mixer with the paddle attachment, beat together 8.75 oz (248 g) of the eggs and 1.4 oz (39 g) of the butter at medium speed until combined. At low speed, add the dry ingredients and mix until combined.

3. In a mixer with the whisk attachment, beat 5.75 oz (163 g) of the egg whites with .87 oz (25 g) of the sugar to stiff peaks. Fold the egg whites into the batter. Spread the cocoa batter evenly over the yellow stenciled stars (it will be a thin layer). Bake for 6 to 8 minutes, until set. While still hot, flip the cake over and peel off the silicone baking mat. Cool completely.

4. Using the 2 3/4" (6.9 cm) triangle template, cut the cake into 48 triangles.

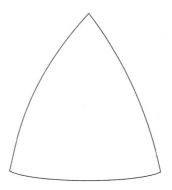

YELLOW JOCONDE

1. In a bowl, sift together the remaining 6.6 oz (188 g) of confectioners' sugar and the remaining 1.75 oz (50 g) of the cake flour. Whisk in the remaining 6.6 oz (188 g) of the almond flour.

2. In a mixer fitted with a paddle attachment, beat together the remaining 8.75 oz (248 g) of the eggs and the remaining 1.4 oz (39 g) of the butter at medium speed until combined. At low speed, add the dry ingredients to the batter and mix until combined. Mix in enough of the yellow food coloring to give the batter an egg yolk hue.

3. In a mixer fitted with a whisk attachment, beat the remaining 5.75 oz (163 g) of the egg whites with the remaining .87 oz (25 g) of the sugar to stiff peaks. Fold the beaten egg whites into the batter. Spread the yellow batter evenly over the cocoa-stenciled stars. Bake for 6 to 8 minutes, until set. While still hot, flip the cake over and peel off the silicone baking mat. Cool completely.

4. Using the triangle template, cut the cake into 48 triangles.

RUM SYRUP	14 oz	397 g	granulated sugar
	8 liq oz	237 ml	water
	1 liq oz	30 ml	Myer's dark rum

1. In a saucepan, combine the sugar and water and cook over medium heat until the sugar is dissolved.

2. Stir in the dark rum and cool.

WHITE-CHOCOLATE AND	8.75 oz	248 g	extra-ripe bananas
BANANA MOUSSE	7 liq oz	207 ml	heavy cream
	.75 liq oz	22 ml	Myer's dark rum
	34 oz	964 g	white chocolate, melted and kept warm

1. In a mixer fitted with the whisk attachment, whip the bananas until smooth. Add the cream and the rum and whip until the mixture forms soft peaks.

2. Fold the banana cream into the melted chocolate and refrigerate until ready to use.

CRUNCHY PRALINE	2.5 oz	71 g	white chocolate
	13 oz	368 g	praline paste
	8.75 oz	248 g	paillete feuilletine

Melt the chocolate with the praline paste. Fold in the paillete feuilletine.

PECAN CAKE	1 lb, 1 oz	482 g	pecans
	2 lbs 9.5 oz	1.17 k	granulated sugar, divided
	2 lbs 2 oz	964 g	all-purpose flour
	1 oz	28 g	baking powder
	2 tsp	14 g	salt
	48 liq oz	1.4 lt	heavy cream
	21 oz	595 g	whole eggs
	2 Tbs	24 g	vanilla extract

1. Line 3 sheet pans with parchment paper. Preheat oven to 350°F (175°F). In a food processor, process the pecans with 3.5 oz (99 g) of the sugar until finely ground; set aside.

2. In a bowl, sift together the flour, baking powder, and salt; set aside.

3. In a mixer fitted with a whisk attachment, whip the cream to soft peaks and refrigerate.

4. In a mixer fitted with a whisk attachment, beat the eggs, the remaining 2 lbs 6 oz (1.07 kg) of sugar, and the vanilla extract at high speed, to the ribbon stage. Fold in the whipped cream. Fold in the dry ingredients and the ground pecans. Divide the batter among the prepared pans and bake the cakes for 8 to 10 minutes. Cool completely.

5. Cut out 24 rounds of the pecan cake, to fit the bottom of the dome molds.

PRALINE RUM SAUCE

17.5 oz	496 g	praline paste
10.5 liq oz	310 ml	heavy cream
5.25 liq oz	155 ml	Myer's dark rum

In a saucepan, bring the cream to a simmer. Whisk in the praline paste until smooth. Stir in the rum.

CHOCOLATE SAUCE

2 oz	57 g	bittersweet chocolate, finely chopped
13.3 oz	378 g	unsweetened cocoa powder, sifted
1 lb	454 g	unsalted butter, cut into cubes
2 lbs	907 g	granulated sugar
32 liq oz	946 ml	heavy cream
24 liq oz	710 ml	water
3.5 oz	103 ml	light corn syrup

1. In a large bowl, stir together the chopped chocolate and cocoa powder.

2. In a saucepan, combine the butter, sugar, cream, water, and corn syrup. Bring to a boil, stirring occasionally. Pour the syrup over the chocolate and cocoa powder. Allow to sit for 10 minutes and then whisk until smooth. Chill.

WHITE CHOCOLATE SAUCE

| 32 liq oz | 946 ml | heavy cream |
| 17.5 oz | 496 g | white chocolate, finely chopped |

1. In a saucepan, bring the heavy cream to a boil.

2. Place the white chocolate in a bowl and pour the hot cream over it. Allow to sit for 10 minutes and then whisk until smooth. Chill.

MANGO PURÉE

| 3 | 3 | mangoes |

Peel and pit the mangoes. Purée in a food processor. Pass the purée through a fine chinois and chill.

RUM MIRROR GLAZE

16 liq oz	473 ml	water
8 liq oz	237 ml	Myer's dark rum
8 liq oz	237 ml	Mount Gay rum
1 lb	454 g	granulated sugar
1.06 oz	30 g	gelatin leaves, bloomed and drained

1. In a saucepan, combine the water, both rums, and the sugar. Cook over medium heat, stirring constantly, until the sugar is dissolved. Do not boil.

2. Add the gelatin and stir until dissolved. Pass the glaze through a fine chinois and reserve.

ASSEMBLY *Sliced bananas*

1. Line the dome molds with 4 cake triangles (stenciled side against the mold), alternating the yellow and cocoa colors.

2. Brush the cake layers with the light rum syrup. Pipe the white-chocolate and banana mousse into the molds until they are three-quarters full. Lay a few slices of fresh banana into the mold and freeze the molds for 3 to 4 hours.

3. Using a small spoon, spread a thin layer of the crunchy praline over the banana layer. Soak the pecan circles with the light rum syrup and place on top of the praline layer. Chill the domes for 1 hour.

4. Unmold the domes and brush with the rum mirror glaze.

5. Place the mold onto a dessert plate and garnish with the chocolate sauce, praline rum sauce, white chocolate sauce, and mango purée. Top the molds with chocolate coils (made with star transfer sheets, if desired).

> *An intriguing pattern will form in a dried banana chip if the banana is used at the proper time, says Chef Edwards; if it is almost ripe, usually two days after the shipment is received, the sugars are at the proper level to yield the visual accent.*

CARAMELIZED BRAEBURN APPLES WITH DATE CRISPS

DONALD WRESSELL

Pastry Chef, *Four Seasons Hotel,
Beverly Hills, California.*

"I always have an apple dessert in the winter and fall menus," says Donald Wressell. "People love them. I don't have to push them. When I recently pulled an apple dessert from the menu, the community revolted. The challenge is to come up with an apple dessert that will make them forget the other apple dessert." Named for the Tatin sisters, who served their upside-down, caramelized tart to guests at their nineteenth century, Loire-region hotel, tarte Tatin is traditionally made with puff pastry or pâte brisé. For his vertical play on the classic, Donald Wressell has chosen layers of date crisps and date purée instead, which is cooked separately from the apples. "We haven't lost anything," he says, "we've gained." Other modernizing touches are the use of crème frâiche ice cream, rather than simple crème frâiche, "which is a nice refreshing taste with the caramelized apples," says Chef Wressell, "and to intensify the apple flavor further, I've made an apple reduction sauce."

YIELD: 10 SERVINGS

CARAMELIZED APPLES			
	10	*10*	*Braeburn apples, about 6.2 oz/177 g each*
	3 oz	*85 g*	*unsalted butter*
	6 oz	*170 g*	*granulated sugar*

1. Peel, halve, and core the apples.

2. Melt the butter and sugar in a large sauté pan over medium heat. Add the apple halves and cook, turning frequently, until the apples are softened and well-caramelized, about 20 minutes.

APPLE CIDER SAUCE			
4	4	Braeburn apples, about 6.25 oz/177 g each
1.5 qt	1.42 lt	apple cider
2 liq oz	59 ml	apple brandy, such as Calvados

1. Peel, core, and cut the apples into 1/2" (1.3 cm) dice.

2. In a large saucepan, combine the cider and diced apples and reduce by two-thirds.

3. Pass the mixture through a fine sieve. Stir in the apple brandy; set the sauce aside.

DATE PURÉE			
3 oz	85 g	pitted Medjool dates (12 to 14 dates)
2	2	3" (7.6 cm) long cinnamon sticks
2 oz	57 g	honey
1/2 tsp	1 g	ground nutmeg
1	1	vanilla bean, split and scraped
6 liq oz	177 ml	water

Combine all the ingredients in a medium saucepan and bring to a boil. Reduce the heat, cover, and simmer for 4 minutes. Purée the date mixture in a food processor or blender. Cool.

DATE CRISPS			
40	40	3 x 3" (7.6 x 7.6 cm) squares phyllo dough
3 oz	85 g	unsalted butter, melted
2 oz	57 g	granulated sugar

1. Preheat oven to 350°F (177°C). Lightly butter a sheet pan.

2. Brush the phyllo squares with butter and sprinkle with some of the sugar. Layer 2 squares together and spread with a thin layer of the date purée. Top with 2 more squares of buttered and sugared phyllo. Repeat to make 10 date crisps.

3. Place the squares on the prepared pan and bake until golden brown and crispy, about 10 to 15 minutes.

CRÈME FRÂICHE ICE CREAM			
8 liq oz	237 ml	milk
2 oz	57 g	light corn syrup
2 oz	57 g	egg yolks
2 oz	57 g	granulated sugar
18 oz	510 g	crème frâiche

1. In a large saucepan, scald the milk and corn syrup.

2. In a bowl, lightly whisk the yolks with the sugar. Temper the yolks with the hot milk mixture and return to the saucepan. Cook the mixture to the custard stage.

3. Remove the custard from the heat; whisk in the crème frâiche. Strain through a chinois. Cool in ice bath. Chill.

4. Process in an ice cream machine according to the manufacturer's instructions.

ASSEMBLY   *10 pulled-sugar spirals*

1. Place one apple half, core side up, in the center of a dessert plate. Top with a date crisp. Place a second apple half, core side up, on top of the crisp. Place a pulled-sugar spiral on the apple and top with a #30 scoop (or 1.5 oz/43 g), of the crème frâiche ice cream.

2. Surround the dessert with some of the apple cider sauce.

WARM RASPBERRY PUDDING WITH SOUR CREAM ICE CREAM TERRINE

RICHARD LEACH

Pastry Chef, *Park Avenue Cafe,*
New York.

"Everything stems from classic recipes," observes Richard Leach. "There's a classic raspberry tart in there, but we've presented it in a different form, that's all." Composed of ricotta cheese, flour, and egg whites, the pudding is a cross between a classic pudding and a bread pudding. Crowning it is the tart, showing through like the hidden image in a Magic Eye 3-D painting. *"I chose the components I wanted on the plate, and we just pieced it together,"* Leach adds. *"The sauce is light because the ice cream is heavy, but then the dessert is swimming in sauce. I like it that way."*

YIELD: 10 SERVINGS

Special Equipment:
1" (2.5 cm) PVC tube
Ten 3 oz (89 ml) ramekins
Cut-off whisk and 2 dowels for spinning sugar

TART DOUGH			
4.5 oz	128 g	*unsalted butter, softened*
2 oz	57 g	*confectioners' sugar*
1.75 oz	50 g	*whole eggs*
2 oz	57 g	*almond flour*
7.5 oz	213 g	*all-purpose flour*

1. Preheat oven to 350°F (175°C). Line a half-sheet pan with parchment paper.

2. In a mixer fitted with a paddle attachment, cream together the butter and confectioners' sugar. Add the eggs and mix until incorporated.

3. On low speed, add the almond and all-purpose flours to the creamed mixture and mix until combined.

4. Shape the dough into a disc and refrigerate for 1 hour.

5. Remove the dough from the refrigerator and roll out to 1/8" (.32 cm) thickness. Using a 3" (7.6 cm) round cutter, cut out 10 rounds of dough and place them on the prepared pan.

6. Bake for 10 to 12 minutes, until lightly browned. Cool on a rack.

| CRÈME FRAÎCHE FILLING | 8 oz | 227 g | *crème fraîche* |
| | 1 Tbs | 14 g | *granulated sugar* |

Whip the crème fraîche with the sugar to stiff peaks. Refrigerate until needed.

WARM RASPBERRY PUDDING	6 oz	170 g	*whole milk ricotta cheese*
	4 oz	113 g	*granulated sugar, divided*
	1.5 oz	43 g	*egg yolks*
	1 oz	28 g	*all-purpose flour*
	6 oz	170 g	*egg whites*
	5 oz	142 g	*fresh raspberries*

1. Preheat oven to 325°F (163°C).

2. In a bowl, combine the ricotta cheese, 2 oz (57 g) of the sugar, and the egg yolks. Whisk in the flour to make a smooth paste.

3. In a mixer fitted with a whisk attachment, whip the egg whites and sugar to soft peaks.

4. Fold the meringue into the cheese mixture. Fold in the raspberries.

5. Fill the buttered ramekins with the raspberry-cheese mixture to two-thirds full. Bake in a water bath for 25 to 30 minutes, until the pudding is set and golden brown.

RASPBERRY SORBET	18 oz	510 g	*fresh raspberries*
	4 liq oz	118 ml	*water*
	13 liq oz	384 ml	*simple syrup*

1. Purée the raspberries with the water in a food processor. Strain the mixture through a chinois to extract the seeds. Combine the raspberry purée with the simple syrup and chill.

2. Process in an ice cream machine according to the manufacturer's instructions.

SOUR CREAM ICE CREAM			
16 liq oz	473 ml	half-and-half
6 oz	170 g	granulated sugar
4 oz	113 g	egg yolks
1 lb	454 g	sour cream

1. In a large saucepan, combine the half-and-half and sugar, and bring to a boil.

2. In a bowl, temper the yolks with hot cream mixture. Return the mixture to the saucepan and whisk in the sour cream. Strain the mixture through a chinois and cool in ice bath. Chill.

3. Process in an ice cream machine according to the manufacturer's instructions.

ALMOND CAKE			
7 oz	198 g	almond paste
7 oz	198 g	sugar
7 oz	198 g	butter, softened
7 oz	198 g	eggs
3 oz	85 g	cake flour

1. Preheat oven to 325°F (163°C). Line 2 half-sheet pans with buttered parchment paper.

2. In a mixer with a paddle attachment, combine the almond paste, sugar, and butter; beat until creamy. Add the eggs and beat until blended.

3. On low speed, add the cake flour and mix to combine.

4. Scrape the batter into the prepared pans and bake until set, about 25 to 30 minutes. Cool the cakes in the pans.

ASSEMBLY

1. Have ready two 7 x 3 1/2 x 2 1/2" (17.8 x 8.9 x 6.4 cm) terrine molds or loaf pans.

2. Measure and cut the almond cake to line the inside of the terrine molds. Fill the lined molds with the sour cream ice cream. Top each mold with a strip of almond cake. Freeze overnight.

RASPBERRY SAUCE			
24 oz	680 g	fresh raspberries
8 oz	227 g	granulated sugar
4 liq oz	118 ml	water
2 Tbs	30 ml	lemon juice

1. In a medium saucepan, combine the raspberries, sugar, and water. Bring to a boil; reduce the heat and simmer for 10 to 15 minutes, or until thickened.

2. Strain through a chinois to extract the seeds. Stir in the lemon juice. Chill.

VANILLA SABAYON SAUCE			
4 oz	113 g	egg yolks
4 oz	113 g	granulated sugar
1	1	vanilla bean, split and scraped
8 liq oz	237 ml	heavy cream
8 oz	227 g	crème fraîche

1. Combine the yolks, sugar, and vanilla bean in a double boiler and whisk until pale and thick, about 4 to 6 minutes. Remove from the heat. Cool.

2. In a mixer fitted with a whisk attachment, whip together the cream and crème fraîche until soft peaks form. Fold into the yolk mixture. Strain through a chinois, discarding the vanilla bean. Place the sauce in a squeeze bottle and chill.

SPUN SUGAR CYLINDERS

14 oz	*397 g*	*granulated sugar*
8 liq oz	*237 ml*	*water*
2 oz	*57 g*	*glucose*

1. Place the sugar and water in a heavy saucepan. Cook over low heat, stirring constantly, until the sugar is dissolved. Add the glucose, stirring until it is combined with the syrup.

2. Increase the heat and bring the syrup to a boil, washing down the sides of the pan with a brush dipped in water occasionally. Bring the syrup to 310°F (154°C). Immediately remove the pan from the heat and plunge the bottom of the pan in cold water to stop the cooking process. Remove the pan from the water and allow the syrup to stand for a few minutes to thicken slightly.

3. Arrange 2 dowels over the edge of a table. Dip a cut-off whisk in the sugar and flick it back and forth over the dowels in a rapid motion to create the spun sugar. When enough of the sugar has formed, immediately wrap it around a 1" (2.5 cm) PVC tube to form a spun-sugar cylinder (see photo to the left). Repeat to form a total of 10 cylinders.

FINAL ASSEMBLY

26 oz/737 g fresh raspberries
Honey
Mint leaves
Pulled-sugar sticks

1. Pool the raspberry sauce on a dessert plate. Squeeze out a few dots of the sabayon sauce onto the plate.

2. Spread a thin layer of crème fraîche filling on the tart shell. Cover the filling with raspberries and drizzle with honey.

3. Place a 1" (2.5 cm) thick slice of sour cream terrine on one side of the plate. Top with a spun-sugar cylinder. Fill the cylinder with raspberries.

4. Unmold a warm pudding onto the other side of the plate. Place a raspberry tart on top of the pudding and top with a small scoop of raspberry sorbet. Place a sprig of mint next to the sorbet.

5. Garnish the plate with pulled-sugar sticks, raspberries, and mint leaves.

RHUBARB AND STRAWBERRY STRUDEL

KRISTA KERN

Pastry Chef, *Three Fish, Westerly, Rhode Island.*

Although strudel is generally considered Austrian in origin, most food historians agree that the original recipe was developed in Hungary and refined by the Austrians. The name comes from the German word for "whirlwind." "There is a reason this dessert looks the way it does," says Krista Kern, who first served it at a restaurant called Bang in Greenwich, Connecticut. "It was Asian cuisine, and a lot of it was vertical. This was my play on a spring roll, using a strudel but standing it up, and the dried rhubarb giving the air of firecrackers." The classic combination of strawberry and rhubarb is given fresh life when combined with bruléed lemon-ricotta cheesecake, lemon sabayon, and lemon meringue discs. Fresh strawberries, rhubarb sorbet, and pink peppercorn berry broth finish the presentation. "The pink peppercorn broth adds heat and spice that really complements rhubarb and strawberry," says Krista Kern. "It also gives it body."

YIELD: 6 SERVINGS

Special Equipment:
9 1/2" (24 cm) loaf pan
Six 1 1/2" (3.8 cm) diameter × 4" (10.2 cm) high stainless-steel tubes

SAUTÉED RHUBARB AND	3 oz	85 g	unsalted butter
STRAWBERRY COMPOTE	10.6 oz	300 g	rhubarb, cut into 1/2" (1.27 cm) pieces
	2.6 oz	74 g	granulated sugar
	1/4	1/4	vanilla bean, split and scraped
	7.4 oz	210 g	strawberries, hulled and halved
	3 grinds	3 grinds	pink peppercorns
	2 Tbs	30 ml	lemon juice

1. In sauté pan over medium-high heat, melt the butter. Add the rhubarb and sauté until tender. Reduce heat slightly and add the sugar and the vanilla bean seeds. Cook until the sugar is completely dissolved.

2. Add the strawberries, a few grinds of pink peppercorns, and the lemon juice; toss well. Remove the mixture from the heat and allow to cool.

CORNMEAL CAKE	7.6 oz	215 g	cornmeal
	7.5 oz	213 g	all-purpose flour
	1 tsp	5 g	baking powder
	1 tsp	5 g	ground cinnamon
	1/4 tsp	1.6 g	salt
	8 oz	227 g	unsalted butter, softened
	8 oz	227 g	light brown sugar
	3.5 oz	99 g	granulated sugar
	2 tsp	4 g	grated lemon zest
	14 oz	397 g	whole eggs
	4 liq oz	118 ml	whole milk
	1.5 liq oz	45 ml	brandy
	1/4	1/4	vanilla bean, split and scraped

1. Preheat the oven to 350°F (175°C). Butter and flour a 9 1/4 x 5 1/4" (23 x 13 cm) loaf pan.

2. Sift together the cornmeal, flour, baking powder, cinnamon, and salt; set them aside.

3. In a mixer fitted with a paddle attachment, beat together butter, sugars, lemon zest, and vanilla bean seeds until light. Beat in eggs, one at a time. Beat in milk and brandy. At low speed, add dry ingredients and mix just until combined.

4. Scrape batter into pan and bake for 45 minutes, until a tester comes out clean. Cool cake in its pan for 15 minutes. Turn it out onto a rack and cool it completely.

5. Slice the crust off the cake on all sides. Slice the cake into 1/2" (1.27 cm) slices, arrange them on a sheet pan and allow them to dry for 30 minutes. Process the cake to fine crumbs in a food processor. Toast the crumbs in a 350°F (175°C) oven just until golden; cool completely.

STRUDEL TUBES	8 sheets	8 sheets	phyllo dough (12 x 17"/30 x 43 cm)
	12 oz	340 g	clarified butter
	5.6 oz	160 g	toasted cake crumbs (above)
	1.05 oz	30 g	egg white, whisked

1. Preheat oven to 400°F (205°C). Place a phyllo sheet on a work surface and brush evenly with some of the clarified butter. Sprinkle one-third of the cake crumbs over the sheet, leaving a 2" (5 cm) crumbless border on one of the long sides. Repeat layering 2 more times, and top with the fourth sheet of phyllo.

2. Repeat the above process to form a second set of phyllo layers.

3. With the sheets facing you horizontally, brush the top three-quarters of the top sheet with clarified butter, and the lower quarter of the top sheet with egg white. Using a pizza cutter, trim all the sides of the layers so that they are even. Cut the layers vertically into 3 3/4" (8.7 cm) wide strips (you will need a total of 6 strips).

4. Starting with a buttered end and ending with an egg-white-coated end, wrap a phyllo strip around one of the stainless tubes, pressing to seal the edge. Repeat with the remaining tubes. Place the tubes standing up on a parchment-lined sheet pan and bake until golden, 15 to 20 minutes.

5. Remove the pan from the oven and very carefully remove each strudel from the steel tubes. Cool the strudel tubes on a wire rack completely.

LEMON MERINGUE DISC			
2 tsp	4 g	grated lemon zest
4 oz	113 g	ground almonds
4.2 oz	119 g	egg whites
6 oz	170 g	granulated sugar

1. Preheat the oven to 300°F (150°C). In a small bowl combine the lemon zest and ground almonds; set aside.

2. In a mixer with a whisk attachment, beat the egg whites to soft peaks. Gradually add sugar and beat to stiff, shiny peaks. Fold almond mixture into whites.

3. Using a medium, plain pastry tip, pipe meringue onto a parchment-lined sheet, into solid 2 1/2" (6.35 cm) triangles. Bake until dry and cool, about 1 hour.

RHUBARB SORBET			
24 oz	680 g	rhubarb
1 pint	473 ml	water
7 oz	198 g	granulated sugar
7.9 oz	224 g	honey
1 Tbs	15 ml	lemon juice
5	5	pink peppercorns

1. Remove the tough outer strands of the rhubarb by "stringing" the stalks (use a paring knife if necessary); set the rhubarb strings aside. In a saucepan, bring the water, sugar, and honey to a boil; boil for 1 minute. Add the reserved rhubarb strings, and allow everything to soak for 10 minutes. Remove the strings to a parchment-lined sheet pan, spreading them out so that they do not overlap. Allow the strings to dry at room temperature overnight, and reserve for garnish.

2. Chop the rhubarb stalks. Add the peppercorns and the chopped rhubarb to the remaining sugar syrup and simmer until the rhubarb is completely soft.

3. Purée the mixture in a food processor; the strain through a chinois. Cover and chill the mixture for several hours. Stir in the lemon juice and process in an ice cream machine according to the manufacturer's instructions.

> *"Dry rhubarb is very simple," says Krista Kern. "Strip it off and let it dry. I hang it off my refrigerator. You can also dip it in sugar syrup before drying it, which makes it a bit more palatable."*

LEMON-RICOTTA CHEESECAKE

1 lb	*454 g*	*cream cheese*
5 oz	*142 g*	*granulated sugar*
1	*1*	*vanilla bean, split and scraped*
4 tsp	*8 g*	*grated lemon zest*
7 oz	*198 g*	*whole eggs*
1.3 oz	*37 g*	*egg yolks*
10 oz	*283 g*	*ricotta cheese*
2 liq oz	*59 ml*	*lemon juice*
6 oz	*170 g*	*crème fraîche*

1. Preheat the oven to 325°F (160°C). In a mixer with a paddle attachment, beat together cream cheese, sugar, vanilla bean seeds, and lemon zest on low speed until smooth. Gradually beat in eggs and yolks (at low speed).

2. In a medium bowl, combine ricotta, lemon juice, and crème fraîche. Add this to the egg mixture and mix at low speed until combined. Scrape batter into a half hotel pan (4"/10 cm deep) and bake in a water bath until just set and slightly golden. Cool completely and refrigerate overnight. Scoop the cheesecake filling into a pastry bag fitted with a plain 1/4 to 1/2" (.6 to 1.3 cm) tip and refrigerate until serving time.

PINK PEPPERCORN BERRY BROTH

4 pts	*1.9 lt*	*overripe strawberries, stemmed*
10.5 oz	*298 g*	*granulated sugar*
1.5 liq oz	*45 ml*	*lemon juice*
6	*6*	*pink peppercorns*

1. In large saucepan, combine strawberries, sugar, lemon juice, and peppercorns. Bring mixture to a boil, stirring to dissolve the sugar. Cool the mixture to room temperature.

2. Pass broth through a chinois. Chill the broth and place in a squeeze bottle. Refrigerate until serving time.

LEMON SABAYON

1.95 oz	*55 g*	*egg yolks*
1.75 oz	*50 g*	*granulated sugar*
1 liq oz	*30 ml*	*lemon juice*
3 tsp	*6 g*	*finely grated lemon zest*
2.1 oz	*60 g*	*crème fraîche*
4 liq oz	*118 ml*	*heavy cream*

1. Strain yolks and sugar into a medium bowl and set over a bain-marie. Add the lemon juice and zest; whisk until thick. Remove the bowl from the bain-marie.

2. In a mixer with a whisk attachment, beat crème frâiche with the heavy cream into soft mounds.

3. Beat the egg mixture over an ice bath until cold. Fold in the whipped cream. Pass the sabayon through a chinois to remove the zest. Transfer sabayon to a squeeze bottle and refrigerate until serving time.

SUGAR GARNISH	*1 lb*	*454 g*	*isomalt*
	5 liq oz	*148 ml*	*water*

1. Line a sheet pan with parchment paper. Place the isomalt and water in a heavy saucepan and stir to combine. Cook over low heat until the isomalt is dissolved.

2. Increase the heat to medium and cook the syrup to 340°F (171°C); immediately plunge the bottom of the pan into cool water to stop the cooking process. Allow the sugar to cool until slightly thickened, about 5 minutes.

3. Using a teaspoon, drizzle the sugar into a free-form circular pattern, 6 to 7" (15.2 to 17.8 cm) in diameter, onto the prepared sheet pan. Repeat to form a total of 6 pieces. Allow the sugar to harden completely.

ASSEMBLY
Fresh strawberries, sliced
Fresh strawberries, diced
Dried rhubarb strings
Grated lemon zest
Confectioners' sugar
Fresh mint

1. Place a strudel tube slightly off-center on a 12" (30.5 cm) dessert plate. Place a lemon meringue triangle to the left of the tube. Pipe about 2 oz (57 g) of the cheesecake filling onto the meringue. Top with 3 strawberry slices. Sprinkle the slices with confectioners' sugar and pipe on a dollop of cheesecake filling. Sprinkle with more confectioners' sugar and caramelize the top lightly with a blowtorch.

2. Heat the rhubarb and strawberry compote. Fill the strudel tube one-quarter of the way with cheesecake filling. Fill the remainder of the tube with the compote and four fresh strawberry slices. Top with a small squirt of cheesecake. Place the sugar garnish on top of the tube.

3. Place a quenelle of rhubarb sorbet to the right of the tube. Sprinkle some diced strawberries between the meringue and sorbet.

4. Arrange 2 rhubarb strands in the tube.

5. Garnish the plate with dots of berry broth and sabayon. Sprinkle confectioners' sugar over the dessert and garnish with mint.

MONT BLANC

MICHAEL HU

Executive Pastry Chef, *Waldorf-Astoria Hotel, New York.*

Named for the snow-capped mountain located at the border between France and Italy, this classic, autumn dessert usually consists of chestnut purée, and is quite heavy. Michael Hu's lighter variation consists of a dome of chocolate sorbet atop a chocolate sable, with chestnut mousse and whipped cream piped at the base, and chocolate sauce splashed in between. A chocolate fence surrounds all. Candied chestnuts in caramel and a white chocolate spiral finish the plate.

YIELD: 10 SERVINGS

Special Equipment:
Ten acetate strips, 1 3/4 x 11 1/2 " (4.4 x 29.2 cm)
Twenty bamboo skewers

CHESTNUT MOUSSE			
1.5 lb	.68 kg	*fresh unshelled chestnuts, about 48 to 52*
1/2 tsp	3.4 g	*salt*
6 liq oz	177 ml	*milk*
6 liq oz	177 ml	*light cream*
3 oz	85 g	*granulated sugar*
1 1/2	1 1/2	*vanilla beans, split and scraped*
9 liq oz	177 ml	*heavy cream*
1.5 Tbs	7.5 ml	*dark rum*

1. Preheat the oven to 375°F (191°C).

2. With the point of a paring knife, make a cross on the round side of each chestnut. Place the chestnuts, flat-side-down on a baking sheet and roast for 10 to 15 minutes or until the shells split apart. Remove the shells and the inner skins while the chestnuts are still warm.

3. Place the shelled chestnuts in a large saucepan and cover with water. Add the salt and bring to a boil. Lower the heat and simmer for 30 to 45 minutes, until the chestnuts are soft and can easily be pierced with a knife. Drain the nuts and purée them in a food processor.

4. In a large saucepan, combine the milk, light cream, sugar, and vanilla beans; bring to a boil. Remove the pan from the heat and let steep for 15 minutes. Discard the vanilla beans and return to a boil. Add the chestnut purée and cook, stirring constantly with a wooden spoon until the mixture is thickened and slightly reduced, about 5 to 7 minutes. Transfer the mixture to a heat-proof container and place a piece of plastic wrap directly on the surface of the mixture to prevent a skin from forming. Let cool to room temperature.

5. In a mixer fitted with a whisk attachment, combine the heavy cream and rum; whip to soft peaks. Lighten the chestnut mixture with some of the whipped cream. Fold in the remaining whipped cream and chill.

CHOCOLATE SHORTDOUGH			
	8.5 oz	241 g	all-purpose flour
	3.25 oz	92 g	cocoa powder
	8 oz	227 g	granulated sugar
	1/2 tsp	3.6 g	salt
	8 oz	227 g	butter, softened
	3.5 oz	99 g	whole eggs
	1.3 oz	37 g	egg yolks

1. In a bowl, sift together the flour, cocoa powder, sugar, and salt.

2. In a mixer fitted with a paddle attachment, cream the butter until light.

3. On low speed, slowly add the sifted dry ingredients to the butter and mix until the mixture is uniform with a crumbly consistency. Add the eggs and yolks; mix to combine. Do not overmix.

4. Shape the dough into a disc, cover in plastic wrap, and refrigerate overnight.

5. Preheat the oven to 350°F (177°C). Line a sheet pan with parchment.

6. Remove the dough from the refrigerator and roll out to 1/8" (.32 cm) thickness. Using a 3" (7.6 cm) round cutter, cut out 10 circles of dough and place on the prepared pan. Refrigerate for at least 30 minutes, then bake for 10 to 12 minutes until done. Cool on a rack.

CHOCOLATE-ORANGE SORBET			
	6 oz	170 g	bittersweet chocolate, finely chopped
	30 liq oz	887 ml	simple syrup
	20 liq oz	591 ml	water
	5 liq oz	148 ml	fresh orange juice
	1.5 oz	43 g	orange zest
	6 oz	170 g	glucose
	1.75 oz	50 g	cocoa powder

1. Place the chopped chocolate in a large bowl.

2. In a large saucepan, combine the simple syrup, water, orange juice, orange zest, glucose, and cocoa powder. Boil for 1 minute.

3. Strain the mixture over the chopped chocolate. Whisk until the chocolate is completely melted and the mixture is smooth. Cool and chill.

4. Process in an ice cream machine according to manufacturer's instructions.

| CHOCOLATE SAUCE | 4 oz | 113 g | *bittersweet chocolate, chopped* |
| | 5 liq oz | 148 ml | *water* |

1. Combine the chopped chocolate and water in a small, heavy-bottom saucepan. Cook over low heat, stirring until the chocolate is melted and the mixture is smooth. Cool.

2. Place in a squeeze bottle and reserve.

| COMBED CHOCOLATE BANDS | 1 lb | 454 g | *dark chocolate, melted and tempered* |

1. Place the acetate strips on a work surface.

2. Using an offset spatula, spread an even layer of chocolate across each strip. Pull a decorating comb horizontally through the chocolate.

3. Fill a parchment cone with some of the chocolate and pipe very thin, crossed diagonal lines over the strips. Allow them to stand until they are almost set.

4. Form each strip into a ring, with the chocolate decoration on the inside. Let them set completely.

CARAMEL-DIPPED CHESTNUTS	20	20	*fresh, unshelled chestnuts*
	16 liq oz	473 ml	*water*
	32 oz	907 g	*granulated sugar*
	7 oz	198 g	*glucose*

1. Preheat the oven to 375°F (191°C). Have ready 20 bamboo skewers and a bowl of cold water to cool the saucepan in which syrup will be cooked. Place a few sheets of parchment paper on the floor in front of the work surface to catch the excess dripping syrup. Place a strip of wood, such as a ruler, at the edge of the work surface, securing it by placing heavy weights at each end of the wood strip.

2. With the point of a paring knife, make a cross on the round side of each chestnut. Place the chestnuts, flat-side-down, on a baking sheet and roast for 10 to 15 minutes or until the cut side of the shells split. Remove the shells and the inner skins while the chestnuts are still warm.

3. Place the shelled chestnuts in a saucepan and cover with water. Lower the heat and simmer until the chestnuts are just beginning to soften. Remove from the heat and drain thoroughly.

4. Insert a bamboo skewer into the flat side of each drained chestnut, penetrating about halfway through the nut.

5. Place the water in a large heavy-bottom saucepan. Add the sugar and glucose and cook the syrup until golden brown. Immediately place the saucepan in a bowl of cold water. Let the caramel cool until thickened but still liquid.

6. Dip a skewered chestnut into the caramel. Lift it out and hold it so that the tapered end is pointing down. Place the flat side of the skewer under the ruler so that it extends out from work surface and the caramel will drip onto the parchment paper on the floor. Repeat this procedure to make 20 caramel-dipped chestnuts.

7. When the caramel on the chestnut has cooled and hardened, use a scissors to cut caramel the tail that has formed to the desired length. Leave the skewer in the chestnut until assembly. (This dipping procedure should be done as close as possible to service since the moisture in the chestnuts can cause the caramel to liquefy.)

ASSEMBLY

Tempered white chocolate triangles
Whipped cream

1. Fill a pastry bag fitted with a large star tip (Ateco #7), with chestnut mousse. Remove the acetate from the combed chocolate bands.

2. Place a chocolate cookie on a dessert plate. Top the cookie with a scoop of chocolate sorbet placed slightly off-center. Pipe some chestnut mousse (about 1/3 cup) next to the sorbet. Surround the cookie with a chocolate band. Spoon some whipped cream over the sorbet and partially over the mousse.

3. Gently remove the skewers from two caramel-dipped chestnuts. Arrange the chestnuts (tail-side-up) and a white chocolate triangle on top of the dessert. Garnish the plate with dots of chocolate sauce.

OPERA AND THE MOSAIC IMPRESSION

STANTON HO

Executive Pastry Chef, *Las Vegas Hilton Hotel.*

"This is an opera cake with variations," says Stanton Ho. "The triangular form contains caramel mousse, which blends with the coffee, white chocolate, and chocolate mousse in the opera. The three work well together. The biscuit joconde flavored with syrup and coffee extract is classic, but I am using mousse rather than the classic buttercream—it is more appealing to the American palate and it's lighter than buttercream."

YIELD: 20 SERVINGS

Special Equipment:
Twenty plastic 3-surface pyramid molds (available at office supplystores), with a triangular base of 1.5 x 1.5 x 1.5 " (3.8 x 3.8 x 3.8 cm),a height of 4" (10.2 cm), and a capacity of 2.5 liq oz (74 ml)
Wagner airless paint sprayer

BISCUIT JOCONDE			
8.75 oz	*248 g*	*almond flour*
8.75 oz	*248 g*	*confectioners' sugar*
2.75 oz	*78 g*	*all-purpose flour*
11.5 oz	*326 g*	*whole eggs*
11.5 oz	*326 g*	*egg whites*
2 oz	*57 g*	*granulated sugar*
2 Tbs	*12 g*	*dried egg whites*
1/2 tsp	*2 g*	*cream of tartar*
1.75 oz	*50 g*	*unsalted butter, melted*

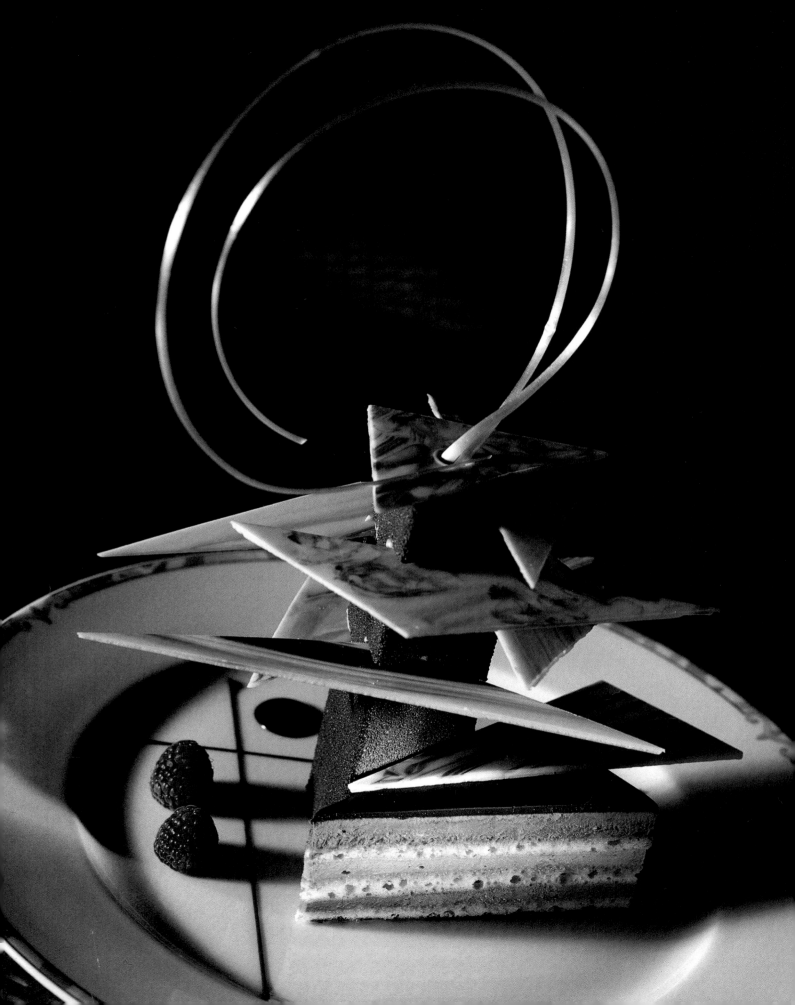

1. Preheat oven to 400° (204°). Line 3 half-sheet pans with silicone baking mats.

2. In a bowl, combine the almond flour, confectioners' sugar, and all-purpose flour. Sift together twice.

3. In a mixer fitted with a whisk attachment, beat the eggs on high speed until doubled in volume. Fold in the sifted dry ingredients in three additions.

4. In a mixer fitted with a whisk attachment, combine the egg whites, one-third of the granulated sugar, the dried egg whites, and cream of tartar. Beat to soft peaks. Slowly add the remaining granulated sugar and beat until firm peaks. Fold the meringue into the egg-flour mixture; then fold in the melted butter.

5. Divide the batter into 3 equal parts and spread evenly onto the 3 prepared pans. Bake for 10 to 12 minutes until set; cool completely.

SEMISWEET CHOCOLATE MOUSSE			
11 liq oz	325 ml	milk
11 oz	312 g	semisweet chocolate, such as Valrhona Extra Noir, finely chopped
.35 oz	10 g	gelatin sheets, softened in cold water
5.5 oz	156 g	egg yolks
5.5 oz	156 g	granulated sugar
18 liq oz	532 ml	heavy cream, whipped to soft peaks

1. In a saucepan, bring the milk to a boil. Add the chocolate; lower the heat and stir until the chocolate is melted. Add the drained gelatin to the chocolate mixture and stir until the gelatin is melted and the mixture is smooth. Remove from the heat.

2. In a large double boiler, whisk together the egg yolks and granulated sugar. Place the bowl over a bain-marie. Whisk until the mixture is pale and thick. Add the chocolate mixture to the egg mixture and whisk until well-combined.

3. Place the mixture over an ice bath and stir with a rubber spatula until it begins to congeal. Remove from the ice bath and fold in one-third of the whipped cream. Fold in the remaining whipped cream in two additions.

CAFÉ-WHITE-CHOCOLATE MOUSSE			
11 liq oz	325 ml	heavy cream
2 Tbs	30 ml	Kahlua liqueur
1 Tbs	15 ml	coffee extract
1 tsp	4 g	instant espresso powder
4 liq oz	118 ml	milk
4 oz	113 g	white chocolate, such as Valrhona Ivoire, finely chopped
.24 oz	6.7 g	gelatin sheets, softened in cold water
2.6 oz	74 g	egg yolks
2.5 oz	71 g	granulated sugar

1. In a mixer fitted with a whisk attachment, combine the cream, Kahlúa liqueur, and coffee extract. Whip to soft peaks. Refrigerate until needed.

2. In a saucepan, bring the milk and espresso powder to a boil. Add the chopped chocolate and, over low heat, stir until the chocolate is melted and the mixture is smooth. Add the drained gelatin and stir until the gelatin is dissolved in the mixture. Remove from the heat.

3. Combine the egg yolks and sugar in a large double boiler and whisk until pale and thick. Add in the melted chocolate mixture and whisk until smooth.

4. Place over an ice bath and stir with a rubber spatula until the mixture begins to congeal. Remove from the ice bath and fold in one-third of the whipped cream combination. Fold in the remaining whipped cream in two additions.

COFFEE AND KAHLÚA SYRUP			
16 liq oz	473 ml	*simple syrup*
6 liq oz	177 ml	*coffee*
1 Tbs	15 ml	*Kahlúa liqueur*

Combine all the ingredients.

GANACHE GLAZE

7 liq oz	207 ml	*heavy cream*
9 oz	255 g	*Valrhona Guanaja chocolate, finely chopped*

1. Place the chopped chocolate in a heat-proof bowl.

2. In a saucepan, bring the cream to a boil over medium-high heat. Pour the boiling cream over the chocolate. Let sit for about 30 seconds; stir with a rubber spatula until the chocolate is completely melted and the ganache is very smooth.

OPERA CAKE ASSEMBLY

1. Place a layer of the joconde on the bottom of a sheet pan. Spread half of the semisweet chocolate mousse evenly over the joconde. Place a second layer of joconde on top of the mousse. Spread the café-white-chocolate mousse over this layer. Top this with the third layer of the joconde and spread the remaining semisweet chocolate mousse over this layer. Freeze the cake for at least 3 hours to firm up the mousse layers.

2. Remove the opera from the freezer and pour the ganache glaze over the top of the cake, spreading it evenly with a metal spatula. (You may not need all of the glaze.) Refrigerate and allow the ganache to set completely.

3. Cut the glazed opera into 2 x 3" (5.1 x 7.6 cm) wedges as needed.

CHOCOLATE TOWERS

3 lbs	1.4 kg	*bittersweet chocolate, melted and tempered*

1. Ladle melted chocolate into a plastic pyramid mold to completely fill. Turn the mold upside down and let the excess chocolate drip back into the bowl containing the tempered chocolate. Repeat to make 20 chocolate-lined towers. (If a second coat of chocolate is desired, repeat the above process after the first coat has set.)

2. Allow the towers to set at room temperature for at least one hour before filling with caramel mousse.

CARAMEL MOUSSE

21 liq oz	621 ml	*heavy cream, divided*
3.5 oz	85 g	*granulated sugar*
2.75 oz	78 g	*glucose*
.5 oz	14 g	*unsalted butter, at room temperature*
3.25 oz	92 g	*egg yolks*
2 liq oz	59 ml	*simple syrup*
.41 oz	11.7 g	*gelatin sheets, softened in cold water*
		Cocoa Barry "prima" coating

1. In a saucepan, scald 6 liq oz (177 ml) of the heavy cream. Keep warm.

2. Whip the remaining 15 liq oz (444 ml) of heavy cream to soft peaks and refrigerate until needed.

3. In another saucepan, cook the granulated sugar and the glucose to a medium caramel color. Remove from the heat and stir in the butter.

4. Return the pan to low heat and slowly add the heavy cream. (The mixture will bubble up.) Stir until the mixture is well-blended and any hardened caramel has melted. Remove the caramel from the heat and set aside.

5. Combine the egg yolks with the simple syrup in a large heat-proof bowl. Place over a bain-marie and whisk until the mixture is thick and pale. Add in the drained gelatin and stir until the gelatin is dissolved and the mixture is smooth. Remove the bowl from the heat and stir in the caramel. Cool over an ice bath.

6. When the mixture starts to congeal, fold in the heavy cream in three stages.

7. Fill a pastry bag fitted with a plain tip with the caramel mousse and pipe the mousse into the chocolate towers. Chill until the mousse is set, about 2 to 3 hours.

8. Remove the filled chocolate towers from the plastic molds. With a heated knife, make 5 slits in each tower. These will eventually hold 5 marbled chocolate triangles. Fill a Wagner airless paint sprayer with Cocoa Barry "prima" and spray a fine mist evenly over the towers.

| MARBLED-CHOCOLATE | 12 oz | 340 g | dark chocolate, tempered |
| TRIANGLES | 2 lbs | 907 g | white chocolate, tempered |

1. On a work surface, randomly drizzle some of the melted dark chocolate. Before it sets and using an offset spatula, spread a thin layer of the white chocolate over the drizzled dark chocolate. This will create a marbled effect. Allow to set.

2. Cut out 140 triangles (7 per tower) of various sizes (see photo, page 82). There should be 20 of each size. Make sure that one of the sizes is such that the triangle will be at least as large as the top surface of the opera wedge. Make sure that one of the sizes is such that the triangle will cover the open end of the chocolate tower; this triangle should have a 1/2" (1.3 cm) hole cut from its center.

ASSEMBLY AND PLATING

20 pulled-sugar spirals
Chocolate sauce
40 fresh raspberries

1. Remove a caramel mousse-filled tower from the refrigerator. Have ready 7 marbled triangles of assorted sizes including one with a cut-out hole. Cut a 2 x 3" (5 x 7.6 cm) wedge from the refrigerated opera cake.

2. Insert a pulled-sugar spiral through the triangle with the hole. Insert 5 assorted triangles into the slits of the prepared tower.

3. On a dessert plate, place the wedge of opera cake slightly off-center. Arrange the assembled tower next to the cake, so that the cake will help support the tower. Top the cake with the triangle of similar size; it should not completely cover the glaze. Top the open end of the tower with the triangle that has the attached sugar spiral; it should completely cover the mousse.

4. Garnish the plate with dots and lines of chocolate sauce and 2 raspberries.

PETITS POTS DE CRÈME D'AUJOURD'HUI

PASCAL JANVIER

Pastry Chef, Instructor, Technical Manager, *Callebaut Barry Training Center, Pennsauken, New Jersey.*

Today's pot de crème "is a reworked version of an old French dessert that I have tried to modernize to suit the expectations of today's customers," says Pascal Janvier. The rich pot de crème recipe is intact, but the top is sprayed with white chocolate and it is further crowned with a chocolate tablet, with chocolate lines arranged in such a way that "I am playing with round, rectangular, and triangular forms," says Janvier. "With this plate you also have a square."

YIELD: 13 SERVINGS

Special Equipment:
Thirteen ramekins, 3 1/2" (8.9 cm) diameter and 1 1/4" (3.2 cm) deep
Wagner airless paint sprayer

POTS DE CRÈME			
	34 liq oz	1 lt	heavy cream
	8.5 oz	240 g	Chocolat-Amer 60% (extra-bitter chocolate)
	5.6 oz	160 g	Grand Caraque (unsweetened chocolate)
	8.5 oz	240 g	large egg yolks
	7 oz	198 g	granulated sugar
	4 drops	4 drops	red food coloring

1. Preheat a convection oven to 210°F (100°C). In a saucepan, bring the cream to a boil. Remove from heat; add the extra bitter and unsweetened chocolates to the hot cream and whisk until the chocolate is melted.

2. In a bowl, whisk the egg yolks and sugar together. Add some of the chocolate mixture to the yolk mixture to temper; add the remaining chocolate mixture. Add the food coloring.

3. Strain the mixture and pour it into the ramekins, filling them. Bake 20 minutes or until barely set (no water bath is needed). Refrigerate.

CHOCOLATE LINES | 9 oz | 255 g | *dark couverture chocolate, tempered*

1. Spread some of the chocolate onto acetate. Scrape with a wide-tooth comb to make 39 lines about 1/4" (.6 cm) thick and 6 1/2" (162.7 cm) long.

2. Let set and remove the strips from the acetate.

CHOCOLATE TABLETS | *Extra Bitter Guayaquil 64%, tempered*

Spread some chocolate onto acetate. When it just starts to set, cut it into thirteen 1 x 1 1/2" (2.5 x 3.7 cm) tablets. Let it set completely and remove from the acetate. (You can also use tablet molds available from Cocoa Barry.)

ASSEMBLY | 4 oz | 113 g | *white chocolate*
| 4 oz | 113 g | *cocoa butter*
| | | *gold leaf*

1. Cover the rims of the ramekins. Melt the white chocolate and cocoa butter together and place in the airless paint sprayer. Carefully spray the pots de crème with the mixture.

2. Place a dot of gold leaf onto the center of each tablet.

3. Place 3 of the chocolate strips into a triangle shape on top of each ramekin. Place a chocolate tablet in the center of each.

CHOCOLATE CROISSANT BREAD PUDDING WITH SPECKY VANILLA ICE CREAM AND CARAMEL

MARSHALL ROSENTHAL

Executive Pastry Chef, *Trump Taj Mahal Hotel and Casino, Atlantic City, New Jersey.*

Bread pudding—an American classic recipe—is updated with croissants rather than brioche. "You have tart and sweet, warm and cold, smooth and crunchy on this plate," remarks Marshall Rosenthal. The classic chocolate and banana combination (via the caramelized bananas) is supported with caramel sauce, raspberry coulis, and vanilla-bean ice cream, for an all-American interplay of neutral, tart, and sweet flavors.

YIELD: 50 SERVINGS

BREAD PUDDING			
	2 lbs, 8 oz	1.13 k	day-old croissants, cut into 1/4" pieces
	24.5 oz	695 g	whole eggs
	5.2 oz	147 g	egg yolks
	1 lb, 4 oz	567 g	granulated sugar
	7.5 oz	213 g	extra-brute cocoa powder, sifted
	2 qts, 8 liq oz	2.13 lt	heavy cream (40%), divided
	2 liq oz	59 ml	bourbon vanilla extract

1. In a 20 qt (18.9 lt) mixer using a whisk attachment, beat the eggs, yolks, sugar, and 1 qt (.9 lt) of the heavy cream at low speed until blended. Gradually add the cocoa powder, vanilla, and the remaining heavy cream; mix until blended.

2. Strain the mixture into a large bowl. Add the croissant pieces, tossing them into the custard until they are well coated. Cover the custard and refrigerate for at least 4 hours.

3. Preheat the oven to 330°F (165°C). Lightly coat 4 oz (118 ml) ramekins with clarified butter. Spoon the custard into the ramekins. Place the ramekins in a hotel pan. Fill the pan halfway with cool water and bake 40 to 45 minutes, until set.

CARAMEL FILLING			
2 lbs	907 g	granulated sugar
2 pts	946 ml	water
1 tsp	3 g	cream of tartar
2 pts	946 ml	heavy cream

1. In a large, heavy saucepan, combine the sugar, water, and cream of tartar. Bring the mixture to a boil, washing down the side of the pot as necessary. Cook the sugar to 328°F (164°C). Remove the pan from the heat and immediately pour in the heavy cream all at once. Allow the mixture to bubble up and then settle.

2. Return the pan to low heat and cook, stirring constantly, until the mixture is dissolved. Cool, place in a plastic squeeze bottle, and refrigerate until ready to serve.

SPECKY VANILLA ICE CREAM			
8 liq oz	237 ml	pasteurized egg yolks
17.5 oz	496 g	granulated sugar
1 qt	.95 lt	milk
1 qt	.95 lt	heavy cream
3 tsp	12 g	Rose brand specky vanilla*

*Available from Rose Brand Corporation, Brooklyn, NY 11238.

1. Whisk all the ingredients together until well blended.

2. Freeze in an ice cream machine following manufacturer's instructions.

PÂTE À CHOUX GARNISH			
8 oz	227 g	unsalted butter, cut into cubes
1 pt	473 ml	water
12 oz	340 g	high-gluten flour
14 oz	397 g	whole eggs
2–3 liq oz	59–89 ml	milk
1 tsp	4 g	almond extract

1. Preheat the oven to 425°F (218°C). In a small saucepan, combine the butter and water; heat until the butter is melted and the mixture comes to a full boil. Reduce the heat to low; add the flour all at once and stir the mixture with a wooden spoon for 2 to 3 minutes, until it comes away from the side of the pan.

2. Transfer the mixture to a mixer fitted with a paddle attachment. Allow the paste to cool slightly, about 5 minutes. Mix in the eggs, one at a time, at low speed. Add as many eggs as the mixture can absorb and still hold its shape when piped. Mix in the extract. When ready to pipe the paste, mix in the milk to thin out the paste.

3. Place the paste into a pastry bag fitted with a small writing tip. Lightly grease a sheet pan. Using the template as a guide, pipe out a filigree garnish for each pudding. Bake the garnishes until they are golden brown, about 5 minutes. Immediately place the garnishes over a curved tuile or baguette pan. Transfer to a rack and cool completely.

ASSEMBLY	
	Chocolate cone
	Caramelized banana slices
	Fresh raspberries
	Confectioners' sugar, for dusting
	Raspberry sauce

1. Invert a warm croissant pudding onto a dessert plate. Push the tip of the squeeze bottle containing the caramel filling into the center of the pudding. Squeeze out about 2 oz (57 g) of the filling into the center of the pudding, so that it spills out onto the plate. Make a cut halfway through the pudding and separate the two wedges slightly. Push the pointed end of one of the chocolate cones into the pudding. Place 2 raspberries into the cone. Dust the dessert with the confectioners' sugar. Place a choux garnish behind the pudding.

2. Garnish the plate with a few caramelized banana slices, a scoop of the specky vanilla ice cream, and the raspberry sauce.

LACE WAVE

PHILIPPE LAURIER

Executive Pastry Chef,
*Patisfrance USA, East Rutherford,
New Jersey.*

The classic miroir (or mirror cake) is given a Modernist makeover—apple-cinnamon mousse with layers of biscuit and succès is "glazed," though food colorings and Calvados are added to this glaze. White chocolate, milk chocolate, and dark chocolate comprise the lace. A chocolate cigarette covered in cinnamon powder, ("We could have used cinnamon sticks," says Chef Laurier, "but you can't eat it."), star-fruit, mini-apples (imported from China), and green-apple coulis finish the presentation.

YIELD: 12 SERVINGS

Special Equipment:
Twelve 3" (7.6 cm) oval ring molds, 1 3/4" (4.4 cm) high, about 6 oz (177 ml) capacity
Silicone baking mat

ALMOND MERINGUE			
	3 oz	*85 g*	*almond flour*
	2.5 oz	*71 g*	*confectioners' sugar*
	4 oz	*113 g*	*egg whites*
	1 oz	*28 g*	*granulated sugar*

1. Preheat oven to 300°F (149°C). Line a half-sheet pan with parchment paper.

2. In a bowl, whisk together the almond flour and confectioners' sugar until thoroughly blended.

3. In a mixer fitted with the whisk attachment, whip the egg whites and granulated sugar to firm peaks. Fold in the almond mixture.

4. Fill a pastry bag fitted with a plain tip (Ateco #4) with the almond meringue. Pipe 3" (7.6 cm) ovals onto the prepared pan. Bake for 25 to 30 minutes, until lightly browned. Let cool completely. Trim the meringues with a serrated knife to uniform size.

HAZELNUT-ALMOND BISCUIT			
	3 oz	85 g	*hazelnut flour*
	2 oz	57 g	*almond flour*
	1 oz	28 g	*all-purpose flour*
	3.25 oz	92 g	*egg yolks*
	1.75 oz	50 g	*whole eggs*
	10 oz	283 g	*granulated sugar, divided*
	5.25 oz	149 g	*egg whites*

1. Preheat oven to 400°F (204°C). Line a half-sheet pan with parchment. Lightly butter the pan.

2. In a bowl, whisk together the hazelnut flour, almond flour, and all-purpose flour until well combined.

3. In a mixer fitted with the paddle attachment, beat the egg yolks, whole eggs, and 9 oz (255 g) of the sugar to a pale ribbon, about 5 to 6 minutes. On low speed, slowly add the dry ingredients until just combined. Do not overmix.

4. In a mixer with a whisk attachment, whip the egg whites with the remaining 1 oz (28 g) of sugar to firm peaks. Fold the meringue into the egg-flour mixture.

5. Spread the batter onto the prepared pan. Bake for 10 to 12 minutes. Allow to cool, then cut the cake into twelve 3" (7.6 cm) ovals.

CINNAMON-BAVARIAN CREAM			
	8 liq oz	237 ml	*milk*
	3 oz	85 g	*granulated sugar, divided*
	.5 tsp	2 g	*ground cinnamon*
	1.95 oz	55 g	*egg yolks*
	.41 oz	11.7 g	*gelatin sheets, softened in cold water*
	14 liq oz	414 ml	*heavy cream, whipped to soft peaks*

1. In a saucepan, bring the milk, 2 oz (57 g) of the sugar, and the cinnamon to a boil.

2. Whisk the yolks with the remaining 1 oz (28 g) of sugar until combined.

3. Temper the yolk mixture with the hot milk. Return to the heat and cook the mixture until it reaches the custard stage. Remove from the heat and stir in the drained gelatin. Pass the custard through a chinois. Cool over an ice bath. Fold in the whipped cream before the custard sets.

GREEN-APPLE SAUCE			
	1.2 oz	34 g	*egg yolk*
	3 liq oz	89 ml	*simple syrup*
	14 oz	397 g	*frozen green-apple purée, thawed*
	2 oz	57 g	*granulated sugar*
	1/2	1/2	*vanilla bean*
	.5 tsp	2 g	*ground cinnamon*
	1	1	*whole clove*

3 oz	85 g	unsalted butter
2 liq oz	59 ml	lemon juice
1.5 oz	44 ml	Calvados
.41 oz	11.7 g	gelatin sheets, softened in cold water

1. In a double boiler, cook the egg yolks with the simple syrup to 165°F (74°C); set aside.

2. In a saucepan, combine the green-apple purée, granulated sugar, vanilla bean, cinnamon, clove, and butter. Bring to a boil, stirring constantly. Remove from the heat and stir in the lemon juice and Calvados. Whisk in the drained gelatin. Before the mixture cools add the yolk-syrup mixture.*

Note. If this sauce is chilled, it will become very stiff and will have to be warmed gently before using.

CALVADOS-MIRROR GLAZE	15 oz	425 g	mirror glaze (from Patisfrance)
	1.5 liq oz	44 ml	Calvados

Melt the mirror glaze in a saucepan. Remove from the heat and stir in the Calvados.

DRIZZLED-CHOCOLATE DECORATION	12 oz	340 g	dark chocolate, tempered
	12 oz	340 g	milk chocolate, tempered
	12 oz	340 g	white chocolate, tempered

ASSEMBLY

1. Arrange twelve oval ring molds on a parchment-lined sheet pan. Place one almond meringue in the bottom of each mold.

2. Fill a pastry bag fitted with a medium plain tip with the cinnamon Bavarian cream. Pipe a 1/2" (1.3 cm) layer of Bavarian cream onto each disc. Top with an oval of hazelnut-almond biscuit and gently press down. Pipe another 1/2" (1.3 cm) layer of Bavarian cream, leaving room for the Calvados-mirror glaze. Smooth over with the bottom of a small spoon. Chill until firm, about 2 hours.

3. If necessary, reheat the Calvados-mirror glaze to a pouring consistency. Cool slightly, so as not to melt the Bavarian cream.

4. Remove the desserts from the refrigerator. Spoon some of the mirror glaze over the Bavarian layer and swirl to create a thin even layer of glaze. Return to the refrigerator for 1 hour or until the glaze sets. (Do not glaze dessert more than one day ahead.)

6. Cut acetate into twelve 5" (125 cm)-long teardrop shapes. Cut additional acetate into 12 rectangular strips with an oval appendage so that it will partially wrap around the dessert (see photo, page 95).

7. Drizzle dark, milk, and white chocolates over the acetate cut-outs.

8. Allow the "rectangular" chocolate decorations to set slightly while unmolding the Bavarian desserts.

9. Wrap the drizzled-chocolate "rectangular" strips around the unmolded desserts and refrigerate until the chocolate is set, at least 15 minutes. Let the drizzled-chocolate ovals set completely at room temperature.

FINAL ASSEMBLY   *Whole mini-apples with stems attached**
                  Star fruit slices
                  Chocolate cigarettes dusted with ground cinnamon

   Note. Mini-apples are available from Patisfrance, (800) PASTRY-1.

1. Remove a dessert from the refrigerator and remove the acetate. Place the ensemble on a dessert plate.

2. Sauce the plate with the green-apple sauce.

3. Remove the acetate from a teardrop decoration and place on the plate. Garnish the plate with two apple halves, a star fruit slice, and the chocolate cigarettes.

CHOCOLATE ANGEL FOOD CAKE

KRISTA KERN

Pastry Chef, *Three Fish, Westerly, Rhode Island.*

A cone of frozen white-chocolate parfait is topped with a Cointreau truffle; a ring of chocolate angel food cake shimmers under stars of sugar and a curl of chocolate tuile. Tangerine sorbet and citrus juices lend tang to this chocolaty plate. "When I first sketched this," reports Krista Kern, "it looked to me like something that hops on Mars. A planet hopper."

YIELD: 6 SERVINGS

Special Equipment: Six individual-size angel food cake pans

CHOCOLATE ANGEL FOOD CAKE			
3.2 oz	91 g	all-purpose flour
1.9 oz	54 g	cocoa powder
10.5 oz	298 g	granulated sugar, divided
10.5 oz	298 g	egg whites
.25 tsp	2 g	salt
1.5 tsp	5 g	cream of tartar
1/4	1/4	vanilla bean, scraped
1/8 tsp	.5 g	almond extract

1. Preheat oven to 350°F (175°C). Sift together three times: the flour, cocoa powder, and half of the sugar; set aside. In a mixer fitted with a whisk attachment, whip the egg whites, salt, and cream of tartar to soft peaks. Slowly add the remaining sugar and beat until stiff and shiny. Mix in the vanilla bean seeds and almond extract.

2. Fold the dry ingredients into the whites. Divide the batter evenly among six ungreased angel food pans. Bake for 20 minutes or until a cake tester inserted comes out dry. Hang the pans upside-down and cool for one hour. To unmold, run a knife around the sides of the pans and invert.

WHITE CHOCOLATE PARFAIT			
.1 oz	3 g	gelatin sheets
1.3 liq oz	38 ml	Cointreau
3.4 liq oz	101 ml	water
22 oz	624 ml	white chocolate, melted
2 oz	57 g	egg yolks
3.2 oz	91 g	egg whites
12 liq oz	355 g	heavy cream, whipped to soft peaks

1. Bloom the gelatin in cold water. In a saucepan, heat together the Cointreau and water. Wring the excess water out of the gelatin and melt it in the warm liqueur.

2. In a large bowl whisk the melted gelatin into the white chocolate. Whisk in the egg yolks and allow the mixture to cool.

3. In a mixer whip the egg whites to stiff peaks. Fold the whites into the white chocolate mixture. Gently fold in the whipped cream. If the mixture is very loose, refrigerate it until it has set just slightly.

4. Pipe the parfait into 2 1/2" (6.3 cm) parchment cones. Freeze overnight. Unwrap when ready to serve.

COCOA MERINGUES			
4.2 oz	119 g	egg whites
3.5 oz	99 g	granulated sugar
2 oz	57 g	confectioners' sugar
.4 oz	11 g	cocoa powder
2	2	tangerines, zest finely grated

1. Preheat oven to 275°F (135°C). In a mixer fitted with a whisk attachment, whip the egg whites to soft peaks. Mix in the granulated and confectioners' sugars. Add the cocoa powder and tangerine zest and whip until stiff and shiny.

2. Pipe the meringue into 3" (7.6 cm) diameter circles on parchment-lined sheet pans. Bake for 35 to 45 minutes or until crisp and dry.

TANGERINE SORBET			
32 liq oz	946 ml	water, divided
10.5 oz	298 g	granulated sugar
3 Tbs	82 g	corn syrup
16 liq oz	473 ml	tangerine juice, strained
1 tsp	1 tsp	lemon juice
to taste	to taste	Cointreau

1. In a saucepan combine 12 liq oz (355 ml) of the water, the sugar, and corn syrup and bring to a boil. Remove from heat and cool completely.

2. Combine the syrup with the tangerine juice and the remaining 20 liq oz (591 ml) of water. Add the lemon juice, adjusting according to taste, and the Cointreau. Refrigerate overnight.

3. Process the mixture in an ice cream machine, according to the manufacturer's instructions.

COINTREAU TRUFFLES

8 oz	227 g	Valrhona Manjari chocolate
1.5 oz	43 g	unsalted butter
4 liq oz	118 ml	heavy cream
2 oz	57 g	granulated sugar
3 liq oz	89 ml	Cointreau
2	2	tangerines, zest finely grated
12 oz	340 g	milk chocolate couverture

1. Melt together the Manjari chocolate and the butter over a double boiler. In a saucepan, heat the cream and sugar and add to the chocolate mixture. Stir until fully incorporated. Add the Cointreau, adjust according to taste, then the tangerine zest. Cover with plastic wrap and freeze until firm.

2. Remove the ganache from the freezer and form truffles with a melon baller. Return truffles to the freezer until firm.

3. Temper the milk chocolate. Either coat the truffles completely or drizzle them with chocolate. Refrigerate until set.

CHOCOLATE TUILES

3.5 oz	99 g	unsalted butter
5.9 oz	167 g	granulated sugar
4.7 oz	133 g	all-purpose flour
.8 oz	23 g	light cocoa powder
.5 tsp	2.5 g	cinnamon
3.8 oz	108 g	egg whites

1. Preheat a convection oven to 350°F (175°C). In a mixer fitted with a paddle attachment, cream the butter and sugar together until light. Sift together the flour, cocoa powder, and cinnamon; add to the butter mixture. Slowly mix in the egg whites.

2. On a silicone sheet pan lined with a baking mat, spread the batter through a stencil with lines 11" (28 cm) long and 1/2" (1.3 cm) wide. Bake for 5 to 6 minutes or until just barely firm. Remove from the oven and immediately wrap each tuile around a cone. Cool until set.

MILK CHOCOLATE SAUCE

1 pt	473 ml	heavy cream
2 oz	57 g	unsalted butter
1	1	cinnamon stick
21.3 oz	605 g	milk chocolate, chopped

1. In a saucepan bring the heavy cream and butter to a boil. Add the cinnamon stick. Remove from the heat, cover with plastic wrap, and let infuse for 15 minutes.

2. Remove the cinnamon stick and reheat the cream. Pour the hot cream over the chocolate and whisk until combined. Pour mixture into a squeeze bottle.

WHITE-CHOCOLATE CREAM	2.5 liq oz	74 ml	heavy cream
	8 oz	227 g	white chocolate, melted
	8 oz	227 g	crème fraîche, at room temperature

1. Heat the cream and add it to the white chocolate. Stir until combined. Stir in the crème fraîche.

2. Pour into a squeeze bottle with a wide tip. Refrigerate until ready to use.

CITRUS JUICE	56 oz	1.6 k	honey mandarins

1. Squeeze the juice from the tangerines and strain out the pulp. Hold in the refrigerator.

2. Let the juice come to room temperature before serving.

CARAMEL SHOOTING STARS	16 oz	454 g	granulated sugar
	8 liq oz	237 ml	water
	3 oz	85 g	glucose

1. Combine the sugar and water in a saucepan and bring to a boil, washing down the sides of the pan as necessary. Add the glucose and cook the sugar to a light caramel. Briefly immerse the bottom of the pan in cold water to stop the cooking process.

2. When the caramel has cooled and thickened just a bit, drizzle it off of a spoon onto parchment paper to create free-hand stars with a tail coming out of one point.

ASSEMBLY	Tempered chocolate discs, 3 " (7.6 cm) diameter
	Spun sugar
	Tangerine segments

1. Place a cocoa meringue in the center of a 12" (30.5 cm) soup bowl and top with three 1 1/2 ounce (43 g) scoops of tangerine sorbet. Place a chocolate disc on the sorbet and top with an angel food cake.

2. Using a melon baller, scoop a small hole out of the fat end of each parfait cone. Place the cone, fat end up, in the center of the cake and stick a truffle in the hole of the cone.

3. Drizzle milk chocolate sauce around the top of the cake, being careful not to get sauce on the parfait.

4. In the center of the cake place a chocolate tuile, narrow end up, a spun-sugar spray, and two caramel shooting stars.

5. Pour citrus juice around the dessert. Squeeze a few white chocolate lines into the juice. Place 5 tangerine segments around the dessert, sprinkle the tuile with confectioners' sugar, and serve immediately.

CHAPTER THREE

EQUIPMENT, MOLDS, AND MODERNISM

MICHAEL HU

Executive Pastry Chef
*Waldorf-Astoria Hotel,
New York.*

BORN: May 1967, Oahu,
Hawaii.
TRAINING/EXPERIENCE: Kapalua
Hotel Company; Michael's (self-
owned), Maui; Chart House
Restaurant Company; Zabar's,
New York; Ritz-Carlton, New
York; Grand Hyatt, New York.

*"In Hawaii as a boy, I spent a lot
of time running from island to
island because my family is so
large. To give you an idea, my
youngest brother got married recently. He couldn't have a big wedding—he could only invite our
family, which meant there were over
two thousand people there. We roasted ten pigs, tapped fifteen kegs of
beer. I come from a family that is
very used to putting on big parties,
so it is only appropriate that I work
for the Waldorf."*

KIM O'FLAHERTY

Pastry Cook
Essex House Hotel, New York.

BORN: February 1967,
Lowell, Massachusetts.
TRAINING/EXPERIENCE:
Newbury College, Boston;
Sweet Creations, Wakefield,
Massachusetts; White Barn Inn,
Kennebunkport, Maine; Ritz-
Carlton, San Francisco; Ritz-
Carlton, Boston.

*"The best advice I ever got? Take
your time. That means two things
to me. First, to create pastry, it
should be built and layered. Too
many chefs try to just throw it
together all at once. It should be
done in stages over a period of
weeks. If you just stop at the initial
stage, it might be fine, but if you
continue to work on it, you will
build a better product. And take
your time with your career. Many
American chefs try to jump into a
chef position without getting the
proper training. I'm taking the
slow route, so that by the time I'm
ready, I'll be a great chef. I got a
pastry chef position early, in 1991.
I didn't know what I was doing.
The customers were happy, but I
was not."*

Pastry chefs are familiar with this scene: you go into
the office of the executive chef or food and beverage
manager and request the purchase of a mold—or a comb or
a lamp or a set of stencils. The questions start coming at
you. The room grows warmer, as the line cooks pass by and
glare at you.

"We in the pastry shop are always being blamed that we
want so many little tools and molds," says Bo Friberg of
The Culinary Institute of America at Greystone in St.
Helena, California. "They say, 'John back there has his pot
and his spoon and his skillet, what do you need all that
stuff for?' But it's just the nature of the business. We do so
many more specialized things than the hot kitchen. If
you're using it to create an incredible dessert that is showy
and sells, why not?"

Some pastry chefs solve this problem by purchasing the
molds they want themselves. "I find it easier to just buy it
myself," says Richard Leach of the Park Avenue Cafe. "If
people are going to pick at me, I'd rather argue about
ingredients." John Degnan of the Lodge at Koele, Lana'i
Hawaii, has a budget to purchase equipment. "But I spend
a lot of my own money on molds and equipment," he says,
citing chocolate molds, small equipment for sugar, lamps,
stencils, silpat mats, and silkscreens. "Quite often I purchase molds that the savory cooks can use," he adds. "The
hot kitchen can use some of the plastic molds for garde-
manger and the pantry area."

It is probably no coincidence that the burst of creativity
in American pastry kitchens is occuring in the wake of
remarkable improvements in equipment. The Modernist
pastry chef, seeking unfamiliar shapes and abstraction,
now has a wealth of it, and can produce in bulk. "What
the equipment enables you to do is do in high volume
what you used to do by hand," says Degnan. "It's an
explosion in new materials and molds," enthuses Bo
Friberg. "It's making things so much easier to make
desserts looks showy." Every menu needs at least one
"wow" dessert, says Friberg, because the restaurant down
the street probably does.

The revolution in plated desserts might not have been possible without the Demarle Company in France. These are
the people who manufacture Silpat and Flexipans, two
pieces of equipment that have changed the way chefs approach their work.

Silpat was actually created in the early 1980s, but has only been in wide use in the United
States for the last few years. Silpat is made from a woven glass fabric covered with F.D.A.-
approved, conformed food-graded silicone. It can be used in either the oven, the freezer, or
the microwave, and is designed to replace paper or fat in a tray or pan. Excellent for use for

chocolate work, sugar- and pastry-making. Silpat is responsible for many of the sinuous, gracefully curved, and exquisitely conformed shapes found in this volume. It also led the way for the second major advance: Flexipans.

Flexipans are made of some of the same materials as Silpat—silicone-coated, spun fiberglass with a knitted fabric underneath—and have comparable tolerances to temperature. Flexipans are sold as full-size cake pans or in single-serving, multicavity sheets, with anywhere from 15 to 30 cavities in each. Forms available include savarin, brioche, mini-cheesecake, muffin, madeleine, timbale, florentine, quichettes, pyramid, muffin, demi-sphere, petit four, cylinder, pomponette, oval, tartlet, Christmas log, heart, dariole, and others. These molds are guaranteed for 2,000 uses, but will probably last longer. They release frozen items and most baked goods extremely well, and clean-up is effortless.

Silicone baking mats are now being manufactured by several companies. Also relatively new in the pastry kitchen are Teflon-coated sheet pan liners; plastic production molds, for assembly; Zig templates, an alternative to the improvised cardboard and fish-tub plastic templates most chefs use. These new products join the armamentarium of molds long available to the pastry chef: tinned-steel molds in all of the forms mentioned above; metal rings, pyramids, demi-spheres, and tartlets; acrylic rings for cold preparations; plastic chocolate molds; wooden graining tools for chocolate work; cake-top stencils; aluminum angel food cake pans and bundt pans.

From this array of equipment, chefs are combining and improvising to create new looks for their desserts. "These molds give you flexibility to create new creations," agrees Philippe Laurier. "For example, you can do a crème brûlée in a Flexipan and put it in the freezer. Then you can use it as a disc inside another dessert, a mousse for example. How could you take it out of any other kind of mold?" Laurier has also cut yule logs and triangular forms into wedges, for fresh components on his plates.

STANTON HO

Executive Pastry Chef
Las Vegas Hilton Hotel.

BORN: April 1952, Honolulu, Hawaii.
TRAINING/EXPERIENCE: Kapiolani Community College (University of Hawaii), culinary program; Ecole Lenôtre, Paris; various hotels and resorts, Hawaii.

"Chefs must make a number of mistakes, major mistakes, as part of the learning process. I have personally learned a lot from mistakes, and that makes you a better person as far as swallowing your pride, admitting your mistake, and correcting it so that in the future it will be easy sailing, production-wise. This is the best way to improve yourself as far as timing, servicing, mise en place, ensuring that you have a lot of backups in your refrigerators—it's a constant awareness of what's around you."

RICHARD LEACH

Pastry Chef
Park Avenue Cafe, New York.

BORN: November 1965, Greenlawn, New York.
TRAINING/EXPERIENCE: The Culinary Institute of America; River Café, Aureole, L'Espinasse, One Fifth Avenue, Symphony Café, La Côte Basque, all in New York.

"I've been lucky. People have given me a chance to do what I want. Charlie Palmer first gave me a chance to try pastry. We started with small, simple stuff, but once we started building vertically, and we saw how people reacted to it, we went nuts for a few years. Some things are vertical, and some aren't. It's not a goal to make things that poke you in the nose. But a lot of the things I did in the beginning I don't do anymore; I found them to be a little heavy and not as refreshing. Now I'm going more toward lighter fruit items when possible. People need lighter food."

This restless search for new forms and new materials also creates new challenges for the chef. "A lot of people don't know the science of conduction of heat," says Judy Prince of J.B. Prince in New York. They need to know the materials (stainless steel is not a great conductor of heat, for example), how the contour and size of a mold will affect the way the ingredients will bake, how the fat content of a recipe will affect its release, and how that changes with the mold material.

Chefs also fashion their own equipment from materials found in hardware stores, plumbing stores, and plastic concerns, presenting yet another challenge to this equipment-intensive industry—many chefs don't know the properties of items they use. PVC piping, so popular among pastry chefs, can leach toxins into foods if not properly wrapped. "You don't want to fool around too much because metals react," says Krista Kern. "You need to know the properties of these metals. I've seen kitchens that use curtain rods. You just can't be sure of the metals the curtain-rod people used."

But the informed chef, master of his materials, is ready to take on the world. Michael Hu's Gianduja Mousse is contained in a unique triangle form—unique in that Hu, executive pastry chef at the Waldorf-Astoria, had a carpenter at his hotel make an original for him to his specifications, and then he made an acetate mold from that. "I was looking for this triangle, not a pyramid," recalls Hu. "You'd think this form could be found on a trophy or on a light fixture somewhere, but it wasn't. So we had the carpenter make it." He uses it to great effect, positioning it at a gentle diagonal, and then making it the eye of raspberry powder undulations, creating an attractive arrangement with an unusual color timbre that calls attention to a classic flavor combination.

Hu's Pineapple Financier is made from a hexagonal mold, and when combined with exotic touches—bubble sugar, slashes of chocolate—the overall effect of a written Chinese character. The fact is, the forms of the chocolate were completely last-minute-plating, and that any exoticism the plate conveys is purely in the eye of the hungry diner.

Kim O'Flaherty takes a wedge out of a familiar ring and stands it on its side for her Midnight Macadamia Torte. The form is echoed by the white chocolate ring, and chocolate lines rise up from the back, as if they are frets, and the entirety is a delicious musical note. Note also how the simple converging lines of powder off to the side add drama, sweep and, contrast to this circle-themed plate.

Pascal Janvier makes his Chocolate Basket from a demi-sphere mold, creating a sphere within a sphere, a cold form and a warm one, with all the homey associations of a basket. Richard Leach juxtaposes the cold, severe Chocolate Box with a loose drizzle of chocolate sauce on the plate, and playful positioning of triangle cookies on a quenelle.

Boundless creativity? A paradise of limitless possibilities? John Degnan is already seeing a sameness, and yet another challenge to the contemporary chef. "The drawback is that a lot of people are doing the same style of pastry with this equipment," he says. "What is emerging is a similarity of look. The challenge is to do something new with it."

BITTERSWEET CHOCOLATE BOXES WITH CHOCOLATE ESPRESSO SORBET

RICHARD LEACH

Pastry Chef, *Park Avenue Cafe,*
New York.

Espresso mousse is enclosed with cubes of chocolate cake in a thin chocolate box, and the flavor is reinforced by the chocolate espresso sorbet atop a chocolate meringue. Dots of espresso sabayon, chocolate tuiles, and drizzles of chocolate sauce finish the presentation. "The smear of white chocolate on the box is just for decoration," says Richard Leach. "When I first did the box it was solid, but then I started fooling around, piping lines and so on. Now I take a brush and swipe it with white chocolate. It breaks it up a bit. It's not enough to affect the taste."

YIELD: 14 SERVINGS

Special Equipment:
Fourteen 2 x 2 x 3" (5.1 x 5.1 x 7.6 cm) plastic boxes (available at office supply stores)
Silicone baking mat
2" (5.1 cm) high x 8 1/4" (21 cm) long triangular stencil

| CHOCOLATE BOXES | 12 oz | 340 g | white chocolate, tempered |
| | 28 oz | 794 g | bittersweet chocolate, tempered |

1. Using a small paintbrush, streak some of the tempered white chocolate on the inside of the boxes. Chill until set, about 15 minutes. Coat the inside of the boxes with tempered bittersweet chocolate. The layer of chocolate should be 1/16 to 1/8" (.16 to .32 cm) thick.

2. Place the boxes on a sheet pan and allow to set.

> *"You have to work clean with chocolate, and be delicate," says Richard Leach. "Polish molds well, and work on a clean, hard surface. The chocolate should be thin and easy for the customer to access. That's the trick to that box."*

Dessert shown on page 104.

CHOCOLATE ESPRESSO SORBET	16 oz	454 g	bittersweet chocolate, chopped
	2 oz	57 g	espresso roast coffee beans, crushed
	4 oz	113 g	granulated sugar
	48 liq oz	1.4 lt	water
	1 Tbs	15 ml	coffee extract

1. Place the chopped chocolate in a bowl.

2. In a saucepan, combine the crushed coffee beans, sugar, water, and coffee extract; cook until the sugar is dissolved and the syrup is boiling.

3. Pour the hot syrup over the chopped chocolate and stir until completely melted.

4. Strain the mixture through a fine chinois and chill.

5. Process in ice cream machine, following manufacturer's intructions.

ESPRESSO SABAYON SAUCE	3 oz	85 g	egg yolks
	3 oz	85 g	granulated sugar
	1.5 Tbs	18 g	ground espresso beans
	6 liq oz	177 ml	heavy cream
	6 oz	170 g	crème frâiche

1. Combine the yolks, sugar, and ground espresso beans in a double boiler and whisk until pale and thick, about 4 to 6 minutes. Remove from the heat. Cool.

2. In a mixer fitted with a whisk attachment, whip together the heavy cream and crème frâiche until soft peaks form. Fold into the yolk mixture. Strain through a chinois; chill.

CHOCOLATE SAUCE	12 oz	340 g	bittersweet chocolate, finely chopped
	2.25 liq oz	67 ml	light corn syrup
	4.5 liq oz	133 ml	heavy cream

1. Place the chopped chocolate in a bowl.

2. In a saucepan, bring the corn syrup and cream to a boil.

3. Pour the hot cream over the chocolate and stir until completely melted.

CHOCOLATE CAKE	9.25 oz	262 g	all-purpose flour
	1 Tbs	12 g	baking powder
	.5 tsp	2.5 g	salt
	5.25 oz	149 g	unsalted butter, at room temperature
	12.25 oz	347 g	granulated sugar
	2.5 oz	71 g	alkalized cocoa powder
	5.5 oz	156 g	eggs
	8 liq oz	237 ml	warm water

1. Preheat the oven to 325°F (163°C). Butter an 8 x 3" (20.3 x 7.6 cm) round cake pan. Dust with flour.

2. Sift together the flour, baking powder, and salt.

3. In a mixer with a paddle attachment, beat the butter until creamy. Gradually beat in the sugar and continue to beat until smooth. Turn the mixer off and add the cocoa powder all at once. On low speed, mix until combined. Gradually add the eggs, then slowly add the sifted dry ingredients and mix until combined. Slowly add the warm water and mix until smooth. Scrape the batter into the prepared pan and bake 60 to 70 minutes, or until the center is set. Cool for ten minutes; remove from pan and cool completely.

4. Cut the cake into small dice.

CUBE MOUSSE			
2.5 liq oz	74 ml	milk
2 oz	57 g	unsalted butter
4 oz	113 g	bittersweet chocolate
2 tsp	4 g	finely grated orange zest
4 tsp	20 ml	coffee extract
3.5 oz	99 g	egg yolks
8 oz	227 g	granulated sugar, divided
20 oz	567 g	crème fraîche
11 liq oz	325 ml	heavy cream
22 oz	624 g	diced chocolate cake

1. Combine the milk, butter, chocolate, orange zest, and coffee extract in a double boiler and cook until the chocolate is melted and the mixture is smooth. Remove mixture from the heat and let it cool.

2. In a mixer fitted with a whisk attachment, whip the yolks and 4 oz (113 g) of the granulated sugar until pale and fluffy. Whisk into the melted chocolate mixture.

3. In a mixer with the whisk attachment, combine the crème fraîche, heavy cream, and the remaining 4 oz (113 g) of granulated sugar. Whip until soft peaks form. Fold into yolk-chocolate mixture. Fold in the diced chocolate cake.

4. Fill the chocolate boxes with mousse, leveling off the top with a spatula. Freeze until the mousse is firm.

DARK COCOA TUILES			
3.35 oz	95 g	all-purpose flour
4 oz	113 g	confectioners' sugar
.75 oz	21 g	dark cocoa powder
4 oz	113 g	unsalted butter, softened
3.25 oz	92 g	honey
2 oz	57 g	egg whites

1. Preheat the oven to 300°F (149°C). Line a half-sheet pan with a silicone mat. Have ready a dowel or pipe for bending the tuiles.

2. Sift together the flour, confectioners' sugar, and dark cocoa powder.

3. In a mixer fitted with a paddle attachment, beat the butter until smooth. Add the honey and beat until pale. At low speed, add the sifted dry ingredients. Gradually beat in the egg whites and mix until the batter is smooth.

4. Place a triangular stencil on the silicone baking mat and spread the tuile batter in a thin layer over the stencil. Remove the stencil and bake the tuiles until set, about 9 to 11 minutes. Remove the tuiles from the oven and bend them, warm, over the pipe. Repeat to make 14 tuiles.

LIGHT COCOA TUILES			
	3.35 oz	95 g	all-purpose flour
	4 oz	113 g	confectioners' sugar
	.75 oz	21 g	light cocoa powder
	4 oz	113 g	unsalted butter, softened
	3.25 oz	92 g	honey
	2 oz	57 g	egg whites

1. Preheat oven to 300°F (150°C). Line a half-sheet pan with a silicone baking mat. Have ready a dowel or pipe for bending the tuiles.

2. Sift together the flour, confectioners' sugar, and light cocoa powder.

3. In a mixer with a paddle attachment, beat the butter until smooth. Add the honey and beat until pale. At low speed, add the sifted dry ingredients. Gradually beat in the egg whites and mix until the batter is smooth.

4. Place the triangular stencil on the baking mat and spread the tuile batter in a thin layer over the stencil. Remove the stencil and bake the tuiles until set, about 9 to 11 minutes. Remove the tuiles from the oven and bend them, warm, over the pipe. Repeat to make 14 tuiles.

COCOA MERINGUES			
	12 oz	340 g	sliced, blanched almonds
	15 oz	425 g	granulated sugar, divided
	1.5 Tbs	18 g	dark cocoa powder
	12 oz	340 g	egg whites

1. Preheat the oven to 250°F (121°C). Lightly oil a baking sheet or line it with parchment.

2. In a food processor fitted with a metal blade, grind together the almonds, 12 oz (340 g) of the granulated sugar, and the cocoa powder.

3. In a mixer fitted with a whisk attachment, beat the egg whites with the remaining 3 oz (85 g) of the granulated sugar until firm peaks form. Fold in the ground almond mixture.

4. Fill a pastry bag fitted with medium plain tip (Ateco #4) with the meringue. Pipe out fourteen 3" (7.6 cm) ovals using a zigzag motion. Bake for 45 minutes, or until dry.

ASSEMBLY

Confectioners' sugar

1. Drizzle some of the chocolate sauce onto a dessert plate. Dot with some espresso sabayon.

2. Hold a cupped hand over the open end of a filled chocolate box. With a sharp thrust, slide the chocolate box out of the plastic mold.

3. Place a chocolate box on the plate, slightly off-center. Arrange 1 cocoa meringue opposite the chocolate box and top with a quenelle of chocolate-espresso sorbet. Dust 1 dark and 1 light tuile with confectioners' sugar. Insert the tuiles into the sorbet so that 1 tuile is resting on the box.

GIANDUJA MOUSSE

MICHAEL HU

Executive Pastry Chef, *Waldorf-Astoria Hotel, New York.*

The European classic favorite of chocolate and hazelnut is contrasted with the slightly acidic tang of passion fruit. Michael Hu is particularly satisfied with the look of the plate: "Visually it is complete," he says. "Everything is working in harmony. There are some smooth dramatic lines in the raspberry powder, the piped sorbet is very flowing, and the sugar connects everything together."

YIELD: 28 SERVINGS

CHOCOLATE-COATED PYRAMID MOLDS

32 oz	907 g	dark chocolate, tempered

1. Using a template, cut out a piece of acetate with an X-acto knife, along the heavy lines (as shown in the diagram below). Lightly score the dotted lines with the X-acto; this makes the folding process easier. Fold along the dotted lines to produce a pyramid with three triangular surfaces. The fourth surface gets folded in for stability. Each triangular surface measures 3 x 3 x 2" (7.6 x 7.6 x 5.1 cm), where the 2" (5.1 cm) side is the base. Repeat to make 28 pyramids molds.

2. Ladle tempered chocolate into a mold to fill it completely. Turn the mold upside-down to allow the excess chocolate to drip back into the bowl of tempered chocolate. Place the mold on its side on a parchment-lined sheet pan. Repeat to make 28 chocolate-coated pyramids molds. Let them set at room temperature for 1 hour.

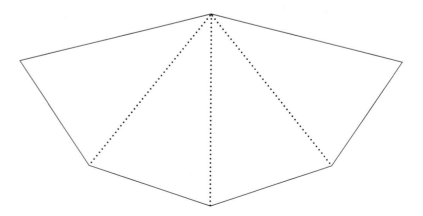

GIANDUJA MOUSSE	13 oz	369 g	Gianduja chocolate, finely chopped
	3 oz	85 g	unsalted butter, cut in chunks
	3 oz	85 g	egg yolks
	2 oz	57 g	granulated sugar, divided
	4.2 oz	119 g	egg whites
	16 liq oz	473 ml	heavy cream, whipped to soft peaks

1. Melt the chocolate with the butter in a double boiler. Remove from the heat and set aside.

2. In a mixer with the whisk attachment, beat the egg yolks with 1 oz (28 g) of sugar to the ribbon stage. Fold into the chocolate mixture.

3. In a mixer fitted with a whisk attachment, whip the egg whites with the remaining 1 oz (28 g) of sugar to firm peaks. Fold the meringue into the chocolate mixture. Fold in the whipped cream.

4. Scrape the mousse into a pastry bag fitted with a plain tip. Pipe the mixture into the chocolate-coated pyramid molds, filling them completely. Level the top of the pyramids with a small spatula and chill until set, at least 4 hours.

PASSION FRUIT SORBET	19 oz	539 g	granulated sugar, divided
	.3 oz	9 g	stabilizer*
	44 liq oz	1.3 lt	water
	8.5 oz	241 g	glucose powder
	2.2 lbs	1 kg	frozen passion fruit purée

*Note. Stabilizer is available from Patisfrance, (800) PASTRY-1.

1. In a bowl, combine 9.5 oz (269 g) of the sugar with the stabilizer.

2. In a large saucepan, bring the water to a boil. Gradually mix the sugar mixture into the boiling water. Stir in the remaining 9.5 oz (269 g) of the sugar and the glucose. Return to the boil and boil for 20 to 30 seconds or until the syrup is clear. Remove from the heat.

3. When the syrup has stopped boiling, stir in the frozen passion fruit purée.

4. Process the mixture in an ice cream machine according to the manufacturer's instructions.

5. If not using immediately, freeze in a covered container. Otherwise, soften the sorbet to a piping consistency. Fill a pastry bag, fitted with a St. Honore tip, with the softened sorbet and pipe 28 servings of sorbet onto a cold parchment-lined tray. Freeze.

| COMBED-CHOCOLATE | 3 lbs | 1.36 kg | white chocolate, tempered |
| TRIANGLES | 1.5 lbs | .68 kg | dark chocolate, tempered |

1. Using an offset spatula, evenly spread a layer of white chocolate, about 1/8" (.32 cm) thick, on a work surface. Let stand for about 3 to 5 minutes until the chocolate is just beginning to set.

2. Drag a pastry comb through the chocolate to create straight lines.

3. Spread a layer of the dark chocolate across the white chocolate, filling the spaces created by the comb. Let chocolate set completely.

4. With a hot knife, cut out 28 triangles (3 x 3 1/2 x 2 1/2" / 7.6 x 8.9 x 6.4 cm).

5. With a hot knife, cut out 28 triangles (1 1/2 x 2 1/2 x 3" / 3.8 x 6.4 x 7.6 cm).

ASSEMBLY

Dehydrated raspberry powder*
28 pink-pulled-sugar curls

> **Note.* Dehydrated raspberry powder is available from Fresh 'n Wild, Box 2981, Vancouver, WA (800) 222-5578.

1. Chill a dessert plate. Have ready two combed-chocolate triangles, one of each size. Take out a mousse-filled pyramid from the refrigerator and remove the acetate. Take out the dessert plate from the refrigerator and, using a decorative stencil, dust the plate with dehydrated raspberry powder.

2. Use a propane torch to heat a flat, heat-proof, metallic surface. Touch one side of the large combed-chocolate triangle to the heated surface. Immediately attach the warm side of the triangle to the cold plate, applying pressure so that it rests slightly elevated from the surface of the plate. Similarly, touch one side of the mousse-filled pyramid to the heated surface. Gently attach the pyramid to the elevated triangle.

3. Place the small triangle on the plate. Remove a serving of passion fruit sorbet from the freezer and place it on the triangle. Garnish the dessert with a sugar decoration. Serve.

MIDNIGHT MACADAMIA TORTE

KIM O'FLAHERTY

Pastry Cook, *Essex House Hotel,
New York.*

O'Flaherty won the "Best Individual Plated Dessert" in the 1997

Patisfrance U.S. Pastry Competition for this dessert, a milk chocolate mousse

with chocolate-covered macadamias and a passion-fruit curd inside. A choco-

late blackout disc forms the base. Given the theme "The Age of Aquarius,"

O'Flaherty reproduced the signs of the zodiac in silkscreen on white chocolate.

"It didn't really take too much time to put the visual design together,"

O'Flaherty recalls. "I love passion fruit, macadamias, and blackout cake, so I

just put my favorite ingredients together."

YIELD: 12 SERVINGS

Special Equipment:
Twelve 3 " (7.6 cm) ring molds
Wagner airless spray gun
Ring-shaped silkscreen (for a 3 " (7.6 cm) ring)
Rubber trowel and decorating comb

CHOCOLATE BLACKOUT CAKE			
8 liq oz	237 ml	brewed coffee
4 oz	113 g	unsalted butter
14 oz	397 g	granulated sugar
7.5 oz	213 g	all-purpose flour
pinch	pinch	salt
1 tsp	5 g	baking powder
2 tsp	10 g	baking soda
1.6 oz	45 g	cocoa powder, sifted
5.25 oz	149 g	whole eggs
8 liq oz	237 ml	buttermilk

1. Preheat oven to 350°F. Lightly grease a half-sheet pan. In a saucepan, combine the coffee and butter; heat until the butter is completely melted. Remove mixture from the heat and set aside.

2. In a mixing bowl, combine the sugar, flour, salt, baking powder, soda, and cocoa powder.

3. In another bowl, whisk together the eggs and the buttermilk. Whisk in the coffee mixture. While slowly whisking the dry ingredients, slowly pour in the liquid mixture. Whisk until all are combined. Pour the batter into the prepared pan and bake until set, about 30 minutes. Cool and cut into 2 1/2" (6.3 cm) discs.

PASSION FRUIT CURD	8.8 oz	250 g	*Ravifruit passion-fruit purée**
	1	1	*vanilla bean, split and scraped*
	10 oz	283 g	*granulated sugar*
	8.75 oz	248 g	*whole eggs*
	1.3 oz	38 g	*pastry cream powder**
	12 oz	340 g	*unsalted butter*

Note. Ravifruit passion-fruit purée and pastry cream powder are available from Patisfrance, (800) PASTRY-1.

1. In a saucepan, combine the passion fruit purée and the vanilla bean scrapings (without the pod). Bring the purée to a boil; remove from heat.

2. In a bowl, whisk together the sugar, eggs, and pastry cream powder. Whisk the hot passion fruit purée into the egg mixture. Return the entire mixture to the saucepan and cook over medium heat, whisking constantly, until the mixture has thickened.

3. Pour the curd into a bowl and add the butter, whisking until melted. Cover the curd and refrigerate until firm.

CHOCOLATE MOUSSE	3.25 oz	92 g	*egg yolks*
	5 oz	142 g	*granulated sugar*
	3 liq oz	89 ml	*water*
	1 lb	454 g	*milk chocolate couverture (Patisfrance), melted*
	24 liq oz	710 ml	*heavy cream, whipped to soft peaks*

1. In a mixer fitted with the whisk attachment, beat the egg yolks on medium speed until pale in color.

2. In a saucepan combine the sugar and water and cook to the soft-ball stage (234 to 240°F/112 to 115°C). While beating at high speed, slowly pour the hot syrup into the yolks. Continue beating until the yolks are cool.

3. Using a whisk, fold 1 cup of the whipped cream into the melted chocolate. Fold in the beaten egg yolks and then the remaining whipped cream.

| CHOCOLATE-COVERED | 4 oz | 113 g | *bittersweet chocolate, tempered* |
| MACADAMIA NUTS | 7.7 oz | 221 g | *macadamia nuts, toasted and cooled* |

1. Line a sheet pan with parchment paper. Dip each nut into the chocolate and place on the prepared sheet pan. Allow the chocolate to set completely.

2. Chop the nuts into medium-size pieces.

ASSEMBLY OF MOLDS   *Simple syrup, for brushing cake*

1. Line each ring mold with a strip of plastic. Place a chocolate blackout disc in the bottom of each mold. Brush the cake rounds with simple syrup.

2. Pipe a thin layer of the passion curd on top of each cake round. Sprinkle a layer of the chocolate-covered macadamia nuts over the curd.

3. Pipe enough chocolate mousse over the nut layer to fill each mold. Scrape the mousse into a smooth layer, even with the top of the mold. Freeze the molds for several hours, until set.

SPRAY COATING

| 16 oz | 454 g | bittersweet chocolate, chopped |
| 16 oz | 454 g | cocoa butter, chopped |

1. Melt the chocolate and cocoa butter in a bowl over simmering water.

2. Transfer the mixture to the Wagner airless spray gun.

3. Unmold the frozen mousse rings. With a knife, cut a slice off the side of each round so that the rings can stand on a plate.

4. With the rings standing on this edge, evenly spray all the sides of the desserts, creating a velvet finish.

PLATE DECORATION

1. Place two long pieces of masking tape on a dessert plate in a narrow triangle pattern (see dessert photograph).

2. Cut out a cardboard stencil in a triangle that will fit inside the masking tape, leaving narrow strips between the masking tape and the stencil. Cover the remainder of the plate with parchment paper.

3. Use the chocolate-cocoa butter coating to spray the plate, so that only the narrow triangular strips are coated. Remove the tape, stencil, and parchment paper and repeat with the remaining plates.

SILK SCREEN RING
GARNISH

| 5 oz | 142 g | bittersweet chocolate, tempered |
| 16 oz | 454 g | white chocolate, tempered |

1. Place the silkscreen over a parchment-lined sheet pan. With a rubber trowel, carefully spread the chocolate over the silkscreen. Repeat to form 12 designs. Allow the chocolate to set completely.

2. Spread the white chocolate over the dark chocolate designs in a thin layer. Allow the chocolate to set.

3. Using a 3" (7.6 cm) round cutter, cut out rounds just outside the edge of the designs. Use a 2" (5 cm) round cutter to cut out the inside of each of the rounds.

CHOCOLATE WAVE
GARNISH

| 1 lb | 454 g | bittersweet chocolate, tempered |

1. Cut out twelve 6" (15 cm) long acetate strips (1 1/2" / 13.8 cm wide). Using a small metal spatula, spread the chocolate onto the strips (work with only a few strips at a time). Allow the chocolate to set a little.

2. Drag a decorating comb horizontally across the strip, leaving a 1" (2.5 cm) edge at one short end, so that the chocolate strips stay attached. Allow the chocolate to set completely.

3. Carefully peel the acetate off the chocolate (the garnish is extremely delicate).

ASSEMBLY *Gold leaf*
Mango sauce

1. Place one of the desserts on its side on a decorated plate. Lean one of the silkscreen rings against the dessert. Stand one of the chocolate wave garnishes vertically behind the dessert, with the attached end toward the plate.

2. Place a few graduated dots of mango sauce inside the triangle. Repeat with the remaining desserts.

CHOCOLATE BASKET WITH PRECIOUS HARVEST

PASCAL JANVIER

Pastry Cook, Instructor, Technical Manager, *Cocoa Barry Training Center, Pennsauken, New Jersey.*

"To me, chocolate should be treated like gold," says Pascal Janvier. Cocoa sorbet rolled in cocoa powder is served in a chocolate basket. *"I tried to do it, simply but nicely, to give a picture of preciousness."*

YIELD: 15 SERVINGS

Special Equipment:
5.5" (14 cm) diameter plastic demisphere molds, available from ABC Emballuxe (514) 381-8845

CHOCOLATE SORBET

5.3 oz	150 g	Cocoa Barry Extra Brute, *cocoa powder*
17.6 oz	499 g	granulated sugar, divided
58 liq oz	1.7 lt	mineral water
4.4 oz	125 g	inverted sugar
0.4 oz	10 g	sorbet stabilizer, such as Gel Glace from Patisfrance

1. In a bowl combine the cocoa powder and 14.1 oz (400 g) of the sugar.

2. In a saucepan, heat the mineral water until simmering. Remove from the heat and add the cocoa mixture, then the inverted sugar. When mixture cools to 113°F (45°C), add the stabilizer and the remaining 3.5 oz (99 g) of sugar.

3. Process in an ice cream machine according to the manufacturer's instructions. Using a 5 to 6 ounce (141 to 170 g) scoop, form the sorbet into perfectly round balls and freeze.

CHOCOLATE LACE DISH

60 oz/1.7kg Chocolat-Amer (extra-bitter) chocolate, tempered

1. Put some of the chocolate in a cornet and pipe 15 to 20 lines going in all directions in the demi-sphere molds.

2. Put the rest of the chocolate in a pastry bag with a 1/8" (.3 cm) star tip and pipe another 15 to 20 lines. Scrape the excess chocolate off the tops of the molds. Refrigerate for 30 minutes or until set, then unmold.

> *The chocolate lace is piped in a demi-sphere mold. Using 2 different pipes, there is a texture to one of the lines. Baking chocolate with a low cocoa butter content is used, so that the tempered chocolate remains thick and holds the line.*

ASSEMBLY

Gold leaf
Extra Brute cocoa powder

1. Cover the rim of each basket with gold leaf. Holding the basket with the rim at a 45° angle, rub the bottom on a warm surface until it just begins to melt. Place the basket on a serving plate and hold until set.

2. Roll the frozen balls of sorbet in cocoa powder and place in the chocolate lace dishes.

RASPBERRY TOWER

STAN HO

Executive Pastry Chef, *Las Vegas Hilton Hotel.*

"All the desserts I make are on the light side," says Stanton Ho. *"It's very appealing after a heavy meal. I try for an eye-catching appearance—the drama of this tower, for example. It's like a sales and advertising gimmick when it passes by the tables."* Here, Italian meringue is folded into the raspberry mousse to give it a light consistency. The raspberry coulis on the bottom enhances the flavor of the fruits as well as the mousse, to create a well-balanced combination. A pulled-sugar floral arrangement completes the picture.

YIELD: 16 SERVINGS

Special Equipment:
Six clear, plastic, fluorescent light-protector tubes, 14" (35.6 cm) long x 1 1/4" (3.2 cm) diameter, available at electrical supply stores
Wagner airless spray gun

RASPBERRY MOUSSE			
12.3 oz	350 g	raspberry purée
.25 oz	7 g	gelatin sheet, softened in cold water
1 Tbs	5 ml	lemon juice
9 liq oz	250 g	heavy cream, whipped to soft peaks
7 oz	198 g	Italian meringue

1. Place about half of the raspberry purée in a large bowl and heat over a water bath.

2. Drain the gelatin sheets and add to warm purée. Whisk the purée until the gelatin is dissolved. Remove from heat and whisk in remaining raspberry purée and lemon juice.

3. Cool over an ice bath.

4. Fold the whipped cream into the cooled raspberry mixture. Fold in the meringue. Refrigerate until set.

> With the high volume Stanton Ho must produce every day for his hotel, the chef must be concerned with freshness and storage. "The Italian meringue stores very well cooked, so that there's less chance of bacterial growth," says Chef Ho. "A percentage of alcohol is a standard item in our recipes. When I have banquets for two thousand or three thousand, I have a tendency to put it in, for flavor and as a preservative."

RASPBERRY COULIS	*17.6 oz*	*500 g*	*fresh raspberries*
	4.6 oz	*130 g*	*granulated sugar*

1. In a food processor with the steel blade, combine the raspberry purée and granulated sugar and process until blended.

2. Refrigerate until needed.

WHITE CHOCOLATE DISCS	*9.7 oz*	*275 g*	*white chocolate, tempered*

1. Spread the tempered white chocolate onto parchment paper evenly to make a 1/8" (.32 cm) thick layer. When slightly set, but still pliable, use a 1 1/2" (3.8 cm) round cutter to cut out 16 discs. Allow to set completely.

MARBELIZED CHOCOLATE	*12 oz*	*340 g*	*white chocolate, tempered*
TOWERS	*3 oz*	*85 g*	*semisweet chocolate, tempered*

1. Using a Wagner airless spray gun, spray some warm semisweet chocolate into both ends of one of the plastic tubes. Once the semisweet chocolate starts to set, quickly pour about 2 oz (57 g) of the warm tempered white chocolate into the tube. Roll the white chocolate around in the tube. The rolling motion achieves both a marbling effect and an even thickness. The chocolate layer should be 1/16" (.32 cm) to 1/8" (.16 cm) thick.

2. Repeat to make 6 marbleized tubes. Chill until set. The chocolate will disengage from the tubing when the chocolate sets. Slide the chocolate out of the tubes and cut into 4" (10 cm) pieces at an angle, using a hot wire cutter. Straighten the cuts by sliding the ends onto a hot flat griddle. At this point, attach a white chocolate disc to the base of each tower.

ASSEMBLY	*Pulled-sugar flowers and flourishes*
	Fresh raspberries and assorted fruit

1. Spoon some raspberry coulis onto a dessert plate to create a triangle extending across the plate.

2. Fill a pastry bag fitted with a medium plain tip (Ateco #4), with raspberry mousse. Pipe the mousse into a chocolate tower. Insert a pulled-sugar flower and a few flourishes into the mousse and garnish the plate with raspberries and assorted fruit.

PINEAPPLE FINANCIER CAKE WITH POPPY SEED PARFAIT AND CHERRY SAUCE

MICHAEL HU

Executive Pastry Chef, *Waldorf-Astoria Hotel, New York.*

The flavors of the Mediterranean and the Tropics blend seamlessly in this refreshing finale. "Poppy seed parfait is definitely one of my favorites," says Michael Hu. "Pineapple goes well with almonds and hazelnuts, and the cherry sauce provides a nice contrast." A screen of bubble-sugar finishes the plate.

YIELD: 28 SERVINGS

Special Equipment:
Twenty-eight 4 oz (118 ml) hexagonal ring molds
Twenty-eight 2 oz pyramid molds
Silicone baking mat

POPPY SEED PARFAIT

5 oz	142 g	*poppy seeds*
4.6 oz	130 g	*egg yolks*
6 oz	170 g	*granulated sugar*
.75 oz	21 g	*honey*
2.5 liq oz	74 ml	*Grand Marnier or other orange-flavored liqueur*
2	2	*vanilla beans, split and scraped*
24 liq oz	710 ml	*heavy cream, whipped to soft peaks*

1. Spread the poppy seeds on a sheet pan and bake in a 350°F (177°C) oven for 15 to 20 minutes. Cool and reserve.

2. Combine the egg yolks, sugar, honey, Grand Marnier, and vanilla seeds in a double boiler and whisk until pale in color and thickened, about 10 minutes. Whisk until cool over an ice bath.

3. Fold in the whipped cream and poppy seeds. Pour into the pyramid molds and freeze.

ROASTED PINEAPPLE

7.5 lb	3.4 kg	*peeled and cored fresh pineapple*
12 oz	340 g	*light brown sugar*
6 oz	170 g	*unsalted butter, melted*

1. Preheat oven to 375°F (191°C). Cut the pineapple into 1" (2.5 cm) chunks.

2. Place the pineapple chunks, sugar, and butter in a large roasting pan and toss to coat.

3. Bake for 25 to 35 minutes or until the pineapple chunks are golden brown and lightly caramelized. Stir occasionally to keep the pineapple chunks from sticking. Let cool.

4. Reserve 84 chunks for the cake and dice the remaining ones for the compote.

PINEAPPLE FINANCIER CAKE

30 oz	850 g	*unsalted butter*
11 oz	312 g	*almond flour*
32 oz	907 g	*confectioners' sugar*
11 oz	312 g	*all-purpose flour*
27 oz	765 g	*egg whites*
2.25 liq oz	67 ml	*dark rum*

1. Preheat oven to 350°F (177°C). Line a sheet pan with a silicone mat. Butter the hexagonal molds and place them on the prepared pan.

2. In a saucepan, melt the butter and cool slightly.

3. In a large bowl, combine the almond flour, sugar, and all-purpose flour.

4. In a mixer fitted with a whisk attachment, whisk the egg whites until foamy. Add the flour mixture and mix until just combined. Gradually add the melted butter and mix until blended. Stir in the rum. Let the batter rest for 1 hour.

5. Place 3 chunks of roasted pineapple in each mold. Fill the molds three-quarters of the way with batter. Bake 25 to 30 minutes or until golden. Remove the cakes from the molds and cool.

CHERRY SAUCE			
2.2 lb	1 kg	cherry purée
4 oz	113 g	glucose
2 liq oz	59 ml	lemon juice

1. In a large saucepan, combine the cherry purée and glucose and boil for one minute. Remove from the heat and stir in the lemon juice.

2. Strain and chill.

SUGAR GARNISH			
4 oz	113 g	isomalt
as needed	as needed	powdered food coloring

1. Preheat oven to 350°F (175°C). Line a half-sheet pan with a silicone baking mat, smooth-side-up. Sprinkle the mat with the isomalt. Sprinkle the isomalt with the powdered food coloring, as desired.

2. Place another baking mat, smooth-side-down, over the isomalt covered mat. Bake the isomalt about 7 minutes.

3. Allow the sugar to cool for 20 minutes. Peel off the top baking mat. Break the bubble-sugar into various shapes and set aside to garnish the desserts.

ASSEMBLY *Tempered chocolate triangles*

1. Decorate a dessert plate with the cherry sauce.

2. Place a financier cake in the center of the plate. Top with about one tablespoon of the compote. Unmold a poppyseed parfait and place it over the compote.

3. Arrange a bubble-sugar garnish and 2 chocolate triangles on the parfait.

Making the bubble-sugar garnish.

C H A P T E R **F** O U R

M O D E R N I Z I N G
G A R N I S H E S

JOHN DEGNAN

Executive Pastry Chef,
The Lodge at Koele, Lana'i, Hawaii.

BORN: 1965, Rockaway Beach, New York.
TRAINING/EXPERIENCE: New York City Technical College; Patisserie Lanciani, Pierre Hotel, Rainbow Room, Ritz-Carlton, Sea Grill, Omni Berkshire Hotel, all in New York.

"I liked the technical side of producing pastry at first. I didn't have a great background in food, so the challenge for me was learning flavors and textures. It's an ongoing education. I learn a lot from chefs, and not just pastry chefs, who teach me about flavors. On the artistic side, I see the forms in my head and I start to play with them. Then I visualize flavors and the dessert kind of hits me. Of course it doesn't necessarily work right the first time. You have to work it three and four times, get the opinions of the other chefs, push it forward until you get it the way you want. Flavor and presentation are both important. Flavor is most important, but you want a 'WOW' factor."

ERIC PEREZ

Executive Pastry Chef,
Ritz-Carlton Tyson's Corners, Virginia.

BORN: June 1964, Toulouse, France.
TRAINING/EXPERIENCE: apprenticeship, various pastry shops, including La Coste in Toulouse; French embassy, Ritz-Carlton Pentagon City, both in Washington, D.C.

"It should taste as good as it looks— that's pretty much the basic philosophy of pastry. You should love eating pastry. You cannot be as involved unless you love to eat food, period. That is the way you develop your palate and your taste. Of course, to become a pastry chef involves a lot of things not pastry—learning to deal with people, psychology. I like that part. You give people the passion— what someone else gave to you, you give to them."

"**S**o you're a pastry chef. Create a dessert for me. See if you can't arrange it so that some components are cold, others hot; some tangy, some sweet. I want smooth textures, but also some crunch. Remember that it must be made in huge numbers by a few people in a small kitchen; that it must be carried intact by a frazzled waiter to a table way upstairs; that it must be priced to earn a profit; and that it must taste wonderful. Oh, and while you're at it, design the plate in a pleasing yet provocative manner. Be mindful of line, form, texture, and color. Remember that line is not simply line. A jagged line can convey energy, a horizontal line power, while a vertical line is strong and formal, and a curved line is sensuous. Nor is color simply color; you must sort out hue, intensity, and value. Remember that hot colors advance while cool ones recede. You want balance, but not blandness. You want informal balance—an aesthetic arrangment of dissimilar forms. You want to evidence variety, emphasis, unity, and spacial order."

Little wonder that many culinary schools, including The Culinary Institute of America, offer a visual composition course. The variety of garnishes available to complement the variety of central forms is enough to test any kitchen artist's mettle.

It is in garnishing that chefs go overboard or go blah, where the plate is ghastly or ga-ga, and where the compositional sense of the chef is tested. We will deal with sauce in its own chapter, but garnishes in general—cookies, fruit, nuts, frozen items, and chocolate in all their forms—are much more important in composition desserts than in rustic desserts or in traditional European slice-and-sauce plates.

So what are some guiding principles to proper garnishing, even in an outlandish Modernist dessert?

"I have no rules about garnishing because garnishing is a very personal feeling about finishing a plate," says Pascal Janvier of Cocoa Barry. "You can give the same ingredients to ten chefs and you would have ten different treasures. I try not to impose any rules, except that ingredients should be fresh."

So there *are* rules to garnishing and the chefs can cite a few, but if the reader's incipient Modernist sensibilities start to twitch at the mention of rules, wait. There will be enough exceptions to each rule to create chaos and tail-chasing.

Keep it simple. "It should promote the dessert and should not overpower," says Jacquy Pfeiffer. "You should not spend 75 percent of your time on the garnish. It should be the other way around. Don't overgarnish. Don't put one garnish atop another. For example, sprinkling something over a rosette—you kill the first with the second."

"Garnishes take a lot of time to make, or some do," says Jemal Edwards, "and if you're pressed for time in the kitchen, you want something that is simple and beautiful and doesn't take a lot of time to do. Something you can make twenty or thirty of at a time."

Everything on the plate should be edible. "Sugar is probably the easiest way to make a WOW dessert for a customer," admits Bo Friberg. "Unfortunately, it's edible but not edible. You can cut your gums on that." "It should be edible," agrees Richard Leach. "Not bulky or thick. Delicate enough so that people can eat it."

Sebastien Canonne of the French Pastry School in Chicago agrees, but can think of an example when a large, overblown, inedible garnish is called for: when the client requests it. "Customers expect a lot of show, and that's why in upscale hotels they ask the chef to come up with some sugar work. A big sugar cage, for example," says Canonne. "If that's what they want, they will be happy. We won't be so happy, but we do it. If it's not really necessary, you try to talk them out of it."

Thaddeus Dubois of the Duquesne Club in Pittsburgh can sympathize. "Pastry chefs are in the hospitality business. We are in the business of pleasing people," he says. "If someone comes in and wants a sugar or caramel thing two feet high, we're in the business of providing it."

Wayne Brachman of Mesa Grill in New York doesn't believe garnishes should just be edible. "They should *taste good*," he says. "Edible is a dime a dozen. Hay is edible."

A garnish should promote harmony in flavor. "I like to follow through," says Krista Kern. "Everything should relate to the primary or secondary flavor." Richard Leach of the Park Avenue Cafe believes that a garnish should "provide an accent flavor for the main component. I go for one component with some small back textures."

"The garnish can contrast the flavor, but it's usually a good idea to remind the diner of the flavor," says Sebastien Canonne. "Apple chips for an apple dessert, or caramel. It is a delicate thing. Try to remind the customer what's inside with the garnish. Sometimes you can play with garnish to contrast. If something is not really sweet, you might have a tuile or sugar to bring sweetness or vice versa."

A garnish should provide a contrast in texture to the main component. "It should provide crispness if the dessert is smooth," says Sebastien Canonne, "but you don't want to add what's not needed. This is one of the biggest mistakes that people without classic training make. If the garnish can add to the dessert without taking over the dessert or becoming the dessert, it's okay. It should be a little thing. If you don't know what you're doing, stay with sautéed fruit, or sauce." Madeleines, tuiles, financier, or macaroons pair well with sorbet or ice cream, he says. With cake, a good sauce. With a warm dessert, a compote.

A garnish should add height. "People put a lot of effort into sauce painting and marbleizing, which is fine, there is no rule that says you can't," explains Stanton Ho of the Las Vegas Hilton. "I would concentrate more of my efforts on height. That way it becomes a saleable marketing device. Sauces can't be seen as they're carried through the dining room."

SEBASTIEN CANONNE

Co-owner, *Ecole de Patisserie Francaise, Chicago.*

BORN: October 1968, Amiens, France.
TRAINING/EXPERIENCE: apprenticeship, École Hotelière, Normandy; apprenticeship, Gaston Lenôtre; La Côte St. Jacques, Burgundy; Beau Rivage Palace, Geneva; Hotel Palace Euler, Basel; St. Germain, Ritz-Carlton Hotel, Chicago.

"In this country, a chef must be both creative and a businessman, and this is very difficult. First, though, you have to love the job. You can't make something nice if you don't feel it. You have to be a craftsman, to like to work with your hands. You have to have a business sense, but you can't be too businesslike to be the best, because this is an art which is a little bit of a science."

DONALD WRESSELL

Executive Pastry Chef, *Four Seasons Hotel, Beverly Hills, California.*

BORN: 1960, Issaquah, Washington.
TRAINING/EXPERIENCE: apprenticeship with Mark Randolph; Washington Athletic Club, Sorrento Hotel, and Westin Hotel, all in Seattle; Watergate Hotel, Washington, D.C.; Breakers Hotel, Long Beach, California; Four Seasons Hotel, Philadelphia.

"I like what I do, and I like the life of the pastry chef. I have exposure to things I wouldn't if I were some other kind of craftsman. I wouldn't travel in Europe and the States, experience life the way I have, eat great meals, meet fantastic people. It's a lifestyle choice more than a job, because the job is never over. You're constantly educating yourself. Mark Randolph (owner of Pastries by Randolph in Virginia) instilled into me that whenever you make a plate or a cake and you think it's really great, you have to find something about it that you would do better next time. You can never say, 'That's great, that's as good as it's ever going to be.' Give it the credit it deserves, but scrutinize it."

RICHARD RUSKELL

Pastry Chef,
The Phoenician,
Phoenix, Arizona.

BORN: November 1956,
Nebraska.
TRAINING/EXPERIENCE: French
Culinary Institute, New York;
Le Royal Grey, France; Hotel
Maxim's, Stanhope Hotel, both
in New York.

"Today's pastry chef tends to want
to include everything on a tiny
plate. I've started to come away
from that, and simplify—going
back and back and back to the
basics. People who come to the shop,
students especially, will say to me,
'Oh I want to make showpieces, I
want to pull sugar, and this and
that. . . .' and I say, 'Yeah, don't
we all want to sit down and pull
sugar? I would rather have you
make a little éclair or tart that is so
perfect, so nice, that I want to eat
the whole thing.'"

Contrast, yes, but harmony too. Simplicity, yes, but showbiz pizzazz as well. Rules, you bet, but exceptions too. To the Modernist chef, there are no absolutes. Only personal taste and customer whims.

But a general statement about the aesthetic value of a composition dessert can be made based on the desserts presented here. It is this: If the main component, or prominent forms, of a dessert are executed with precision and professionalism, the eye will forgive—it will admire—some looser forms and compositions on the plate. If the cuts are straight on a cake or cookie, the sugar can be haywire; if the surfaces are smooth on a glazed piece, the sauces can be splattered at random; if the fruits are fresh and chosen for perfect form, then they can be arranged in an asymmetrical way. One other observation: it is common for chefs to include a sugar spiral or rod to subtly bind disparate forms together.

Examples? The perfection of Sebastien Canonne's Raspberry Vanilla Blossom and the chocolate leaf that crowns it allows the eye to enjoy, and accept, the odd puff of sugar, the jumbled arrangement of chips, fruit, a coil of sugar, a berry impaled on a silly fork. Likewise, the precision of Kim O'Flaherty's Almond Sourdough Cake, the craft of the cookie that crowns it, allows us to accept the anarchic saucing as artful.

In this chapter you see many familiar forms—demi-spheres and rings particularly—that are enhanced by the accompaniment of more dramatic, severe, risky forms. See how the clever, if ordinary, ring that makes up Eric Perez's Chocolate and Pear Mousse is completely upstaged by the magnificent, towering chocolate cone, the chocolate curl that hugs it, the chocolate sphere that crowns it. Or how Stanton Ho's Dome of White Chocolate Mousse is lent an exotic air by the "serpentine" cookie that coils around it. Likewise, the simple geometric form of Richard Ruskell's Chocolate Cone is given delirious motion by wheel cookies artfully placed at odd angles.

A brownie, a homespun dessert if ever there was one, is rendered mysterious and powerful through an ultra-modern treatment: Philippe Laurier has elected to dress it up with sinister tendrils of chocolate, a looming cookie, and a pool of sauce, giving the plate a wild, hypnotic appeal.

Sometimes form simply follows function: The "sail" cookie dominates John Degnan's Asian Rice Torte for the simple reason that the chef wanted to hide the iffy attractiveness of rice in a dessert.

The chefs offer startling Modernist imagery: Sebastien Canonne's Sweet Dream Parfait, with its cookie-as-a-warped-clock-hand and the cocoa dusting of clock numbers vanishing dramatically; Norman Love's Banana Mousse and its pure geometric forms—cones so severe they are vanishing into lines, a demi-sphere with chocolate glazed to perfection, a curl of chocolate dangling in air to lessen the severity; John Degnan's Passion Fruit Mousse, perched on a chalice-like pedestal, and partially rimmed by a soaring cookie, like an earthquake remnant.

"The first thing the customer will buy with is his eyes, but the second time he will buy with his mouth," says Bo Friberg of The Culinary Institute of America. "So if it looks great but doesn't taste good, he will not buy it again. It should be showy but also taste great. There is, sometimes, a compromise situation." Sometimes, but not here. These plates exhibit take-no-prisoners, pedal-to-the-metal brashness; full flavor, startling presentation, weary kitchen staff.

PASSION FRUIT MOUSSE ON A CARAMEL CONE

JOHN DEGNAN

Executive Pastry Chef, *The Lodge at Koele, Lana'i, Hawaii.*

Flavors from the same region generally blend well, as this dessert attests: Pâte à cigarette-decorated joconde encircles, and forms the base for, the light, airy, and refreshingly tart mousse. The sweetness of the mangoes blends well with the mousse, while the coconut sauce enhances both flavors and provides visual punch. "I served this at my wedding and at the James Beard House," says John Degnan. "It's always been a favorite."

YIELD: 16 SERVINGS

Special Equipment:
Sixteen ring molds, 2 1/2" (6.25 cm) diameter x 1 1/2" (3.75 cm) high
Wagner airless paint sprayer
5" (125 cm) metal cream horns

PÂTE À CIGARETTE

4 oz	113 g	unsalted butter, melted
4 oz	113 g	confectioners' sugar
3.25 oz	92 g	cake flour
1 oz	28 g	cocoa powder
4 oz	113 g	egg whites

1. In a mixer fitted with a paddle attachment, mix together the butter and sugar. Sift the flour and cocoa powder together and add half to the butter mixture. Mix until combined and scrape down the side of the bowl. Slowly add the egg whites and mix until fully incorporated. Add the remaining dry ingredients and mix just until combined.

2. Put the batter in a cornet. On a half-sheet silicone baking mat pipe rows of triangles across the shorter side, staying within 1" (2.5 cm) columns. Freeze until ready to use.

JOCONDE

6.4 oz	182 g	eggs
4.5 oz	128 g	granulated sugar
4.6 oz	130 g	almond flour
3.9 oz	110 g	egg whites
1.2 oz	34 g	unsalted butter, melted
2 oz	57 g	cake flour

1. Preheat the oven to 375°F (190°C). In a mixer combine the eggs, sugar, and almond flour; whip until very thick and light in color. Whip the egg whites to soft peaks and fold into the flour mixture. Fold in the melted butter followed by the cake flour.

Dessert shown on page 132.

2. Place the silicone baking with the pâte à cigarette on a half-sheet pan and line another half-sheet pan with parchment. Divide the joconde batter evenly between the two pans and spread into very thin layers. Bake for 8 to 10 minutes or until the joconde is a light golden color and feels springy when touched. Remove from the pans and cool completely.

PASSION FRUIT MOUSSE

1 pt	473 ml	heavy cream
4 oz	113 g	granulated sugar
2.1 oz	60 g	egg whites
.3 oz	8 g	gelatin sheets
12 liq oz	355 ml	passion fruit purée, divided

1. Whip the cream to soft peaks and set aside. In a mixer bowl combine the sugar and egg whites and heat over a double boiler, whisking, until warm to the touch. Place the bowl in the mixer and whip mixture to stiff peaks.

2. Soften the gelatin sheets in cold water. Heat the gelatin with about 4 liq oz (118 ml) of the passion fruit purée just until the gelatin melts.

3. Fold the remaining 8 liq oz (236 ml) of the purée into the meringue. Fold in the purée with the gelatin, followed by the whipped cream.

MOUSSE ASSEMBLY

1. Line the ring molds with acetate. Cut the joconde sheet with the triangles into 1" (2.5 cm)-wide strips, cutting between the rows of triangles. Trim each strip to 7.75" (19.4 cm) in length. Cut the other joconde sheet into 2 1/4" (5.6 cm) diameter circles.

2. Line each ring with a strip of joconde so that the triangles are facing outward. Place a joconde circle in the bottom of each ring. Pipe in the passion fruit mousse to the top of the joconde. Refrigerate to set.

CARAMEL CONES

1 lb	454 g	granulated sugar
8 liq oz	237 ml	water
3 oz	85 g	glucose

1. Combine the sugar and water in a saucepan and bring to a boil, washing down the side of the pan as needed. Add the glucose and cook to a light caramel. Quickly plunge the bottom of the pan into cold water to stop the cooking process.

Making the caramel cones.

2. When the caramel has thickened and cooled a bit, drizzle thin lines down and around lightly oiled 5" (12.7 cm) metal cream horns. Pour a thin layer of caramel into lightly oiled ring molds, 2 1/2" (6.3 cm) in diameter. Let set and remove caramel from molds.

3. Dip both ends of the caramel cone in caramel and attach a caramel circle to each end.

TUILES	4.5 oz	128 g	unsalted butter, melted
	9.25 oz	262 g	confectioners' sugar
	5.75 oz	163 g	all-purpose flour
	.75 tsp	4 g	salt
	7 oz	198 g	egg whites

1. Preheat oven to 350°F (175°C). In a mixer with the paddle attachment, combine the melted butter with the sugar. Combine the flour and salt and add half to the butter mixture. Mix until combined. Slowly add the egg whites and mix until fully incorporated. Add the rest of the dry ingredients and mix just until combined. Refrigerate until firm.

2. Make a stencil of a right triangle 8" (20.3 cm) high with a 6" (15.2 cm) base. Spread the batter thinly through the stencil on to a silicone-baking-mat-lined sheet pan. Freeze until set.

3. Use a small spatula to scrape "windows" into the tuile. Bake for 8 to 10 minutes or until light brown. Place each tuile over a 4" (10 cm)-diameter cylinder and let set.

| CHOCOLATE BASES | 8 oz | 227 g | bittersweet couverture chocolate (58%), tempered |

1. Spread the chocolate on a sheet of acetate and let it set until it has just barely started to firm.

2. Cut the chocolate into crescent shapes with rounded edges, following the curve of the tuiles. The bases should be slightly longer than the tuiles.

| COCOA SAUCE | 8 oz | 227 g | cocoa powder |
| | 20 liq oz | 591 ml | simple syrup (2 parts sugar to 1 part water) |

1. Put the cocoa powder in a food processor. In a saucepan bring the syrup to a boil.

2. Pour the syrup down the feed tube of the processor while the machine is running. Process until well combined.

| CHOCOLATE SPRAY | 1 lb | 454 g | milk chocolate (38%) |
| COATING | 4 oz | 113 g | cocoa butter |

1. Melt together the chocolate and cocoa butter over a double boiler.

2. Pour the mixture into a Wagner airless paint sprayer and keep in a warm place until ready to use.

DESSERT ASSEMBLY

Melted bittersweet chocolate
3 mangoes, peeled and diced
Caramel rods

1. Dip the base of each tuile in melted chocolate and attach it to a chocolate base. Let set, then spray with the chocolate mixture.

2. Fill the ring molds to the top with diced mangoes. Unmold and place the mousse on a caramel cone with the wide end on top. Place the cone on the left side of the plate. Pipe dots of chocolate sauce in a semicircle behind the cone. Place a tuile in front of the cone in the center of the plate. Garnish with caramel rods.

ASIAN RICE TART

JOHN DEGNAN

Executive Pastry Chef, *The Lodge at Koele, Lana'i, Hawaii.*

Asian cuisine presents a challenge to the pastry chef. "I've always wanted to use rice in a dish without using rice pudding, so we made a flavorful rice, using Japanese rice, and coconut milk, but no eggs." The rice is contained in a feuille de brick shell. "We hide the rice because it's so plain," says Degnan, "but the caramelized bananas and coconut flavor blend very well with it."

YIELD: 12 SERVINGS

Special Equipment: Twelve tart molds, 3" (7.5 cm) diameter x 2" (5 cm) high

PASTRY SHELL	12 oz	340 g	feuille de brick
	4 oz	113 g	unsalted butter, melted
	1 oz	28 g	raw sugar

1. Preheat oven to 350°F (175°C). Cut the feuille de brick into 7" (17.8 cm) diameter circles. Brush each circle with melted butter and sprinkle with raw sugar.

2. Press each circle into a greased tart mold. Place a slightly smaller cup or mold in the middle to keep the sides from falling inward. Bake for 15 minutes or until golden.

FEUILLE DE BRICK GARNISH	5.9 oz	170 g	feuille de brick
	4 oz	113 g	unsalted butter, melted
	1 oz	28 g	raw sugar

1. Preheat oven to 350°F (175°C). Cut the feuille de brick into isosceles triangles with 4 1/2" (1.3 cm) sides. Also cut some smaller right triangles. Brush each triangle with melted butter and sprinkle with raw sugar.

2. Place the triangles on a sheet pan lined with a silicon baking mat and top with another baking mat. Bake for 10 to 15 minutes or until golden.

RICE FILLING	4 oz	113 g	Japanese rice
	16 liq oz	473 ml	whole milk
	16 liq oz	473 ml	coconut milk
	1	1	vanilla bean, scraped
	4 oz	113 g	granulated sugar
	.25 tsp	2.5 g	salt

1. Preheat oven to 375°F (190°C). Combine all ingredients in a 9 x 13" (22.3 x 33 cm) baking pan and cover tightly with aluminum foil.

2. Bake, stirring occasionally, for 1 to 1 1/2 hours or until the rice is soft and the liquid has thickened.

| CARAMELIZED BANANA | 6 | 6 | *medium bananas, sliced* |
| SLICES | *2 oz* | *57 g* | *raw sugar* |

Sprinkle the banana slices with sugar. Heat with a torch until the sugar is melted but not burned.

| ASSEMBLY | *Caramel* |
| | *Mango purée* |

1. Place one large feuille de brick triangle flat with the top pointing forward. Stand another large triangle on top of it about 1 1/2" (3.8 cm) behind the point. Dip the two sides of a small right triangle in caramel and glue it behind and perpendicular to the upright triangle to hold it in place.

2. Fill the pastry shell with warm rice filling and place it in the center of a dessert plate. Fan a few caramelized banana slices over the filling and top it with a feuille de brick triangle assembly. Garnish the plate with caramelized banana slices and mango purée.

DOME OF WHITE CHOCOLATE MOUSSE
WITH SERPENTINE OF CASSIS

STANTON HO

Executive Pastry Chef, *Las Vegas Hilton Hotel.*

Although the white chocolate mousse is a neutral flavor, notes Stanton Ho, the griottine cherries add the necessary flavor burst. "No sauce is needed to contradict the flavor," he says. "This is a great treat after a heavy meal, and it can be simple, production-wise. The serpentines can be made well ahead of time." The dome sits on a coconut sablé cookie; the serpentine of cassis is something of a hybrid of fruit leather and tuile.

YIELD: 12 SERVINGS

Special Equipment:
Two half-sheet silicone mats
Twelve 2 3/4" (7 cm) diameter
Flexipan demi-sphere molds
Small hand brush or compressed air spray gun

BISCUIT JOCONDE			
5.75 oz	163 g	almond flour
5.75 oz	163 g	confectioners' sugar
2 oz	57 g	all-purpose flour
7.5 oz	213 g	whole eggs
7.5 oz	213 g	egg whites
1.5 oz	43 g	granulated sugar
4 tsp	8 g	dried egg whites
.25 tsp	1 g	cream of tartar
1.25 oz	35 g	unsalted butter, melted

1. Preheat oven to 400°F (204°C). Line two half-sheet pans with silicone baking mats.

2. In a bowl, combine the almond flour, confectioners' sugar, and all-purpose flour. Sift together twice.

3. In a mixer fitted with a whisk attachment, beat the eggs on high speed until doubled in volume.

4. By hand, fold in the sifted dry ingredients in three additions.

5. In the bowl of a mixer with the whisk attachment, combine the egg whites, one-third of the granulated sugar, the dried egg whites, and cream of tartar. Beat to soft peaks. Slowly add the remaining granulated sugar and beat until firm peaks form. Fold the meringue into the egg-flour mixture. Fold the melted butter into the mixture.

6. Spread the batter evenly onto the prepared pans and bake for 10 to 12 minutes until set and golden. Cool completely.

SERPENTINE OF CASSIS

1.5 oz	43 g	*unsalted butter, melted*
3.5 oz	99 g	*confectioners' sugar*
1.75 oz	50 g	*cassis purée*
1 oz	28 g	*all-purpose flour*

1. Line 2 half-sheet pans with silicone mats. Have ready a rolling pin for shaping.

2. In a mixing bowl, combine all the ingredients and mix by hand to a smooth paste. Refrigerate for at least one hour.

3. Preheat the oven to 350°F (177°C).

4. Spread a thin layer of cassis paste on the prepared pans and bake for about 10 to 12 minutes. Do not overbake (the baked paste should be the color of the fruit). Let rest for one minute.

5. Turn the silicone mat with the baked paste onto parchment paper. While still warm and pliable, cut the paste into 24 "serpentinelike" triangular shapes. Wrap one end around the rolling pin. Cool.

Making the serpentine cookies.

WHITE CHOCOLATE
MOUSSE

9 liq oz	266 ml	*milk*
8.75 oz	248 g	*white chocolate, such as Valrhona Ivoire, finely chopped*
.24 oz	6.7 g	*gelatin sheets, softened in water*
4.25 oz	120 g	*egg yolks*
1.5 oz	43 g	*granulated sugar*
7 liq oz	207 ml	*heavy cream, whipped to soft peaks*

1. In a saucepan, bring the milk to a boil. Add the chopped chocolate, lower heat, and stir until the chocolate is melted. Add the drained gelatin to the melted chocolate and stir until dissolved. Remove from heat.

2. In a medium bowl, whisk together the yolks and sugar. Place the bowl over a hot water bath. Whisk the mixture to the ribbon stage.

3. Whisk the melted chocolate mixture into the egg mixture until combined.

4. Place the mixture over an ice bath and stir with a rubber spatula until it just begins to set. Remove the bowl from the ice bath and fold in one-third of the whipped cream. Fold in remaining whipped cream and chill.

WHITE CHOCOLATE DOMES	3 oz	85 g	semisweet chocolate, tempered
	9 oz	255 g	white chocolate, tempered

1. Freckle the tempered semisweet chocolate onto the Flexipan demi-sphere molds with a hand brush or a compressed air spray gun. Allow to set.

2. Place a thin, even coat of tempered white chocolate over the semisweet chocolate speckles to make a 1/16 to 1/8" (.16 to .32 cm) thick layer. Allow to set.

COCONUT SABLÉ COOKIES	11.5 oz	325 g	all-purpose flour
	2.75 oz	77 g	almond flour
	2.75 oz	77 g	flaked coconut
	.5 tsp	2.5 g	salt
	11.5 oz	325 g	unsalted butter, softened
	5.25 oz	149 g	confectioners' sugar
	1.75 oz	50 g	eggs

1. In a bowl, combine together the all-purpose and almond flours, coconut, and salt.

2. In a mixer fitted with a paddle attachment, cream together the butter and confectioners' sugar. Add the eggs and mix until incorporated.

3. On low speed, add the dry ingtredients to the creamed mixture, and mix until combined.

4. Shape the dough into a disc and refrigerate for at least one hour.

5. Preheat the oven to 375°F (191°C). Line a sheet pan with parchment paper.

6. Remove the dough from the refrigerator and roll out to 3/16" (.45 cm) thickness. Using a 3 1/4" (7.6 cm) fluted, round cutter, cut out 12 rounds of dough and place them on prepared pan.

7. Bake for 10 to 12 minutes, or until lightly browned. Cool on a rack.

ASSEMBLY	48 griottine cherries (about 3.75 oz /106 g)*

 *Note. Griottine cherries are available from Patisfrance, (800) PASTRY-1.

1. Cut out twelve 3 1/2" (8.9 cm) rounds from the joconde. Cut out twelve 1 3/4" (4.4 cm) rounds from the remaining joconde. Line demi-sphere molds with the larger round of joconde.

2. Pipe white chocolate mousse into the cake-lined molds. Arrange 4 griottines in each mold in a random fashion. Top with the smaller round of joconde. Refrigerate until set.

ASSEMBLY	48 griottine cherries (about 3.75 oz /106 g)
	Pulled-sugar sticks

1. Place one coconut sablé cookie onto the center of a dessert plate.

2. Remove a mousse-filled mold from the refrigerator and unmold onto a coconut sablé. Arrange 4 griottines around the cookie.

3. Place a pulled-sugar stick onto the middle of the chocolate dome and garnish the plate with 2 cassis serpentines.

ALMOND SOURDOUGH CAKE WITH PLUM COMPOTE AND LEMON CRÈME

KIM O'FLAHERTY

Pastry Cook, *Essex House Hotel, New York.*

"*I developed this recipe while I was living in San Francisco,*" says Kim O'Flaherty. "*A friend had tried incorporating a sour mix into a chocolate cake, so I tried it on an almond cake and it went really well. We always kept a sourdough starter in the kitchen. You have to take it out once a week. It's like having a pet.*" The lemon crème fraîche ice cream adds a subtle tangy note, with the plum compote sounding sweet counterpoint. Flaherty uses "*a lot of vanilla bean*" in many of her desserts. "*Tahitian Gold is my favorite,*" she confides. "*I'd love to sleep with it under my pillow every night, I think it's so beautiful.*"

YIELD: 15 SERVINGS

SOURDOUGH STARTER			
	1 Tbs	10 g	*active dry yeast*
	16 liq oz	473 ml	*water*
	8.5 oz	242 g	*all-purpose flour*

1. Dissolve the yeast in the water. Stir in the flour.

2. Let the starter sit at room temperature for 2 to 3 days in a nonmetal container covered lightly with plastic wrap. Stir every few hours.

> *To keep the starter alive longer, store it in the refrigerator. Once a week take it out and let it come to room temperature. Add equal amounts of flour and water and return it to the refrigerator.*

ALMOND SOURDOUGH CAKE			
	7.5 oz	213 g	*almond paste*
	7 oz	198 g	*granulated sugar*
	1	1	*vanilla bean, split and scraped*
	6 oz	170 g	*unsalted butter, softened*
	7.9 oz	225 g	*eggs, slightly beaten*
	6 oz	170 g	*cake flour*
	2 Tbs	7 g	*baking powder*
			a pinch of salt
	2.4 oz	68 g	*sourdough starter*

1. Preheat oven to 350°F (175°C). Combine the almond paste and sugar in a food processor and process until fine. Transfer this to a mixing bowl and add the vanilla bean seeds and butter. Using a mixer, beat with the paddle attachment until pale in color.

2. Slowly add the eggs (the mixture may appear broken at this point). Scrape down the side of the bowl.

3. Sift together the flour, baking powder, and salt. Slowly add the flour mixture to the almond mixture. Add the sourdough starter and mix just until combined. Pour the batter into a greased half-sheet pan and bake for 20 to 30 minutes or until it is golden brown and a cake tester comes out clean.

PLUM COMPOTE			
15	15	plums, cut into 1/2" (1.3 cm) dice
8 liq oz	237 ml	raspberry purée
49 oz	1390 g	granulated sugar
12 liq oz	355 ml	peach nectar juice
3	3	vanilla beans, scraped
1 Tbs	1 Tbs	lemon juice

1. Combine all the ingredients in a large saucepan and cook over medium heat for about 10 to 15 minutes or until the plums are soft but still hold their shape.

2. Strain the plums, reserving the syrup, and pour on to a sheet pan to cool.

ALMOND TUILES			
3 oz	85 g	almond paste
18 oz	510 g	granulated sugar
15 oz	425 g	all-purpose flour
10.6 oz	300 g	eggs

1. Preheat oven to 350°F (175°C). Put a sheet pan in the oven to warm it. Combine the almond paste and sugar in a Robocoupe and process until fine. Add the flour and mix. Add the eggs one at a time while the machine is running and process until combined. Strain through a tamis to remove any lumps.

2. Put the batter into a cornet. On a silicone baking mat, pipe right triangles 7" (17.8 cm) long and 4" (10 cm) high with a lattice pattern. Transfer the baking mat to the warm sheet pan and bake for 5 to 6 minutes or just until set. Immediately wrap the 7" (17.8 cm) side of each tuiles around a 2" (5 cm) cylinder and let set.

LEMON CURD			
8 liq oz	273 ml	lemon juice
1	1	vanilla bean, scraped
10 oz	283 g	granulated sugar
8.8 oz	250 g	eggs
12 oz	340 g	unsalted butter, cut in cubes

1. In a large saucepan, combine the lemon juice and vanilla bean seeds and bring this to a boil. Whisk together the sugar and eggs and temper into the hot lemon juice. Cook, whisking constantly, until the mixture has thickened.

2. Pour the lemon curd into a bowl. Add the butter and whisk until completely combined. Cover the surface of the curd with plastic wrap and refrigerate until firm.

LEMON CRÈME FRAÎCHE	*8 liq oz*	*237 ml*	*whole milk*
ICE CREAM	*8 liq oz*	*237 ml*	*heavy cream*
	8 oz	*227 g*	*granulated sugar*
	1/2	*1/2*	*vanilla bean, split and scraped*
	6.5 oz	*184 g*	*egg yolks*
	17 oz	*482 g*	*crème fraîche or sour cream*
	7 oz	*198 g*	*lemon curd*

1. In a saucepan combine the milk, cream, sugar, and vanilla bean seeds and bring to a boil. Temper in the egg yolks and cook until the mixture coats the back of a wooden spoon. Strain over an ice bath and cool. Whisk in the crème fraîche and lemon curd.

2. Process in an ice cream machine according to the manufacturer's instructions.

ASSEMBLY	*8 plums, sliced*
	Fresh mint

1. Poach the plums in the syrup reserved from the plum compote just until soft.

2. Cut the cake into 3" (7.5 cm) circles. Place each circle on a dessert plate and top with plum compote. Place a 1 1/2 oz (42.5 g) scoop of ice cream in the center of the compote and top with another scoop. Place a tuile around the ice cream.

3. Garnish the plate with a mint sprig and poached plum slices with syrup.

CHOCOLATE AND PEAR MOUSSE ENSEMBLE

ERIC PEREZ

Executive Pastry Chef, *Ritz-Carlton Tyson's Corners, Virginia.*

Chocolate, pear, and caramel are the classic flavor combinations at the core of this dessert, which Eric Perez has refined from a presentation that he frequently serves at the Ritz-Carlton in Virginia: chocolate and pear mousse with caramelized pears, layered in the middle, sits on a flourless chocolate biscuit. The dessert is encased by an almond pistachio biscuit. Caramel-pistachio ice cream is enclosed in the marbled chocolate sphere.

YIELD: 20 SERVINGS

Special Equipment:
Twenty ring molds, 3" (7.5 cm) diameter x 2" (5 cm) high
2" (5 cm) demi-sphere molds

CARAMELIZED PISTACHIOS

10.6 oz	300 g	whole pistachios
4 oz	113 g	granulated sugar
.5 liq oz	15 ml	water
.4 oz	12 g	unsalted butter

1. Slightly warm the pistachios in an oven. In a copper pot cook the sugar and water to 240°F (115°C). Add the nuts and stir until the mixture appears to crystallize. Continue cooking until the sugar melts and caramelizes evenly around the nuts. Quickly add the butter and mix well.

2. Pour the nuts out onto a silicone baking mat and separate each nut. Let cool.

ALMOND BISCUIT

10.5 oz	298 g	egg whites
4 oz	113 g	granulated sugar
3.5 oz	99 g	almond flour
3.5 oz	99 g	confectioners' sugar
1.8 oz	50 g	all-purpose flour, sifted
1.5 Tbs	22 ml	heavy cream
1.8 oz	50 g	caramelized pistachios, chopped

1. Preheat oven to 425°F (220°C). Spray 2 half-sheet pans with vegetable spray and line the bottoms with parchment paper. Whip 7.5 oz (213 g) of the egg whites to soft peaks while gradually adding the sugar. Combine the almond flour, confectioners' sugar, and flour; gently fold into the whites. Fold in the remaining 3 oz (85 g) of egg whites (unwhipped) and the cream.

2. Divide the batter into 2 half-sheet pans and spread evenly. Bake for 8 minutes or until the center springs back when gently pressed with a finger. Remove from the pans and cool completely.

CHOCOLATE BISCUIT

6 oz	170 g	Valrhona Pur Caraibe chocolate
3 oz	85 g	unsalted butter
10 oz	284 g	egg whites
3.5 oz	99 g	granulated sugar
2.5 oz	72 g	egg yolks

1. Preheat oven to 425°F (220°C). Spray a half-sheet pan with vegetable spray and line the bottom with parchment paper. Combine the chocolate and butter and melt over a double boiler.

2. In a mixer, whip the egg whites to soft peaks while slowly adding the sugar. Quickly incorporate the egg yolks and melted chocolate.

3. Spread the batter onto the prepared pan. Bake for 10 to 12 minutes or until the cake springs back when gently pressed with a finger. Remove from the pan and cool. (The cake will be extremely moist.)

CARAMELIZED PEARS

4	4	pears, cut into quarters and poached
2.5 oz	71 g	unsalted butter
4 oz	113 g	granulated sugar
		Poire William, to taste

1. Cut pears into 1/4" (.6 cm) slices and cut in half. Melt the butter in a large skillet. Add the pears and cook over medium heat, stirring, for about 5 minutes or until slightly softened.

2. Add the sugar and Poire William, with the pan off the heat, and mix well. Continue to cook, stirring, until the pears are caramelized but still firm.

CHOCOLATE MOUSSE

13 oz	369 g	Valrhona Pur Caraibe chocolate
4 oz	112 g	egg yolks
1.8 oz	50 g	eggs
4 oz	113 g	granulated sugar
3 liq oz	89 ml	water
1 qt	946 ml	heavy cream, whipped to soft peaks

1. Melt chocolate over a double boiler and remove from the heat.

2. In a mixer on medium-high speed whip the yolks and the egg. While the yolks are whipping, cook the sugar and water to 244°F (118°C). Carefully pour the cooked sugar into the whipping eggs and increase to high speed. When foamy and light, reduce the mixer speed to medium and continue whipping until cool.

3. Gently fold the chocolate into the whipped cream. Fold the cream into the pâte à bombe.

PEAR MOUSSE

.4 oz	12 g	gelatin sheets
2 liq oz	59 ml	Poire William
16 liq oz	473 ml	pear purée
2 oz	57 g	egg whites

3.5 oz	99 g	granulated sugar
2.5 liq oz	74 ml	water
16 liq oz	473 ml	heavy cream, whipped to soft peaks

1. Soften the gelatin in cold water. In a saucepan warm the gelatin and Poire William just until the gelatin melts.

2. Place the egg whites in a mixer fitted with the whip attachment. In a saucepan cook the sugar and water to 240°F (116°C), brushing down the side of the pan as needed. When the sugar reaches 230°F (110°C), start whipping the egg whites. The egg whites should reach soft peaks when the sugar is ready. Reduce the mixer speed and slowly pour in the cooked sugar. Increase the speed to high until the whites form stiff, shiny peaks, then reduce speed until cool.

3. Combine the melted gelatin and pear purée. Cool over an ice bath if it is still warm. Fold the meringue into the purée, then gently fold in the whipped cream.

WHITE CHOCOLATE CONES

| 8 oz | 227 g | white chocolate, tempered |

1. Make acetate cones 8" (20 cm) long with a 1" (2.5 cm) opening at the base. Coat the insides with the tempered chocolate and tap out the excess.

2. Let the chocolate set completely and remove the acetate.

CHOCOLATE TWISTS

| 8 oz | 227 g | dark chocolate, tempered |

1. Cut acetate into triangles 10" (25 cm) high with a 1" (2.5 cm) base. Spread with a thin coat of tempered chocolate and let it set just a little bit.

2. Wrap the triangle around PVC pipe 1" (2.5 cm) in diameter, forming a spiral about 8" long (20 cm). Let set completely and remove.

CHOCOLATE SPHERES

a few drops	a few drops	Chefmaster oil-based red and green food coloring
16 oz	454 g	cocoa butter, melted
6 oz	170 g	dark chocolate, tempered
12 oz	340 g	white chocolate, tempered

1. Add the red food coloring to half the cocoa butter and green food coloring to the other half. Spray 2" (5 cm) demi-sphere molds with the red cocoa butter. Let it set and spray with the green cocoa butter. Let set, again.

2. Splatter the molds with dark chocolate using a pastry brush. When the dark chocolate has set, coat the molds with white chocolate. Let set completely and unmold.

CARAMEL ICE CREAM

14 oz	397 g	granulated sugar
1 qt	946 ml	milk
1 qt	946 ml	heavy cream
10.5 oz	298 g	egg yolks, beaten
7 oz	198 g	caramelized pistachios

155

1. Cook the sugar until caramelized. Boil the milk and cream together and carefully add to the caramel off the heat. Temper in the egg yolks and cook to 185°F (85°C). Strain over an ice bath, cool completely, and refrigerate overnight.

2. Process in an ice cream machine according to the manufacturer's instructions. Add the caramelized pistachios to the ice cream as it is coming out of the machine.

CHOCOLATE SAUCE			
20 *liq oz*	*591 ml*	*water, divided*
6.75 *oz*	*191 g*	*granulated sugar*
5 *oz*	*142 g*	*bittersweet chocolate*
1.5 *oz*	*43 g*	*cocoa powder*
.5 *oz*	*14 g*	*cornstarch*

1. Boil 16 liq oz (473 ml) of the water with the sugar. Add the chocolate and cook until completely melted.

2. Combine the cocoa powder, cornstarch, and remaining 4 liq oz (119 ml) of water. Temper into the melted chocolate and boil for 3 minutes. Cool.

CAKE ASSEMBLY			
16 *oz*	*454 g*	*dark couverture*
16 *oz*	*454 g*	*cocoa butter*

1. Line the ring molds with acetate. Cut the almond biscuit into strips 9 1/2" (23.8 cm) long and 1" (2.5 cm) wide and line the ring molds. Cut the chocolate biscuit into 2 3/4" (6.9 cm) circles and place a circle in the bottom of each ring. Pipe pear mousse to fill half the mold, then top with a layer of caramelized pears. Pipe the chocolate mousse into the rest of the mold. Smooth the top and chill until set.

2. Melt together the chocolate and cocoa butter. Remove the cake rings from the freezer. While still frozen, spray the tops with the chocolate-cocoa butter mixture. Unmold.

DESSERT ASSEMBLY

White chocolate ribbons
Chocolate cigarettes
Poached Seckel pears

1. Attach the bottom of the chocolate twist to the base of the chocolate cone. Rub the base of the cone on a warm surface until it just starts to melt. Place on a dessert plate and let set.

2. Heat the tip of a knife or a small pastry tip and make a small hole in a chocolate demi-sphere. Place on the point of the cone. Fill the demi-sphere with caramel ice cream and top with another demi-sphere.

3. Place a mousse cake on the dessert plate. Top with a white chocolate ribbon. Garnish with a chocolate cigarette and a poached Seckel pear.

SWEET DREAM PARFAIT

SEBASTIEN CANONNE

Co-owner, *Ecole de Patisserie Francaise, Chicago.*

"This is the dessert we did for the World Pastry Cup in 1997," says Sebastien Canonne. It is a bombe glace—strawberry sorbet, vanilla parfait, caramelized almonds, and almond dacquoise. Sautéed apricots in syrup are also part of the ensemble. The clock hand is formed with a honey wheat tuile, and the numbers are a chocolate mixture sprayed through a stencil. "The dome is like the actual clock, the cookie is the minute hand, the sugar wire is the second hand. It is time exploding," Canonne explains cryptically.

YIELD: 24 SERVINGS

Special Equipment:
Twenty-four 3" (7.6 cm) demi-sphere molds
Wagner airless paint sprayer
Two 5/8" (1.6 cm) diameter plexiglass modular molds
Clock-hand-shape template
Clock stencil

ALMOND DACQUOISE	9.5 oz	270 g	TPT*
	3 oz	87 g	almond flour
	7.6 oz	215 g	egg whites
	1.9 oz	55 g	granulated sugar

*Note. TPT (tant-pour-tant) is a mixture consisting of 50% almond flour and 50% confectioners' sugar. You can make it by combining 4 3/4 oz (135 g) whole blanched semi-roasted almonds and 4 3/4 oz (135 g) confectioners' sugar in a food processor and grinding it to a fine powder.

1. Preheat the oven to 425°F (220°C). Combine the TPT and almond flour. In a mixer with the whisk attachment, whip the egg whites and sugar to soft peaks. Gently fold in the almond mixture.

2. Pipe the mixture into two 5/8" (1.6 cm) diameter Plexiglas modular molds. Smooth the tops, remove the molds, and bake for about 15 minutes or until just golden. If you do not have modular molds, spread the batter onto a parchment-lined half-sheet pan and after baking cut into two 1/2" (1.3 cm) circles.

CARAMELIZED ALMONDS

10.6 oz	300 g	whole almonds, lightly roasted
4 oz	113 g	granulated sugar
.5 liq oz	15 ml	water
.4 oz	12 g	unsalted butter

1. Slightly warm the almonds in an oven. In a copper pot, cook the sugar and water to 240°F (115°C). Add the nuts and stir until the mixture appears to crystallize. Continue cooking until the sugar melts and caramelizes evenly around the nuts. Quickly add the butter and mix well.

2. Pour the nuts out onto a silicone baking mat and separate each nut. Let them cool.

HONEY WHEAT TUILES

2.6 oz	75 g	unsalted butter (82%)
3.9 oz	110 g	confectioners' sugar
2.6 oz	75 g	lavender honey
2.9 oz	83 g	egg whites
3.9 oz	110 g	whole wheat flour
1 tsp	5 g	ground ginger

1. Preheat the oven to 325°F (160°C). In a mixer fitted with a paddle attachment, cream together the butter, confectioners' sugar, and honey. Add half the egg whites, then half the flour. Add the remaining egg whites and flour. Add the ginger, and mix just until combined.

2. On a sheet pan lined with a silicone baking mat, spread the batter in a thin layer through a clock-hand-shape template. Bake for 8 to 10 minutes or until set. Immediately place over a 1" (2.5 cm) diameter cylinder to shape.

STRAWBERRY SORBET

2.6 liq oz	77 ml	water
3.7 oz	104 g	granulated sugar, divided
2.1 oz	60 g	atomized glucose
.5 tsp	2 g	sorbet stabilizer
26.7 oz	756 g	strawberry purée (10% sugar)

1. In a saucepan, combine the water, 3.3 oz (94 g) of the sugar and the glucose. Bring to a boil and add the stabilizer mixed with the remaining .3 oz (10 g) of sugar. Return the mixture to a boil and immediately remove from the heat and cool. Chill for at least 3 hours.

2. Combine the syrup with the strawberry purée. Pass through a chinois and process in an ice cream machine according to the manufacturer's instructions.

VANILLA PARFAIT

12 liq oz	355 ml	heavy cream (35% butterfat)
5.8 liq oz	172 ml	whole milk (3.6% butterfat)
3 1/2	3 1/2	Tahitian vanilla beans
4.9 oz	139 g	granulated sugar
4.3 oz	123 g	egg yolks
1.1 oz	31 g	inverted sugar

1. Whip the cream to soft peaks and set aside. Microwave the milk and vanilla beans on high power for 30 seconds or until the beans puff. Scrape the seeds into the milk, cover with plastic wrap, and let steep for 30 minutes.

2. In a saucepan, combine the milk mixture with the sugar and egg yolks. Cook gently, stirring, until the mixture reaches 185°F (85°C). Strain through a chinois and whip until cool. Mix in the inverted sugar. Gently fold in the whipped cream.

SAUTÉED APRICOT BRUNOISE			
	5 oz	142 g	unsalted butter
	1	1	vanilla bean
	5	5	apricots, cut into 1/8" (.3 cm) dice
	3 oz	85 g	brown sugar

1. In a large skillet cook the butter with the vanilla bean to a light noisette.

2. Add the apricots and brown sugar and sauté very quickly. Remove from the heat immediately.

BOMBE ASSEMBLY

1. Line the demi-sphere molds with strawberry sorbet, pressing it in tightly to make sure there are no air bubbles. Pipe in the parfait almost to the top of the mold. Cover the parfait with a layer of caramelized almonds and top with a dacquoise circle. Freeze until set.

2. To unmold, run the mold under warm water just until the sides loosen.

CHOCOLATE SPRAY MIXTURE			
	8 oz	227 g	semisweet chocolate, chopped
	8 oz	227 g	cocoa butter

1. Melt the chocolate and cocoa butter over simmering water. Transfer the mixture to the Wagner airless paint sprayer.

2. Lay a clock stencil over a dessert plate. Spray the plate with the chocolate mixture. Remove the stencil and allow the chocolate to set. Repeat with the remaining plates.

ASSEMBLY

Pulled-sugar second hands
Mint leaves

1. Place the bombe in the center of the plate. Arrange some of the apricot brunoise and some of the syrup on the side of the bombe.

2. Garnish the bombe with a tuile, pulled-sugar, and a mint leaf.

CHOCOLATE CONE WITH CINNAMON BAVARIAN
AND FLYING WHEELS

RICHARD RUSKELL

Pastry Chef, *The Phoenician,*
Phoenix, Arizona.

A *cinnamon Bavarian is sprayed with a chocolate mixture, to form the center-piece of the dessert. It is served with wheels of white and chocolate tuile batter, chocolate-chip whipped cream, and clear caramel sauce. "It was originally presented as a sundial,"* says Richard Ruskell. *"We sprayed the numbers of the clock around the plate and cast a shadow with cocoa, using a powergun. Now it really doesn't look like anything, which I kind of like. I don't like to specify when people ask me 'What is it?' It can be anything you want it to be."*

YIELD: 12 SERVINGS

Special Equipment:
Twelve cone-shaped paper drinking cups (2 1/2" / 6.3 cm diameter opening and 4" / 10 cm height)
Wagner airless spray gun

CINNAMON BAVARIAN

16 liq oz	*473 ml*	*milk*
4 sticks	*4 sticks*	*cinnamon*
5.2 oz	*147 g*	*egg yolks*
3.5 oz	*100 g*	*granulated sugar*
1 tsp	*3.1 g*	*powdered gelatin*
16 liq oz	*473 ml*	*heavy cream, whipped to soft peaks*

1. In a saucepan, bring the milk and cinnamon to a boil. Remove the pan from the heat and allow to infuse for 30 minutes. Remove the cinnamon sticks.

2. In a mixer with a whisk attachment, whip the yolks with the sugar until very pale.

3. Return the milk to the heat and bring to a boil. Whisk a few ounces of the hot milk into the yolks to temper them. Return the entire mixture to the saucepan and cook, stirring constantly, until the mixture coats the back of a spoon (do not allow the mixture to boil).

4. Soften the gelatin in 1 Tbs (14.8 ml) water. Whisk the softened gelatin into the hot custard until dissolved.

5. Place the custard over an ice bath and stir until it is cold, but not set. Fold in the whipped cream. Pipe the Bavarian into the cone-shaped paper drinking cups, and freeze until set.

6. When the cones are frozen, peel off the paper and place the cones upside down on a parchment-lined sheet pan. Return the cones to the freezer.

VANILLA AND CHOCOLATE	8 oz	227 g	*confectioners' sugar*
FLYING WHEEL TUILES	4.5 oz	128 g	*unsalted butter, melted*
	5.5 oz	156 g	*all-purpose flour*
	6.3 oz	179 g	*warmed egg whites*

1. Preheat oven to 350°F (175°C). In a mixer fitted with a paddle attachment, combine the sugar, butter, and flour. Add the egg whites gradually, at low speed, and mix until smooth. Place the batter into a pastry bag fitted with a 1/8" (.3 cm) plain tip.

2. For the chocolate tuiles, make the above recipe and add 2 oz of cocoa powder (if the batter is too stiff to pipe, add a little more egg white). Enlarge the templates of the flying wheels on a copy machine so that one wheel is 8" (20 cm) in diameter, one is 6" (15 cm) in diameter, and one is 3" (7.6 cm) in diameter.

3. Place the templates under a piece of parchment paper and pipe out twelve 3" (7.6 cm) chocolate tuiles, twelve 6" (15 cm) vanilla tuiles, twelve 8" (20 cm) vanilla tuiles, and twelve 8" (20 cm) chocolate tuiles. Bake the tuiles until set, about 10 minutes.

To make the flying wheels: "We have a template that we put under the Silpat and then we just pipe white and chocolate tuiles with a cone," says Richard Ruskell. "We bake them off, and that's it. The templates have different interior circumferences, to accommodate the cone."

| CHOCOLATE SPRAY | 8 oz | 227 g | *bittersweet chocolate, chopped* |
| COATING | 8 oz | 227 g | *cocoa butter, chopped* |

1. Place the chocolate and the cocoa butter in a bowl and melt over simmering water. Place the warm mixture into the spraygun.

2. Remove the cones from the freezer. Spray them evenly with the chocolate mixture.

3. Place a 6" (15 cm) round template or plate in the center of a dessert plate. Spray the plate lightly with the chocolate mixture. Remove the template and repeat with the remaining dessert plates.

ASSEMBLY   Place a Bavarian cone in the center of one of the plates. Place the two 8" (20 cm) wheels at an angle over the point of the cone. Place the 6" (15 cm) wheel and then the 3" (7.6 cm) wheel over the point, at opposite angles.

> *"To make the chocolate-chip whipped cream, we put melted chocolate into the cream as it is beating, and it hardens up right away,"* says Richard Ruskell. *The chocolate should be cold.*

SHORT STACK OF HAZELNUT GRIDDLE CAKES, POACHED FALL PEARS, AND BITTERSWEET CHOCOLATE SORBET

DONALD WRESSELL

Executive Pastry Chef, *Four Seasons Hotel, Beverly Hills, California.*

"When I was a kid, my brother and I would torture the hell out of our mom, just grind her down until she would give up and make pancakes for us for dinner," recalls Donald Wressell. "It was such a coup to get Mom to make breakfast for dinner. That's the inspiration. I wanted the flavors of a warm pancake and pears." Wressell adds maple-syrup powder to the hazelnut pancake mix, drenches the entirety in maple syrup, and dresses the side with chocolate sorbet. He then adds poached pears and a hazelnut tuile wafer.

YIELD: 10 SERVINGS

Special Equipment: Large decorating comb with 3/8" (.95 cm) slats

CHOCOLATE SORBET			
15.5 liq oz	458 ml	simple syrup	
6 liq oz	177 ml	water	
8 oz	227 g	unsweetened chocolate, such as Valrhona Cacao de Pâte, finely chopped	
4 oz	113 g	bittersweet chocolate, finely chopped	
2 liq oz	59 ml	orange juice	
1.5 liq oz	44 ml	lemon juice	

1. In a saucepan, bring the simple syrup and water to a boil.

2. Reduce the heat to low and add the chopped chocolates to the saucepan. Stir until completely melted.

3. Remove from the heat. Whisk in the orange and lemon juices.

4. Strain the mixture through a fine chinois and chill.

5. Process in ice cream machine according to the manufacturer's instructions.

POACHED PEARS			
50.5 liq oz	1.5 lt	Riesling wine (2 bottles)	
16 oz	454 g	granulated sugar	
1	1	vanilla bean, split and scraped	
1	1	3" (7.6 cm) cinnamon stick	
1	1	star anise	
1 tsp	2 g	grated lemon zest	
1 tsp	2 g	grated orange zest	
20	20	black peppercorns	
10	10	Bartlett pears, peeled, halved, and cored, (about 7 to 8 oz / 198 to 226 g each)	

1. In a large saucepan, combine all the ingredients except the pears. Bring to a boil; add the pears. Cook the pears in the simmering syrup until tender.

2. Cool the pears in the syrup.

3. With a 2 1/4" (5.7 cm) cutter, stamp out 40 discs of poached pear of 1/4" (.64 cm) thickness.

4. Purée the pear trimmings in a food processer. Thin to the desired consistency with some of the poaching syrup.

HAZELNUT TUILE WAFERS	5 oz	141 g	unsalted butter, softened
	9 oz	255 g	confectioners' sugar
	5 oz	141 g	egg whites
	1 tsp	4.9 ml	vanilla extract
	7 oz	198 g	all-purpose flour
	pinch	pinch	salt
	2 oz	57 g	hazelnut flour

1. Preheat the oven to 350°F (177°C). Have ready a cylinder, 2" (5 cm) in diameter, for bending the wafers.

2. In a mixer fitted with a paddle attachment, cream the butter and confectioners' sugar. Gradually add the egg whites and mix until incorporated. Add the vanilla. Blend in the flour and salt. Do not overmix.

3. Spread a thin layer of wafer paste onto a silicone mat. Use a decorating comb to create 3/8" (.95 cm) wide strips. Sprinkle with hazelnut flour (about 2 Tbs /14 g per half-sheet pan). Bake until golden and set, about 8 to 10 minutes. Cut the strips to desired length and drape around the cylinder, creating a "tail." Repeat to make 40 wafers.

HAZELNUT PANCAKE BATTER	7 oz	198 g	all-purpose flour
	5.75 oz	163 g	hazelnut flour
	1 oz	28 g	maple syrup powder
	1 tsp	5 g	baking powder
	1/2 tsp	2.5 g	baking soda
	pinch	pinch	salt
	14 liq oz	414 ml	milk
	5.25 oz	149 g	eggs
	1.5 oz	43 g	honey
	1.5 Tbs	7.4 ml	vanilla extract
	1.5 oz	43 g	melted butter

1. In a large bowl, sift together the all-purpose and hazelnut flours, maple syrup powder, baking powder, baking soda, and salt.

2. In a separate bowl, whisk together the milk, eggs, honey, and vanilla. Add to dry ingredients and stir until blended. Mix in the melted butter and allow the batter to rest at least 15 minutes.

| ASSEMBLY | Maple syrup |
| | Chocolate zigzags |

1. Using about 1 Tbs (14 g) of batter for each pancake, cook four pancakes on a hot, lightly greased, griddle, or sauté pan. The pancakes should be about 2 1/4" (5.7 cm) in diameter.

2. On a dessert plate, alternately layer four hot pancakes with four slices of poached pear, starting with a pancake and ending with a slice of poached pear.

3. Randomly dot 2 Tbs (14 g) of pear sauce next to the stack of pancakes. Arrange 3 small scoops of chocolate sorbet around the griddle cakes.

4. Drizzle the pancake-pear stack with maple syrup. Garnish the plate with four hazelnut wafers.

CHOCOLATE RIBBON

THADDEUS DUBOIS

Pastry Chef, *Duquesne Club,
Pittsburgh, Pennsylvania.*

White-chocolate-passion-fruit mousse and blackberry sorbet are served with strips of toasted sesame seed honey cake, caramel rum sauce, and a strip of rhubarb leather, which contains fresh fruit. This dessert is actually served on a mirror at the Duquesne Club. "I found about sixty of them sitting around," says Thaddeus Dubois. "I wanted to serve it on a mirror because of all the sharp lines on it."

YIELD: 25 SERVINGS

Special Equipment: Twenty-four 1 1/2" (3.8 cm) diameter x 2" (5 cm) high metal ring molds

BLACKBERRY SORBET			
16 liq oz	*473 ml*	*sorbet syrup*
32 liq oz	*946 ml*	*water*
.5 liq oz	*15 ml*	*lemon juice*
.5 oz	*14 g*	*grated orange zest*
35.3 oz	*1 kg*	*Boiron blackberry purée*
2 liq oz	*59 g*	*blackberry liqueur*

1. Whisk together all the ingredients; chill well.

2. Process in an ice cream machine according to the manufacturer's instructions.

RHUBARB LEATHER			
5 lbs	*2.27 k*	*fresh rhubarb, cut into 2" (5 cm) pieces*
4 liq oz	*118 ml*	*water*
1 lb	*454 g*	*granulated sugar*
1 liq oz	*30 ml*	*Midori melon liqueur*

1. In a large pot, combine the rhubarb pieces and water. Bring to a simmer and cook, uncovered, until tender, about 20 minutes. Cool.

2. Process the cooked rhubarb in a food processor until puréed. Add the sugar and liqueur and process just until combined.

3. Line a sheet pan with a silicone baking mat. Spread the rhubarb mixture onto the mat. Place in an oven with only the pilot light on, for 16 hours, or until dry. Cut the rhubarb leather into variously sized triangles to garnish the plate.

SESAME SEED CAKE			
	2 lbs	907 g	unsalted butter
	1 lb	454 g	dark brown sugar
	1 lb	454 g	clover honey
	15.75 oz	447 g	whole eggs
	8 liq oz	237 ml	milk
	1 lb	454 g	egg whites, at room temperature
	8 oz	227 g	granulated sugar
	2 lbs	907 g	cake flour, sifted
	1 oz	28 g	baking powder
	8 oz	227 g	sesame seeds, lightly toasted

1. Preheat oven to 360°F (180°C). Grease and flour three 12" (30 cm) loaf pans. In a mixer fitted with a paddle attachment, cream the butter, brown sugar, and honey at high speed until light.

2. In a bowl, whisk together the eggs and milk and slowly add to the butter mixture, while beating at medium speed.

3. Fold the flour, baking powder, and sesame seeds into the batter. In a mixer fitted with a whisk attachment, beat the egg whites and sugar to medium peaks. Gently fold into the batter. Scrape the batter into the prepared pans and bake until a cake tester comes out clean, about 45 minutes. Cool slightly; remove from pans. Cut one of the cakes into 1/4" (.64 cm) slices. Cut 1/4" (.64 cm) wide crosswise strips from the slices. Toast the strips lightly and set aside to garnish the plates.

CARAMEL RUM SAUCE			
	16 liq oz	473 ml	heavy cream
	8 oz	227 g	unsalted butter, cut into cubes
	2 lbs	907 g	granulated sugar
	8 liq oz	237 ml	water
	1.5 liq oz	44 ml	dark rum

1. In a saucepan, combine the cream and butter. Cook over medium heat until the butter is melted and the mixture comes to a simmer. Remove from the heat.

2. In another saucepan, combine the sugar and water. Cook over high heat to a medium-dark caramel, washing down the sides of the pan as necessary to prevent crystals from forming. Remove the pan from the heat.

3. While stirring constantly, slowly and carefully pour the warm cream mixture into the caramel. Cool slightly; stir in the dark rum. Cool completely. Cover tightly with plastic wrap and set aside.

WHITE-CHOCOLATE– PASSION-FRUIT MOUSSE			
	3.9 oz	111 g	egg yolks
	1 liq oz	30 ml	water
	1 liq oz	30 ml	glucose
	3 oz	85 g	nonfat milk powder
	12 oz	340 g	white chocolate, melted
	12 oz	340 g	passion fruit purée
	.26 oz	7.5 g	gelatin leaves, bloomed
	32 liq oz	946 ml	heavy cream, whipped to soft peaks
	1 lb	454 g	bittersweet couverture, melted
	1 lb	454 g	white chocolate couverture, melted

1. Line twenty-five 1 1/2" (3.8 cm) diameter x 2" (5 cm) high metal ring molds with plastic strips or grease and sugar the interiors. Place the molds on a parchment-lined sheet pan and place a cake round in the bottom of each mold.

2. In a bowl, whisk together the egg yolks, water, glucose, and milk powder. Set the bowl over a pot of simmering water and, whisking constantly, heat to 185°F (85°C). Strain the yolk mixture and place in mixer fitted with a whisk attachment. With the plastic shield attachment in place on the mixer, whip the yolks on medium-high speed until cool.

3. Heat the gelatin until dissolved. Meanwhile, warm the passion fruit purée slightly and whisk into the melted white chocolate. Whisk in the dissolved gelatin.

4. Gently fold the cooled egg mixture into the chocolate mixture until almost mixed. Fold in the whipped cream and reserved cake cubes. Scrape the mousse into a tipless pastry bag; pipe the mousse into the prepared molds. Freeze the molds for several hours, until firm.

5. Unmold each mousse ring and return to the freezer.

6. Cut out 25 strips of acetate to fit around the ring molds. Dip a small scrub brush (the kind used for cleaning fruit) into the bittersweet couverture and spread a thin layer over one of the strips (the layer should be thin enough so that you can see through it). Then spread a thin layer of white chocolate over the strip, covering it completely. Remove one of the mousse rings from the freezer and wrap the strip, chocolate side against the mousse, around the ring. Refrigerate until serving.

CHOCOLATE RIBBON   2 lbs   907 g   *bittersweet chocolate, melted and tempered*

1. Cut 25 strips of acetate 12 to 14" (30 to 35 cm) long and 3" (7.6 cm) wide. Cut the short ends on an angle.

2. Place some of the chocolate in a small parchment cone. Pipe diagonal lines of chocolate in a heavy crosshatch pattern over the length of one of the strips. Let set slightly; form a teardrop-shaped loop with the strip, pressing it together at the ends. Place the ribbon in a container that is at least as tall as the ribbon. Let it set completely; then carefully remove the acetate. Repeat with the remaining strips. (If any of the ribbons happen to break during the peeling process, you can use the broken pieces of ribbon as additional garnish on the plate.)

SPUN-SUGAR GARNISH   as needed   as needed   *red powdered food coloring*
3 lbs   1.36 k   *isomalt sugar*
1 pt   473 ml   *water*

1. Combine a small amount of the food coloring with a little water.

2. In a heavy pot, combine the isomalt sugar and water and bring to a boil. Continue to cook to 266°F (130°C). Stir in enough of the coloring to reach a deep pink color. Continue cooking the sugar to 338°F (170°C). Immediately plunge the bottom of the pot into cold water to stop the cooking process. Without stirring, allow the sugar to stand for about 5 minutes to thicken to the proper viscosity.

3. Position 2 metal or wooden skewers over the edge of a table, with something heavy on top of them to hold them in place. Place two sheet pans on the floor below. Dip a cut-off whisk or spun-sugar nail device into the sugar. Spin the sugar with quick swinging motions between the two skewers. If the sugar begins to thicken, heat it briefly, without stirring it. Continue this process until you have made enough sugar to garnish the plates.

ASSEMBLY · *Melted chocolate*

1. Place some of the spun sugar on one side of the plate. Place a rhubarb leather triangle on the other side of the plate. Place a scoop of the sorbet onto the triangle and fold one corner on top of it. Wrap another triangle on top of the sorbet.

2. Place a dab of the melted chocolate onto the plate and carefully set the chocolate ribbon on top of the shard. Set one of the passion fruit mousse tubes on its side in the opening of the ribbon. Garnish the plate with dots of the caramel sauce.

CHARTREUSE SUNDAE WITH MACADAMIA BROWNIES

PHILIPPE LAURIER

Executive Pastry Chef,
*Patisfrance USA, East Rutherford,
New Jersey.*

Philippe Laurier's mission was to take an American dessert and dress it up, European-style. He has accomplished this with a basic brownie, baking it in a teardrop mold and pebbling it with macadamia nuts and raisins macerated with Chartreuse and candied ginger, and crowning it with a dollop of Chartreuse ice cream. A florentine cookie with macadamias and chocolate tendrils round off the plate.

YIELD: 12 SERVINGS

Special Equipment:
Silicone baking mat
Curved triangular stencil 9" (22.8 cm) long x 6" (15.2 cm) high
Oval ring mold, 2 1/2 oz (70 g) capacity
Small gold-flecked transfer sheets

CHARTREUSE ICE CREAM			
20 liq oz	*591 ml*	*milk*
7 liq oz	*207 ml*	*heavy cream*
1	*1*	*vanilla bean, split and scraped*
4.6 oz	*130 g*	*egg yolks*
7 oz	*198 g*	*granulated sugar*
1.5 liq oz	*44 ml*	*Chartreuse liqueur*

1. In a large saucepan, scald the milk with the cream and vanilla bean. Remove from the heat. Cover and allow to infuse for 1 hour. Discard the vanilla bean.

2. In a bowl, whisk together the egg yolks and sugar. Temper the yolks with the reheated milk mixture. Return to the saucepan and cook until thickened. Strain the custard and cool in an ice bath. Chill.

3. Process in an ice cream machine, adding liqueur during the last 5 minutes of churning.

MACADAMIA BROWNIE			
1.5 oz	*43 g*	*golden raisins*
1.5 liq oz	*44 ml*	*Chartreuse liqueur*
3.5 oz	*99 g*	*all-purpose flour*
pinch	*pinch*	*salt*
1/8 tsp	*1.8 g*	*baking powder*
9 oz	*255 g*	*unsalted butter, melted*
7 oz	*198 g*	*granulated sugar, divided*
9 oz	*255 g*	*bittersweet chocolate, finely chopped*
.5 oz	*14 g*	*crystallized ginger, finely minced*
3.5 oz	*99 g*	*lightly toasted macadamia nuts, finely chopped*
3 oz	*85 g*	*egg whites*

1. Macerate the raisins in the Chartreuse liqueur for at least one hour. Drain.

2. In a bowl, combine the flour, salt, and baking powder.

3. In a medium saucepan, over low heat, melt the butter and 4 oz (113 g) sugar. Add the chopped chocolate and stir until completely melted. Remove from the heat, transfer to a large bowl, and let cool.

4. Add the dry ingredients to the cooled chocolate mixture. Stir in the drained raisins, minced ginger, and chopped nuts.

5. In a mixer fitted with a whisk attachment, whip the egg whites with the remaining 3 oz (85 g) of the sugar to firm peaks. Fold the meringue into the chocolate-flour mixture.

| MACADAMIA NUT TUILE | 5 oz | 142 g | bee sting powder mix* |
| | 2 oz | 57 g | macadamia nuts, finely chopped |

*Note. Bee sting powder mix is available from Patisfrance, (800) PASTRY-1.

1. Preheat the oven to 400°F (204°C). Line a baking sheet with a silicone baking mat.

2. In a bowl, mix the bee sting powder with the chopped macadamia nuts.

3. Place the stencil on the silicone mat. Spread a thin layer of powder-nut mixture inside the stencil. Remove the stencil. Bake until golden, about 6 to 8 minutes. Form into the desired shape. Repeat to make 12 tuiles.

| CHOCOLATE STICKS | 8 oz | 227 g | bittersweet chocolate, tempered |

1. Spread the chocolate thinly and evenly over small gold-flecked transfer sheets. Allow the chocolate to partially set.

2. With a paring knife, cut thin, wavy strips from the chocolate, 4 to 8" (10 to 20 cm) in length. Allow the chocolate to set completely. Peel off the strips and set aside for garnish.

ASSEMBLY | *Chocolate-dipped sliced almonds*
Crème anglaise
Chocolate sauce

1. Preheat the oven to 300°F (149°C). Lightly butter the oval ring mold.

2. Place 2.5 oz (71 g) of the brownie mixture into the mold. Bake the brownie for 20 to 25 minutes. Unmold onto a dessert plate. Top the brownie with a scoop of Chartreuse ice cream. Place a chocolate-dipped almond slice on the ice cream. Insert several chocolate sticks into the brownie.

3. Garnish the plate with crème anglaise and chocolate sauce and serve immediately.

BANANA MOUSSE WITH BITTERSWEET CHOCOLATE BRÛLÉE

NORMAN LOVE

Corporate Pastry Chef, *Ritz-Carlton Hotel Company, Naples, Florida.*

"There was no inspiration for this dessert, except that I saw a cone mold sitting on a dome mold in my kitchen," says Norman Love. *"From there, it was make it up as you go."* The result is a chocolate-glazed banana mousse, which encloses a bittersweet chocolate crème brûlée; an orange cinnamon biscuit forms the base, and there are dots of a sour caramel sauce; the sauce employs sour cream rather than heavy cream. *"It has a noticeable tang,"* says Love.

YIELD: 24 SERVINGS

Special Equipment:
Twenty-four 4 oz (118 ml) demi-sphere molds
Three 18 x 24" (45.7 x 61 cm) sheets of acetate, plus more acetate for forming cones.

ORANGE-CINNAMON BISCUIT			
6.25 oz	177 g	*almond flour*
6.25 oz	177 g	*confectioners' sugar*
1 tsp	4 g	*ground cinnamon*
2 Tbs	8 g	*finely grated orange zest*
6.3 oz	179 g	*egg whites*
2.5 oz	71 g	*granulated sugar*

1. Preheat the oven to 375°F (191°C). Line three half-sheet pans with parchment paper.

2. In a large bowl, sift together the almond flour, confectioners' sugar, and cinnamon. Mix in the orange zest.

3. In a mixer fitted with the whisk attachment, beat the egg whites with the granulated sugar until stiff peaks form. Fold the meringue into the flour mixture in two additions.

4. Scrape the batter into a pastry bag fitted with a medium plain tip (Ateco #5) and pipe twenty-four 2 3/4" (7 cm) rounds on the prepared pan. Bake for about 10 minutes or until lightly browned. Cool on a wire rack.

CHOCOLATE CRÈME BRÛLÉE			
32 liq oz	946 ml	*heavy cream*
1	1	*vanilla bean, split and scraped*
5.2 oz	147 g	*egg yolks*
8 oz	227 g	*granulated sugar*
5 oz	142 g	*Valrhona Pur Caraibe chocolate, finely chopped*

1. Preheat oven to 300°F (149°C). Line a half hotel pan or a deep-sided 10 x 10" (25.4 x 25.4 cm) baking pan with plastic wrap.

2. In a large saucepan over medium heat, bring the heavy cream and vanilla bean to a low boil.

3. Meanwhile, in a large heatproof bowl, mix the egg yolks and sugar until blended, making sure to incorporate as little air as possible.

4. Temper the yolk-sugar mixture with the hot cream, stirring gently. Add the chopped chocolate and mix until the chocolate is completely melted and the mixture is smooth.

5. Strain the chocolate-brûlée mixture through a fine sieve into the prepared pan; the depth of the brûlée mixture should be about 3/4" (1.9 cm). Place the filled pan in a water bath and bake for 75 to 90 minutes or until the brûlée is set. (The center may still be a bit wobbly, but will set up upon cooling.) Cool completely.

6. Place the cooled brûlée in the freezer for about 2 hours or until the mixture is semi-frozen.

7. Remove the brûlée from the freezer. Using a 1 1/2" (3.8 cm) cutter, cut out 24 rounds of the brûlée, placing them on a parchment-lined tray. If the banana mousse is prepared and the molds are ready to be assembled, do so at this time. Otherwise, place the tray of brûlée rounds in the freezer.

BANANA MOUSSE	17 oz	482 g	*fresh banana purée*
	2 liq oz	59 ml	*lemon juice*
	.6 oz	17 g	*gelatin sheets, softened in cold water*
	4 liq oz	118 ml	*water*
	12 oz	340 g	*granulated sugar*
	5.25 oz	149 g	*egg whites*
	17 liq oz	503 ml	*heavy cream, whipped to soft peaks*

1. Place about half the banana purée, the lemon juice, and the drained gelatin sheets in a saucepan. Cook over medium heat, stirring constantly, until the gelatin is melted and the mixture is smooth. Remove from the heat and transfer the banana mixture to a large bowl. Stir in the remaining banana purée.

2. In a saucepan, boil the water and sugar to 248°F (120°C).

3. Meanwhile, in a mixer fitted with a whisk attachment, beat the egg whites to soft peaks; slowly add the sugar syrup and beat on low speed until the meringue is cool.

4. Fold the whipped cream into the banana mixture; then fold in the meringue.

5. Remove 24 chocolate crème brûlée rounds from the freezer. Fill the demi-sphere molds half way with banana mousse. Place a round of brûlée inside the mold and press down lightly to secure it. Top off the molds with more mousse allowing space for the orange-cinnamon biscuit. Cover each mold with a round of biscuit, trimmed to fit, pressing it into the mold.

6. Freeze the filled molds until firm, about 3 to 4 hours.

CHOCOLATE GLAZE	16 liq oz	473 ml	*milk*
	7.9 oz	225 g	*unsalted butter, cubed*
	7.9 oz	225 g	*granulated sugar*
	4.4 oz	125 g	*alkalized cocoa powder, sifted*
	13.2 oz	375 g	*bittersweet chocolate couverture, chopped*
	4.4 oz	125 g	*pâte à glacé, chopped*

1. In a saucepan, whisk together the milk, butter, sugar, and cocoa powder over medium heat; bring to a boil.

2. Add the couverture and pâte à glacé and whisk until smooth. Cool the glaze to about 85°F (29°C).

3. Remove the banana mousse molds from the freezer and unmold onto a wire rack set over a sheet pan. Pour a thin layer of chocolate glaze over each frozen mousse, letting the excess drip off into the sheet pan. Place the glazed desserts on a tray and refrigerate until ready to serve.

SOUR CARAMEL SAUCE			
2.5 *liq oz*	*74 ml*	*water*
7.5 *oz*	*213 g*	*granulated sugar*
2 *oz*	*57 g*	*unsalted butter*
9 *oz*	*255 g*	*sour cream*

Combine the water and sugar in a heavy-bottomed saucepan. Dissolve the sugar over medium heat. Increase the heat to high and cook the mixture until it is a medium colored caramel. Remove from the heat and whisk in the butter. Return the pan to low heat; slowly add the sour cream and whisk until the sauce is well blended and smooth and any hardened caramel has melted. Strain the sauce and allow to cool.

CHOCOLATE STENCILING			
36 *oz*	*1 kg*	*bittersweet chocolate, tempered*
72 *oz*	*2 kg*	*milk chocolate, tempered*

1. Place a line-patterned silkscreen stencil on a piece of acetate. Spread some of the bittersweet chocolate over the stencil and allow it to set. Remove the stencil and repeat this procedure twice more.

2. Spread some of the milk chocolate over the entire surface of each of the three stenciled acetate sheets. Allow to set completely.

3. Cut out twenty-four 5 1/2" (14 cm) rounds, twenty-four 2" (5 cm) rounds, and twenty-four 1 1/2" (3.8 cm) rounds from the stenciled chocolate. Using a 1/2" (1.3 cm) cutter, cut out circles from the centers of the smallest rounds.

CHOCOLATE CONES			
48 *oz*	*1.4 kg*	*bittersweet chocolate, tempered*

1. Using acetate, form a cone that measures 7" (175 cm) in height with a 1" (2.5 cm) opening. Repeat to make 24 cones.

2. Using acetate, form a cone that measures 10" (25 cm) in height with a 1/2" (1.3 cm) opening. Repeat to make 24 cones.

3. Completely fill a cone with the tempered chocolate. Turn it upside down and allow the excess to drip out into the bowl containing the tempered chocolate. Place the cone, on its side, on a parchment-lined sheet pan. Repeat this process for all the cones.

4. Allow the cones to set completely at room temperature for at least one hour.

PLATING   *Melted chocolate (for "gluing")*
24 chocolate "ribbons"

1. Center a 5 1/2" (13.7 cm) stenciled chocolate round on a dessert plate. Remove a glazed banana mousse dessert from the refrigerator and place it on top of the round of chocolate. Top the mousse with a 2" (5 cm) chocolate round.

2. Remove the acetate from one 7" (175 cm) chocolate cone and from one 10" (25 cm) chocolate cone. Arrange one small ring-shaped round over the 7" (175 cm) cone and carefully place that cone on top of the 2" (5 cm) chocolate round.

3. Place the tip of the 10" (25 cm) chocolate cone on the dessert plate. Place a dot of melted chocolate about two-thirds of the way up on the 10" (25 cm) cone and attach it at this point to the shorter cone so that the longer one is standing at an angle.

4. Sauce the plate with graduated circles of sour caramel sauce. Partially insert a chocolate "ribbon" inside the opening of the 10" (25 cm) cone.

RASPBERRY VANILLA BLOSSOM

SEBASTIEN CANNONE

Co-owner, *Ecole de Patisserie Francaise, Chicago.*

A medley of textures—buttery shortdough, creamy Bavarian, and chewy dacquoise—deliver tart raspberry and smooth vanilla flavors. Layers of vanilla Bavarian, raspberry gelée, and dacquoise sit atop a vanilla shortdough cookie, and the entirety is enclosed in a white biscuit marbled with pâte à cigarette. Crowning the dessert is a chocolate shell that contains a medley of fruits in cherry coulis. Mango chips, spun sugar, pâte de fruit, a tuile fork, and a gooseberry finish the plate.

YIELD: 24 SERVINGS

Special Equipment:
Twenty-four ring molds, 2 1/4" (5.7 cm) diameter x 2" (5 cm) high
1 3/4" (4.4 cm) diameter Plexiglas modular molds

VANILLA SHORTDOUGH			
4.4 oz	126 g	unsalted butter (82%)
1	1	vanilla bean, scraped
1.9 oz	55 g	confectioners' sugar
3	3	hard-boiled egg yolks
5.6 oz	160 g	cake flour
1/3 tsp	2 g	baking powder

1. In a mixer fitted with a paddle attachment, cream the butter. Add the vanilla bean seeds and sugar, and pass through a tamis.

2. Pass the yolks through a tamis and weigh out 1.5 oz (44 g). Add to the butter mixture.

3. Sift together the cake flour and baking powder and add to the butter mixture. Mix until just combined. Form the dough into a disc, wrap it in plastic, and refrigerate for 30 minutes or until chilled.

4. Preheat the oven to 325°F (165°C). On a floured surface, roll out the dough to 1/8" (.3 cm) thick. Cut dough into circles using a 1 3/4" (4.4 cm) diameter cutter. Place the circles on a parchment-lined half-sheet pan and bake for about 12 minutes or until the edges are golden.

ALMOND DACQUOISE	9.5 oz	270 g	TPT*
	3 oz	87 g	almond flour
	7.5 oz	215 g	egg whites
	1.9 oz	55 g	granulated sugar

*Note. TPT (tant-pour-tant) is a mixture consisting of 50% almond flour and 50% confectioners' sugar. You can make it by combining 4 3/4 oz (135 g) whole blanched semi-roasted almonds and 4 3/4 oz (135 g) confectioners' sugar in a food processor and grinding it to a fine powder.

1. Preheat oven to 425°F (220°C). Combine the TPT and almond flour. In a mixer, whip the egg whites and sugar to soft peaks. Gently fold in the almond mixture.

2. Pipe the mixture into 1 3/4" (4.4 cm) diameter plexiglass modular molds. Smooth the tops, remove the molds, and bake for about 15 minutes or until just golden. If you do not have modular molds, spread the batter onto a parchment-lined half-sheet pan and after baking cut into 1 3/4" (4.4 cm) circles.

PÂTE À CIGARETTE	3.5 oz	100 g	unsalted butter (82%)
	3.5 oz	100 g	confectioners' sugar
	3.2 oz	90 g	egg whites
	2.6 oz	75 g	cake flour
	as needed	as needed	red food coloring

1. In a mixer fitted with a paddle attachment, cream the butter. Mix in the confectioners' sugar. Add half the egg whites and half the flour, mix well, then mix in the remaining egg whites and flour. Add the desired amount of food coloring.

2. Spread the batter unevenly on to 3 silicone baking mat-lined half-sheet pans. Freeze until ready to use.

BISCUIT	1.8 oz	50 g	confectioners' sugar
	1.8 oz	50 g	almond flour
	2.9 oz	82 g	cake flour
	14.5 oz	412 g	eggs
	2.1 oz	60 g	unsalted butter (82%), melted and warm
	8.8 oz	250 g	egg whites
	1.3 oz	37.5 g	granulated sugar

1. Preheat oven to 425°F (220°C). In a mixer, whip the confectioners' sugar, almond flour, cake flour, and eggs until they are very light and airy; about 12 minutes. Mix in the butter.

2. Whip the egg whites and sugar to soft peaks. Gently fold the whites into the yolks.

3. Divide the batter into thirds and spread evenly in the pans prepared with pâte à cigarette. Bake for about 8 to 10 minutes or until the cake springs back when gently pressed with a finger.

4. Let cool for a couple of minutes, then run a knife around the edge of the pan and invert the cake onto a cooling rack. Carefully peel off the silicone baking mat and cool completely.

RASPBERRY GELÉE	.2 oz	6 g	*gelatin sheets*
	7.9 oz	225 g	*fresh raspberry purée (10% sugar)*
	2.6 oz	75 g	*inverted sugar*
	2.6 oz	75 g	*dextrose*
	1 liq oz	34 ml	*raspberry liqueur*

1. Bloom the gelatin in cold water. In a microwave oven on medium power, heat the gelatin with one-fourth of the raspberry purée just until melted, about 15 seconds.

2. Add the inverted sugar, dextrose, and remaining purée. Mix in the liqueur.

RASPBERRY MEDLEY	8.7 oz	250 g	*fresh raspberries*
	4.4 oz	100 g	*fresh raspberry purée*

Toss the berries in the purée and mix well. Set aside.

VANILLA BAVARIAN	15 liq oz	444 ml	*heavy cream (35%)*
	.3 oz	8 g	*gelatin sheets*
	2	2	*Tahitian vanilla beans*
	9 liq oz	266 ml	*whole milk (3.6%)*
	4.8 oz	137 g	*granulated sugar*
	2.3 oz	65 g	*egg yolks*

1. Whip the cream to soft peaks and reserve in the refrigerator. Bloom the gelatin in cold water. Put the vanilla beans in water and microwave on high power for about 15 seconds or until puffy. Cut the beans in half, scrape, and combine them with the milk in a saucepan. Add half the sugar and cook to 158°F (70°C). Remove from heat, cover with plastic wrap, and infuse for 30 minutes.

2. Combine the rest of the sugar with the egg yolks and temper into the milk. Cook gently, stirring with a wooden spoon until the mixture reaches 185°F (85°C). Add the gelatin and strain through a chinois over an ice bath. Let cool and gently fold in the whipped cream.

BLOSSOM ASSEMBLY

1. Line the molds with acetate strips and place them on a sheet pan lined with plastic wrap. Cut the biscuit into strips 7" (17.5 cm) long by 2" (5 cm) wide. Place a strip in each ring mold with the colored side facing out. Fill the molds one-third of the way with Bavarian. Cover the Bavarian with a layer of raspberry medley, and top with a layer of raspberry gelée. Freeze until gelée is set.

2. Place a dacquoise circle on top of the gelée. Fill molds almost to the top with Bavarian. Place a shortdough circle on top and freeze until set.

RASPBERRY PÂTE	26 oz	750 g	raspberry purée
DE FRUIT	10.6 oz	300 g	fresh raspberries
	.8 oz	22 g	pectin
	43.9 oz	1.2 kg	granulated sugar, divided
	7.9 oz	225 g	glucose
	.7 oz	19 g	tartaric acid solution*
	.7 oz	19 g	framboise d'Alsace

*Note. To make tartaric acid solution, dissolve tartaric acid powder in an equal amount of boiling water and strain through two layers of cheesecloth.

1. Combine the raspberry purée and fresh raspberries and heat to 104°F (40°C). Mix together the pectin and 4 oz (113 g) of the sugar and add to the raspberries. Bring to a boil and add the remaining 39.9 oz (1130 g) of the sugar and the glucose. Cook to 223°F (106°C). Add the tartaric acid solution and framboise d'Alsace.

2. Pour into a parchment-lined half-sheet pan. Cool completely, cut into 1" (2.5 cm) squares, and coat with granulated sugar.

TUILES	4 oz	113 g	unsalted butter
	5 oz	142 g	confectioners' sugar
	4.1 oz	117 g	egg whites
	5 oz	142 g	bread flour

1. Preheat oven to 350°F (175°C). In a mixer fitted with a paddle attachment, cream the butter and sugar. Slowly add the egg whites alternately with the bread flour.

2. Make a 6" (15 cm) long fork-shaped stencil. Spread a thin coat of the batter through the stencil onto a silicone baking mat-lined sheet pan. Bake for 6 to 7 minutes or just until firm. Let cool on sheet pan.

MANGO CHIPS	2	2	firm mangoes
	16 liq oz	473 ml	water
	33.3 oz	944 g	granulated sugar

1. Peel the mangoes and slice them very thinly on a mandoline. Combine the water and sugar in a large saucepan and bring to a boil. Pour the warm syrup over the mango slices and let steep overnight.

2. Preheat a convection oven on low fan to 250°F (120°C). Place the mango slices on a silicone baking-mat-lined sheet pan and bake for about 30 to 40 minutes or until crisp.

| CHERRY JUICE | 18 liq oz | 532 ml | liquid from poached cherries in syrup |
| | 1 Tbs | 10 g | cornstarch |

1. In a saucepan bring the liquid to a boil. Dissolve the cornstarch in cold water and add it to the juice.

2. Continue to boil for a few minutes, adjusting the amount of cornstarch if necessary to reach the desired consistency.

CHOCOLATE SHELLS   *2 lbs*   *907 g*   *dark chocolate, tempered*

1. Spread the chocolate very thinly on marble. When the chocolate just begins to set, scrape it with a 3 1/4" (8.2 cm) diameter round metal cutter to form a curl.

2. Pinch one end of the curl to form a shell shape.

DESSERT ASSEMBLY   *Assorted fresh fruit*
Blackberries
Gooseberries
Spun sugar
Pulled-sugar curls

1. Invert the blossom so that the shortdough is on the bottom and unmold it onto a dessert plate. Top the blossom with a chocolate shell. Fill the shell with assorted fresh fruit tossed in cherry juice.

2. Sauce the plate with cherry juice. Place a blackberry upside down and stick a tuile fork in it.

3. Garnish the plate with a gooseberry, a mango chip, pâte de fruit, spun sugar, and a pulled-sugar curl.

Making the chocolate shells (see above).

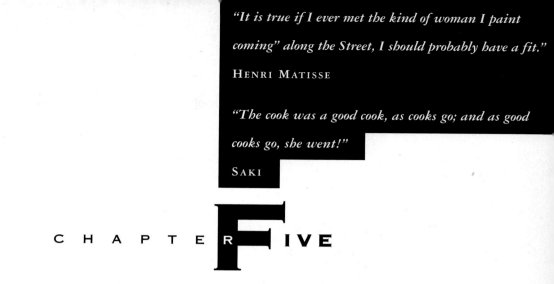

CHAPTER **F**IVE

MODERNIST
SAUCE PAINTING

LINCOLN CARSON

Pastry Chef,
*The Highlands Inn, Carmel,
California.*

BORN: March 1969,
Beirut, Lebanon.
TRAINING/EXPERIENCE: pastry
program, Johnson and Wales,
Rhode Island; Le Pactole, Le
Bernadin, Peacock Alley
(Waldorf-Astoria), Luxe, Four
Seasons Hotel, Cascabel, La
Côte Basque, all in New York.

*"I've had some lucky breaks. I
worked for some excellent people. I've
received a lot of great advice and
good training. Some of that training was under traditional French
management, which is based on fear.
I'm very serious about what I do,
but I'm not a screamer. My feeling
is, work harder than anyone working for you, and they'll do it for
you. Don't lose sight that there are
more outlets, creative and otherwise,
in your life. When you leave work,
leave work."*

Sauce paintings are an exquisite, accessible, affordable way to dress a dessert. The col-ors of sauces are so spectacular, and the colors of many main components are so drab, that chefs will be tempted to choose sauces for their color rather than their flavor. "Don't," says Wayne Brachman of the Mesa Grill in New York. "One drop of sauce can radically change the flavor of something. In the hands of a careful chef, each bite of a sauced dessert will be slightly different, and all of them satisfying.

The Modernist chef has the option of making his or her own sauces from fresh fruit or mak-ing them from purchased, frozen purées—or both. "We keep fruit that is not perfect," says Thomas Worhach of the Four Seasons Hotel in Palm Beach, Florida, "although berries should be unblemished. Once a week we cook them, adding a little sugar. The sugar is what helps preserve the fruit. Refrigerated, they will last two weeks, but the flavor really is perfect only for a week, so we use them up in a week." Maintaining the sauces' consis-tency is not a problem, says Worhach. "We thicken it with cornstarch if we have to. You don't want it too thick. You just want it to sit on the plate without the water running out."

"You want to leave the sauce as natural as possible," says Michael Hu of the Waldorf-Astoria in New York. "Some sauces have a better consistency than others—cherry sauces and other sauces with more sugar in them."

There are alternatives beyond those of purchased purées and conventional fruit purées. Donald Wressell of the Four Seasons Beverly Hills does not consider sauce painting "the forward motion" for many of his plate designs, but he is still intrigued by sauces. "I'm becoming more interested in sauces that are clear rather than cream-based or purée-based," he says. "Burnt orange sauce is something I've evolved into. I like the look better. It fits my plates better. I like reduction sauces too."

"Purées are a lot of work to do yourself," admits Thomas Worhach, "but a lot of these are readily available now." Even chefs who make their own sauces will supplement their own product with purchased purées. Improvements in shipping, manufacture, and customer service have vastly improved the quality of these purées.

In the premium packaged brands, fruits are frozen as soon after harvesting as possible to eliminate any degradation of color or flavor. No colorings or additives are used. A flash pas-teurization process may be employed to control bacteria and oxidation once the purée is defrosted. Many of the purées contain no added sugar, while a few do add some 10 percent sugar. A knowledgeable chef can control the sweetness of each preparation.

Thomas Worhach is one of the acknowledged masters of this type of plate presentation; it has become his signature. At banquets, he will try to arrange it so that every person at a table will have a different sauce design around their dessert. It creates a sensation. This is how it works in his kitchen:

Worhach always uses white plates. "Using showplates with all this saucing makes a plate too busy," he says. Most of the time, his sauces are contained within a design piped in chocolate with a paper cone. Worhach does every design free-hand. "I used to do free sauces, twirling them, shaking the plate," he says, "but I wanted something a little more precise." Why, then, does he go free-hand rather than employing templates? "I don't use anything that could make it a perfectly designed sculpture"—in other words, Worhach feels that much of the beauty in his designs lies in their inexactitude.

Worhach can do the chocolate lines well ahead of time. Then during service, he and other members of his team will fill in the sauces. He puts the plate on a turntable and sauces the broad areas with a squeeze bottle, then extends it into the fine area with a wooden pick. "I don't want the dessert swimming in sauce. I want it only as part of the garnish," he says.

"The sauces can be done an hour ahead or so," he says. "They hold up that well." With Worhach doing the chocolate outlines and five of his people doing the saucing, it takes about an hour to do 110 desserts.

Modernists generally work clean, with sharp, distinct lines, though loose saucing is, of course, valid and beautiful. In this chapter we showcase the work of three chefs with three distinct approaches to saucing. "I have four people in my kitchen," says Lincoln Carson of The Highlands Inn in Carmel, California. "It's ludicrous for me to assume that every plate that goes out will be exactly like the way I'd put it out. It's important for them to get the style, the feel of the way I do things, but I tell them, play with it. I'm there during production, so I know the flavors will be there."

Here we have examples of the beauty of controlled sauce painting, as realized by Tom Worhach; looser saucing, as displayed by Lincoln Carson; and a third, hybrid style demonstrated by Wayne Brachman—precision saucing used to create an overall loose, freewheeling design. Any of these approaches can work, and additional sauce displays are seen throughout this volume.

Tom Worhach continues the triangular theme created by his Chocolate Almond Cappuccino Kaleidoscope—the slice is echoed by the triangles in the sauce painting. Tropical fruit purées are paired with the chocolate, almond, cappuccino flavor in the tart. In his Crispy Caramel Crab Apple Crysanthemum, the sauce portrait is in keeping with the floral/coral visual effect. Sauce flavors include mango, raspberry, papaya, and green apple. A floral theme accompanies his Kaffir Lime Tart. Mango, cactus pear, and kiwi coulis' match the lime tart flavor-wise and create an interesting color when blended.

Lincoln Carson chooses tequila orange sauce and cassis purée to accompany his Lemon Europa, a frozen lemon soufflé. The sauces echo the colors of the main ingredient and provide a nice planetary, galactic swirl to realize the theme that Carson had loosely in mind. (Europa is a moon of Jupiter where life might be found.) Caramel and chocolate sauces are arranged haphazardly around Carson's Hazelnut Mousse, in a brutal color combination. But, as was stated earlier in the book, the precision of the forms—Carson's mousse ring, the triangular cookies, the elegant coil of caramel—imply beauty and artistry in the loose saucing.

The flavors of these sauces blend beautifully with the main components. So how does that happen? "You can't intellectualize about flavor," says Wayne Brachman. He minimizes the importance of books, charts, and flavor wheels. "It is extremely primal," he says. "There's

THOMAS WORHACH

Executive Pastry Chef,
*Four Seasons, Palm Beach,
Florida.*

BORN: March 1952,
Danville, Pennsylvania.
TRAINING/EXPERIENCE: The
Culinary Institute of America;
Hotel Bel Air, Los Angeles;
Ritz-Carlton Hotel, Houston;
Ritz-Carlton Hotel,
Philadelphia; Mansion on Turtle
Creek, Dallas.

"Doing desserts for a book is one thing, to become a good pastry chef is another. Making desserts is just a small part of it, though it takes a lot of time. There's so much to learn—with the sugar, the chocolate, the baking, the banquet presentations. You have to be a good manager. You have to be respected, you have to know how to treat people, communicate with people. A good way to learn is to jump from job to job, see different environments, learn different styles and ways to do things. But it's also a good learning experience—and rewarding in itself—to build a relationship, to build a team."

WAYNE BRACHMAN

Executive Pastry Chef,
*Mesa Grill and Bolo,
both in New York.*

BORN: April 1951, Queens,
New York.
TRAINING/EXPERIENCE: various
restaurants in New York and
Massachusetts; Odeon, Arizona
206, both in New York.
Author: *Cakes & Cowpokes*
(William Morrow & Co., 1995).

"Pastry is one of the few jobs that almost works on a guild system, meaning old-fashioned standards of developing skills. It's mostly craft, but it has a smathering of artistry. The skill of what you're doing turns you on rather than the money. It had better because you're underpaid for what you do. You're in the production end, which never pays as much as sales. You work with waiters who get paid twice as much and don't need to care or take the work home. You will always be the back-up, the man or woman behind the executive chef. But you do it because you're driven, because you love it. Some jobs, you go into work, you sit in front of a computer and your life is on hold. But working in a kitchen is the same as living. It's aggravating at times, rewarding at times; you hang out, you work hard, but you keep communicating."

only one way to learn flavor—keep tasting things over and over. Don't just eat when you're hungry. Train your palate. Don't be too influenced by your personal preferences." In general, he says, if a dessert you're trying for the first time compels you, and other chefs, to have a second bite, it is a success.

Brachman also believes that chefs should taste a dessert as the customer would—sitting down, at leisure. "Chef tastings, where people stand around and try it, are very deceptive. A customer doesn't isolate flavors the way chefs might do it," he advises. "When you pierce something from the top it will be different than if you attack it from the side, as a customer would. Sit down and eat. Never pick at things."

Is it true, Chef Brachman, that Modernist desserts are heading in the direction of simplicity and pure flavors? "The only direction pastry should be heading is in your mouth," he says.

CHARLOTTE'S WEB

THOMAS WORHACH

Executive Pastry Chef, *Four Seasons, Palm Beach, Florida.*

Guanabana, or sour sop, is a tree fruit grown in Florida and the Caribbean; with few seeds, the white flesh is juicy, with an aroma and flavor on the tangy side of pineapple. It imparts a unique sour-sweetness to this surprising dessert. Ladyfingers form the base of the charlotte, which consists of a sour sop frappé—not a typical mousse. Chef Worhach uses sweetened condensed milk instead of sugar for the sweetness.

YIELD: 12 SERVINGS

Special Equipment:
Twelve 4 oz (118 ml) demi-sphere molds
Propane torch

CRISPY LADYFINGERS	.5 oz	14 g	*confectioners' sugar*
	7 oz	198 g	*granulated sugar, divided*
	1.95 oz	55 g	*egg yolks*
	.25 tsp	1.25 ml	*vanilla extract*
	6 oz	170 g	*all-purpose flour, sifted*
	3.2 oz	91 g	*egg whites*
	.25 tsp	1.7 g	*salt*

1. Preheat the oven to 375°F (191°C). Butter and flour a sheet pan. In a small bowl, combine the confectioners' sugar and 1 oz (28 g) of the granulated sugar. Set aside.

2. In a mixer fitted with a whisk attachment, beat the egg yolks, vanilla extract, and 3 oz (85 g) of the granulated sugar until pale and thick.

3. In a mixer with the whisk attachment, beat the egg whites and salt until stiff peaks form. Fold into the yolk mixture. Fold in the flour.

4. Scrape the batter into a pastry pag fitted with a 1/2" (1.3 cm) plain tip (Ateco #6) and pipe 3" (7.6 cm) long ladyfingers on the prepared pan, leaving 1 1/2" (3.8 cm) between them. Sift over half the reserved sugar mixture and let stand for 15 minutes. Sift over the remaining sugar mixture and bake for 8 to 10 minutes or until the edges of the ladyfingers are golden brown. Cool on a wire rack.

PASTRY NESTS	6 oz	170 g	*kataifi dough**
	3 oz	85 g	*unsalted butter, melted*

*****Note.*** Kataifi dough is available from Patisfrance, (800) PASTRY-1.

Dessert shown on page 188.

1. Preheat oven to 375°F (191°C). Butter a sheet pan.

2. Divide the kataifi dough into 12 bunches to resemble nests. Each nest should be about .5 oz (14 g). Place on the prepared pan and brush with some melted butter. Bake until golden, about 10 to 12 minutes. Let cool.

GUANABANA (SOURSOP) FRAPPÉ	*2.6 oz*	*74 g*	*egg yolks*

2.6 oz	*74 g*	*egg yolks*
14 oz	*397 g*	*sweetened condensed milk*
8 liq oz	*237 ml*	*fresh guanabana purée*
4.2 oz	*119 g*	*egg whites*

1. In a large bowl, combine the egg yolks with the condensed milk. Stir in the guanabana purée.

2. In a mixer with the whisk attachment, beat the egg whites to firm peaks. Fold into the guanabana mixture.

3. Fill the 4 oz (118 ml) demi-sphere molds halfway with the guanabana mixture. Top with a layer of crispy ladyfingers, trimmed to fit the mold. Gently press down on the ladyfinger layer. Fill the molds to the top with the guanabana mixture; level off with a small spatula. Freeze until firm.

5.2 oz	*147 g*	*egg yolks*
8 oz	*227 g*	*granulated sugar*
8 liq oz	*237 ml*	*fresh lemon juice*
.75 oz	*21 g*	*lemon zest, in large strips*
3 oz	*85 g*	*unsalted cold butter, cut into 1/2" (1.3 cm) chunks*
.35 oz	*10 g*	*gelatin sheets*

LEMON CURD GLAZE

1. In a large heatproof bowl, whisk the egg yolks with the sugar until blended. Add the lemon juice, lemon zest, and butter; mix to combine. Place the bowl over a bain-marie and cook, stirring constantly, until the mixture is thickened. Add the drained gelatin and stir until melted.

2. Remove the bowl from the heat and strain, discarding the lemon rind. If not using the glaze immediately, cool and chill in the refrigerator, pressing a piece of plastic wrap directly on the surface of the lemon curd.

ASSEMBLY

Scrivosa writing chocolate*
Mango purée
Cactus pear purée
Orange segments
Melted dark chocolate
Decorative fresh flowers
Fresh mint
Pomegranate seeds
Spun-sugar rings

*Note. Scrivosa writing chocolate is available from Swiss Chalet, (800) 359-4226.

1. Fill a small parchment cone with the Scrivosa dark chocolate. On a dessert plate, make an outline of a spider's web and fill in the outline with the mango and cactus-pear purées. Brown the orange segments with a propane torch and place the segments between the spokes of the web. Set the pastry nest on the plate.

2. Gently rewarm the lemon curd, if necessary, until it is of a pourable consistency.

3. Remove the guanabana frappé from the freezer and unmold onto a rack. Pour the warmed lemon curd over the frozen frappé, letting the excess drip off. Allow the frappé to set for one minute. Drizzle with the melted chocolate and place the frappé on a pastry nest.

4. Garnish with a fresh flower, a sprig of mint, and a few pomegranate seeds. Gently press a spun-sugar ring onto the glazed frappé.

FROZEN HAZELNUT MOUSSE

LINCOLN CARSON

Pastry Chef, *The Highlands Inn,*
Carmel, California.

The frozen mousse is studded with truffle pieces and is served with a chocolate cookie. "With the caramel and chocolate sauces, there are a lot of reinforcing flavors on the plate," says Lincoln Carson. "It reminds me of an ice cream sandwich—crunchy on the outside, smooth and cool on the inside. Sometimes I'll make things and I'll start getting flavors reminiscent of my childhood or my family, and I'll go for that—there's got to be some reason why I'm remembering things from twenty years ago. There is something pleasant associated with it."

YIELD: 6 SERVINGS

Special Equipment: Six 5 oz (140 g) oval ring molds

CHOCOLATE TRUFFLE

10 oz	*283 g*	*bittersweet chocolate, finely chopped*
2 oz	*57 g*	*unsalted butter, cut into cubes*
8 liq oz	*237 ml*	*heavy cream*

1. Place chocolate and butter in a bowl. In a saucepan, bring the cream to a boil; slowly pour the hot cream over the chocolate and butter, whisking until the chocolate is completely melted.

2. Line a 9" (23 cm) square baking pan with plastic wrap. Pour in the truffle mixture. Freeze the truffle mixture until set.

3. Remove the truffle mixture from the pan and chop into 1/4 to 1/2" (.63 to 1.27 cm) pieces. Return the pieces to the freezer.

HAZELNUT MOUSSE

24 liq oz	*710 ml*	*heavy cream*
12 oz	*340 g*	*hazelnut paste (100% pure)*
2 liq oz	*59 ml*	*water*
8 oz	*227 g*	*granulated sugar*
6.5 oz	*184 g*	*egg yolks*

1. Line a sheet pan with parchment paper and place the oval ring molds on it.

2. In a mixer fitted with a whisk attachment, whip the cream to soft peaks. Add the hazelnut paste and whip to stiff peaks. Refrigerate.

3. In a small saucepan, combine the water and the sugar. Meanwhile, in a mixer with a whisk attachment, begin beating the yolks at low speed.

4. Cook the sugar mixture over high heat until it reaches 240°F (115°C). Increase the mixer speed to medium and add the hot sugar syrup to the whipping yolks. Increase the speed to high and continue to whip the yolks until they are cool.

5. Gently fold the yolk mixture into the hazelnut cream. Scrape the mousse into a pastry bag fitted with a medium plain tip. Pipe the mousse into the molds, filling them halfway. Evenly distribute 5 to 6 truffle pieces over the surface of the mousse in each mold. Pipe more mousse over the truffles, filling the molds completely. Tap the sheet pan firmly against a work surface to remove any air bubbles. Freeze the mousse for several hours.

CHOCOLATE COOKIES			
8 oz	227 g	*unsalted butter, slightly softened*
8 oz	227 g	*granulated sugar*
3.5 oz	99 g	*whole eggs*
8 oz	227 g	*unsweetened cocoa powder*
2 liq oz	30 ml	*water*
10 oz	283 g	*all-purpose flour*

1. In a mixer fitted with a paddle attachment, beat the butter at medium speed until smooth. Gradually add the sugar and continue beating until the mixture is light.

2. Add the eggs and mix until incorporated. Reduce the speed to low and mix in the cocoa powder. Mix in the water, then the flour. Mix just until an even-colored mass of dough has formed. Wrap the dough in plastic wrap and chill for at least 1 hour.

3. Preheat oven to 350°F (175°C). On a work surface that has been dusted with confectioners' sugar, roll the dough out to 1/8" (.3 cm) thick. Using a pastry or pizza wheel, cut out 12 triangles, each measuring 7 x 7 x 2 1/2" (18 x 18 x 6 cm). Transfer the triangles to a parchment-lined baking sheet and sprinkle the cookies with granulated sugar. Bake for 8 minutes, until set. Allow the cookies to cool on the pan.

CARAMEL SAUCE			
14 oz	397 g	*granulated sugar*
8 liq oz	118 ml	*water, divided*

1. In a heavy saucepan, combine the sugar and 4 liq oz (118 ml) of water. Cook over medium heat, stirring constantly, until the mixture comes to a boil and the sugar dissolves. Continue to boil the syrup until it almost reaches a medium brown caramel.

2. Remove the pan from the heat and cover the pan (or use a sheet pan as a cover). Very carefully slide the cover off just enough to create a small opening and slowly pour in the remaining water. Return the pan to the heat and bring the sauce to a boil.

3. To check the consistency of the sauce, pour a small amount onto a cold plate. The sauce should neither be too thick nor too runny. Allow the sauce to cool.

CHOCOLATE SAUCE	3.75 oz	106 g	cocoa powder (Cocoa Barry, Extra Brute)
	1 pt	473 ml	water
	1 lb	454 g	granulated sugar
	1.5 oz	43 g	bittersweet chocolate (64%), finely chopped

1. Place the cocoa powder in a large bowl. In a saucepan, bring the water and sugar to a boil. Remove the pan from the heat and slowly whisk enough of the syrup into the cocoa powder to create a thick paste. Whisk in more of the syrup, and then return the entire mixture to the saucepan, whisking until smooth. Bring the sauce to a boil.

2. Place the chopped chocolate in a bowl. Pour the hot sauce over the chocolate. Allow the mixture to stand for a few minutes to melt the chocolate. Whisk the mixture until smooth. Pass the sauce through a fine sieve.

ASSEMBLY

Chocolate cigarettes
Caramel circle decorations

1. Garnish a dessert plate with a swirled pattern of the chocolate and caramel sauces. Place a chocolate triangle on the plate. Lay one of the frozen mousses on its side, on top of the triangle. Place another chocolate triangle on top of the mousse. Stab the mousse with a chocolate cigarette, pushing it through the mousse from top to bottom.

2. Garnish the dessert with a caramel circle decoration.

LEMON EUROPA

LINCOLN CARSON

Pastry Chef, *The Highlands Inn,*
Carmel, California.

Unremittingly lemon, this is a Meyer lemon semi-freddo with pieces of lemon inside and cassis sauce frozen on the outside, with cassis and orange tequila sauces in support. The lemon chips are lightly poached in sugar and dried. The lemon and cassis cookie reinforces the theme. "The name came to me the week that scientists discovered the possibility of life on Europa, a moon of Jupiter," says Lincoln Carson. "I thought that was extremely cool and this looked very planetary."

YIELD: 24 SERVINGS

Special Equipment: Twenty-four Flexipan 4 oz (118 ml) dome molds

BASE			
8 liq oz	237 ml	cassis purée
6	6	Meyer lemons
1 qt	946 ml	heavy cream
3.5 oz	99 g	whole eggs
3.25 oz	92 g	egg yolks
8 oz	227 g	granulated sugar

1. Pass the cassis purée through a fine chinois. Using a small brush, paint some of the cassis purée in a random design onto the interior of the dome molds, so that it beads. Freeze the molds to set the purée. Reserve the remaining purée to garnish the dessert plates.

2. Grate the zest of the lemons and reserve. With a sharp knife remove the lemon peels completely and cut out the individual lemon segments. Dice the lemon sections. Squeeze the juice from the remaining lemon membranes, and reserve.

3. In a mixer fitted with the whisk attachment, whip the cream to medium peaks. Add the lemon zest and whip to firm peaks. Reserve the whipped cream in the refrigerator.

4. In a mixer fitted with the whisk attachment, whip the eggs, egg yolks and sugar at high speed until tripled in volume. Fold the egg mixture into the whipped cream in two batches. Fold in the juice and the diced lemon segments. Fill the frozen dome molds with the lemon mousse. Freeze the molds for several hours, until hard.

LEMON SABLÉ	8 oz	227 g	unsalted butter
	8 oz	227 g	granulated sugar
	4	4	lemons, zested
	1	1	vanilla bean, split and scraped
	3.5 oz	99 g	whole eggs
	14 oz	397 g	cake flour

1. In a mixer fitted with the paddle attachment, cream the butter, sugar, lemon zest, and vanilla beans just until smooth. Beat in the eggs, scraping down the side of the bowl as necessary. At low speed, mix in the flour. Form the dough into a ball and chill the dough for at least 2 hours.

2. Preheat the oven to 350°F (175°C). Roll the dough out to 1/8" (.3 cm). Using a 4" (10 cm) round cutter, cut out 48 crescent shapes. Place half of the crescent shapes onto a silicone-lined sheet pan. Using the cutter, trim off the bottom third of the crescents. Places the remaining crescents on the pan and trim off the bottom two-thirds of these crescents. Bake until lightly browned, about 10 minutes.

LEMON CHIPS	6	6	Meyer lemons
	2 qts	1.9 lt	simple syrup
	3 oz	85 g	glucose

1. Slice the lemons very thinly. In a pan, combine the syrup and glucose. Add the lemon slices and gently poach them until they are translucent.

2. Preheat the oven to 220°F (105°C). Transfer the poached slices to a silicone baking-mat-lined baking sheet. Bake until crisp, 1 hour 45 minutes to 2 hours, turning the slices over occasionally.

TEQUILA-ORANGE SAUCE	1 tsp	2.5 g	cornstarch
	1 qt	946 ml	orange juice, divided
	2 oz	57 g	granulated sugar
	2 liq oz	59 ml	Sauza Commemerativo tequila

1. In a small bowl, dissolve the cornstarch in 2 Tbs (30 ml) of the orange juice; set aside.

2. Place the orange juice in a saucepan and bring to a boil over medium-high heat; boil the juice until it is reduced by half. Stir in the sugar.

3. Add the dissolved cornstarch mixture to the juice and bring it to a boil. Allow to boil for 1 minute. Remove the sauce from the heat and stir in the tequila. Chill.

ASSEMBLY

1. Unmold a frozen lemon soufflé onto a dessert plate. Pool some of the tequila-orange sauce around the dessert. Squeeze a random design of cassis purée onto the orange sauce.

2. Arrange a large lemon sablé and a smaller one on top of the dome, in a spiral pattern. Arrange 3 lemon chips on top of the dome. Repeat with the remaining soufflés and serve immediately.

KAFFIR LIME TART

THOMAS WORHACH

Executive Pastry Chef, *Four Seasons, Palm Beach, Florida.*

Although more aromatic than a Key lime, a Kaffir lime's flavor is delicate. Here, it is featured as a filling in a graham cracker crust, accompanied by coconut rum ice cream, passion fruit sorbet, mango and papaya slices, pineapple crisps, and cinnamon-coated, deep-fried angel hair pasta.

YIELD: 12 SERVINGS

Special Equipment:
Twelve 2" (5 cm) diameter × 1 1/8" (2.9 cm) high stainless steel ring molds
Silicone baking mat

COCONUT-RUM ICE CREAM

28 oz	794 g	Coco Lopez cream of coconut
20 liq oz	591 ml	milk
1 liq oz	30 ml	rum

1. Combine all the ingredients in a large bowl. Whisk until blended. Chill.

2. Process in an ice cream machine according to the manufacturer's instructions.

PASSION FRUIT SORBET

16 liq oz	473 ml	water
12 oz	340 g	granulated sugar
3 oz	85 g	glucose
32 oz	907 g	frozen passion fruit purée, thawed
2 liq oz	59 ml	lemon juice

1. In a large saucepan, bring the water, sugar, and glucose to boil. Remove from the heat and stir in the passion-fruit purée and lemon juice. Cool and chill.

2. Process in an ice cream machine according to the manufacturer's instructions.

PINEAPPLE CRISPS

7 oz	198 g	trimmed, peeled, whole pineapple
4 liq oz	118 ml	simple syrup

1. Preheat the oven to 150°F (66°C). Line a baking pan with a silicone mat.

2. Cut the pineapple into 12 very thin slices, about 1/16 to 1/8" (.16 to .32 cm) thick. If desired, remove the cores with a small cutter.

3. Brush both sides of the pineapple slices with simple syrup. Place the slices on the prepared pan and bake for 3 to 4 hours or until dry and crisp.

4. Transfer to a rack and cool completely.

GRAHAM CRACKER CRUST

4 oz	113 g	graham cracker crumbs
2.25 oz	64 g	unsalted, roasted cashew nuts, finely ground
2.75 oz	78 g	granulated sugar
3 oz	85 g	unsalted butter, melted

1. Preheat the oven to 350°F (177°C). Line a baking pan with a silicone mat. Place the ring molds on a lined pan.

2. In a medium bowl, combine the graham cracker crumbs, ground nuts, and sugar. Stir in the melted butter and mix until well-blended.

3. Place about 2 to 3 tsp of crumb mixture into each ring mold and press down firmly to form a crust about 1/4" (.6 cm) thick. Bake for 6 to 8 minutes until golden and set. Let cool completely. Keep on the prepared pan.

KAFFIR LIME FILLING

2.6 oz	74 g	egg yolks
16 liq oz	473 ml	sweetened condensed milk
4 liq oz	118 ml	fresh Kaffir lime juice (regular lime juice can be substituted)

1. Preheat the oven to 350°F (177°C).

2. In a bowl, mix the yolks and condensed milk until just combined. Add the lime juice and blend until smooth.

3. Fill the prepared molds with the lime mixture. Bake until set, about 20 minutes. Cool slightly at room temperature; unmold and chill.

MANGO AND PAPAYA SLICES

3	ripe mangoes, about 10 oz (283 g) each
2	ripe papayas, about 12 oz (340 g) each

1. Peel the mangoes and thinly slice them on a mandoline.

2. Peel the papayas and thinly slice them on a mandoline.*

Note. If this is being prepped ahead of time, arrange the slices, in one layer, on a tray lined with plastic wrap. Press the plastic wrap on top of the slices. Repeat the layering, separating each layer with plastic wrap. Chill.

ASSEMBLY

Mango coulis
Kiwi coulis
Cactus pear coulis
Deep-fried angel hair pasta drizzled with chocolate

1. Remove the lime tart from the refrigerator and place on a dessert plate painted with fruit coulis. Place one slice of pineapple crisp on top of the tart.

2. With a #30 scoop, place one scoop of coconut-rum ice cream on top of the tart. Top with a #30 scoop of passion fruit sorbet. Arrange 3 slices of mango over sorbet. Top with one slice of papaya.

3. Garnish with three sticks of angel hair pasta inserted into the top of the dessert.

CRISPY CARAMELIZED CRAB APPLE CHRYSANTHEMUM WITH BONNY DOON SORBET

THOMAS WORHACH

Executive Pastry Chef, *Four Seasons, Palm Beach, Florida.*

"It sounds good," says Tom Worhach, *"and that's part of the dessert experience—how it's worded on the menu. It needs to sound as interesting as it looks. Especially the desserts today, the three-dimensional desserts. If there's nothing standing up on the plate, it's almost a disappointment to the customer."* The spectacular forms also hide the flavor carriers—under the apple tuile is the iced wine sorbet, and inside the feuille de brick chrysanthemum are caramelized crab apples in pastry cream.

YIELD: 8 SERVINGS

Special Equipment: Two half sheet silicone baking mats

BONNY DOON ICE WINE SORBET	25.4 liq oz	750 ml	Bonny Doon Muscat Vin de Glaciere
	24 oz	680 g	stemmed champagne grapes
	8 liq oz	237 ml	simple syrup

1. In a large nonreactive saucepan, combine the wine and grapes, and boil for 5 minutes. Remove from the heat and allow to steep for 30 minutes.

2. Place the wine-grape mixture in a blender or food processor and blend until smooth. Strain through a chinois to extract the grape skin and seeds. Add the simple syrup and chill.

3. Process in an ice cream machine according to the manufacturer's instructions.

CARAMELIZED CRAB APPLE FILLING	2 oz	57 g	golden raisins
	2 liq oz	59 ml	Grand Marnier liqueur
	32	32	crab apples, peeled, quartered, and cored
	2 liq oz	59 ml	lemon juice
	1 Tbs	12 g	ground cinnamon
	1 tsp	5 ml	vanilla extract
	.5 tsp	2 g	ground nutmeg
	4 oz	113 g	light brown sugar
	4 oz	113 g	unsalted butter
	4 liq oz	118 ml	apple brandy, such as Calvados
	2 oz	57 g	chopped walnuts

1. In a small saucepan, cook the raisins and the Grand Marnier until the raisins are plump.

2. In a large bowl, toss the crab apples with the lemon juice, cinnamon, vanilla, nutmeg, and brown sugar.

3. Melt the butter in a large sauté pan and sauté the apples until the sugar melts and the apples begin to soften. Off the heat, add the apple brandy. Return to the heat and continue to sauté until the apples are lightly caramelized, cooked through, but still firm.

4. Remove from the heat. Fold in the cooked raisins and walnuts. Set aside to cool.

VANILLA BEAN PASTRY CREAM			
4 oz	113 g	egg yolks
5.5 oz	156 g	granulated sugar, divided
1 oz	28 g	all-purpose flour
16 liq oz	473 ml	whole milk
1	1	vanilla bean, split and scraped

1. In a bowl, whisk together the egg yolks and 2.75 oz (78 g) of the sugar until smooth. Whisk in the flour to make a smooth paste.

2. In a saucepan, over medium heat, bring the milk, vanilla bean, and 2.75 oz (78 g) of the sugar to a boil. Remove from the heat and allow to steep for 30 minutes. Discard the vanilla bean.

3. Temper the yolks with half of the reheated hot milk mixture. Add the tempered yolks to the saucepan.

4. Continue cooking over medium heat, whisking continuously, until the mixture comes to boil. Cook for 1 minute. Cool over ice bath. Chill.

APPLE TUILES	3	3	medium Granny Smith apples

1. Preheat the oven to 175°F (80°C). Line 2 half-sheet pans with silicone mats.

2. Peel and thinly shave the apples. Press the shaved apple onto the silicone mats. Bake until dry and crispy, about 3 hours. Cool.

3. Break into large pieces and store in an airtight container.

POACHED SPICED CRAB APPLES			
1	1	vanilla bean, split and scraped
1	1	whole nutmeg, cracked
2	2	3 " (7.6 cm) long sticks of cinnamon, broken
24 liq oz	710 ml	simple syrup
4 liq oz	118 ml	brandy
8	8	crab apples

1. In a large saucepan, bring all the ingredients except the apples to a boil. Reduce the heat and simmer for 15 minutes. Remove from the heat and strain.

2. Return the syrup to the saucepan. Bring to a boil and add the apples. Cook the apples in the simmering syrup until tender, about 5 to 7 minutes.

3. Cool the apples in the syrup.

ASSEMBLY
24 sheets feuille de brick
Confectioners' sugar
Mango coulis
Raspberry coulis
Papaya coulis
Green apple coulis

1. Preheat the oven to 400°F (205°C). Line two half-sheet pans with parchment paper.

2. Lightly butter 3 sheets of feuille de brick. Stack the buttered sheets and place 2 Tbs pastry cream in the center of the stack. Top with 2 Tbs of the caramelized crab apple filling. Bring the edges of the sheets together to enclose the filling. Tie with some kitchen twine just above enclosed filling. Fold out the edges of feuille de brick to resemble a chrysanthemum. Bake for 10 to 12 minutes or until the chrysanthemums turn golden brown. Dust with confectioners' sugar.

3. On a dessert plate, place one warm apple chrysanthemum, one poached crab apple, and a scoop of Bonny Doon sorbet. Place pieces of apple tuile around the sorbet.

4. Garnish the plate with the mango, raspberry, papaya, and green apple coulis.

CHOCOLATE ALMOND KALEIDOSCOPE

THOMAS WORHACH

Executive Pastry Chef, *Four Seasons,
Palm Beach, Florida.*

"This basically is a chocolate almond mousse on flourless chocolate cake," says Thomas Worhach. Affixed to the side are chocolate-dipped almonds, and finishing the dessert are cappuccino ice cream wrapped in gold leaf and white chocolate diamonds. As for the name? "My daughter received a kaleidoscope for Christmas," says Worhach. "It reminded me a lot of my sauce paintings. Then, looking through it, I got ideas."

YIELD: 16 SERVINGS

Special Equipment:
Sixteen 2 3/4" (7 cm) triangular molds (1" / 2.5 cm high)
Small gold-flecked transfer sheets
Diamond-shaped template with 2 1/2" (6.3 cm) sides

CHOCOLATE-ALMOND MOUSSE

9 oz	225 g	semisweet chocolate, finely chopped
3 oz	85 g	unsalted butter
3 oz	85 g	granulated sugar
1 liq oz	30 ml	water
7.5 oz	213 g	whole eggs
8 liq oz	237 ml	heavy cream, whipped to soft peaks
3 oz	85 g	toasted blanched almonds, finely diced

1. Melt the chocolate and butter in a double boiler.

2. In a small saucepan, combine the sugar with the water. Cook to 240°F (116°C).

3. Meanwhile, in a mixer with the whisk attachment, whip the eggs until foamy. Slowly pour the syrup over the eggs and whip until cool.

4. Add the chocolate-butter mixture to the yolks and mix until smooth. Fold in the whipped cream and diced nuts.

5. Fill the molds with mousse and freeze for 2 to 3 hours, or until set.

CAPPUCCINO ICE CREAM

2.25 oz	64 g	espresso roast coffee beans
24 liq oz	710 ml	heavy cream
8 liq oz	237 ml	milk
4.6 oz	130 g	egg yolks
4 oz	113 g	granulated sugar
1 tsp	4 g	finely ground espresso beans
1.5 liq oz	44 ml	chocolate flavored liqueur

1. Crack the coffee beans by lightly rolling over them with a rolling pin.

2. In a saucepan, scald the cream, milk, and cracked coffee beans. Remove this from the heat, cover, and allow to infuse for 1 hour. Strain through a chinois and discard the coffee beans.

3. Place the sugar and eggs in a bowl and whisk to blend. Temper the yolks with the reheated milk mixture. Return to the saucepan and cook until thickened. Strain the custard and cool in ice bath. Chill.

4. Process in an ice cream machine according to the manufacturer's instructions, adding the liqueur during the last 5 minutes of processing.

SPRAYED WHITE CHOCOLATE DIAMONDS			
3 oz	85 g	*bittersweet chocolate, tempered*
1 lb	454 g	*white chocolate, tempered*

1. Place the bittersweet chocolate in a small parchment cone and drizzle it randomly onto a small gold-flecked transfer sheet. Allow the chocolate to set.

2. Spread some of the tempered white chocolate over the dark chocolate drizzle in an even layer. Allow the chocolate to set slightly. Using the diamond template as a guide, cut out at least 24 diamond shapes with an X-acto knife. With both ends of a medium plain pastry tip, cut out a few circles from each diamond. Cut 8 of the diamonds in half vertically.

3. Using some of the tempered white chocolate, glue one diamond half onto each of the 16 whole diamonds (see photo on facing page). Allow the kaleidoscope garnishes to set completely.

ASSEMBLY

Melted dark chocolate
Assorted fruit purées
Sliced toasted almonds (15 to 18 per serving)
Gold leaf squares
Fresh raspberries
Mint leaf

1. Place some melted chocolate in a small parchment cone. Make a freehand outline of a star design on the dessert plates, leaving the center of the plate empty. Fill in the outlines with assorted fruit purées. Dip the sliced toasted almonds in melted chocolate so that 1/3 of each almond is covered with chocolate.

2. Unmold a mousse onto the center of a dessert plate and arrange some of the chocolate dipped almonds around the base of the dessert. Top with a small scoop of cappuccino ice cream. Gently drop a square of gold leaf over the ice cream (it should wrap around the scoop on its own).

3. Place a kaleidoscope garnish on top of the gold-wrapped ice cream scoop, pushing it gently into the ice cream so that it is secure. Garnish with a few raspberries and a mint leaf.

BUTTER PECAN CUSTARD CAKE

WAYNE BRACHMAN

Executive Pastry Chef, *Mesa Grill and Bolo, both in New York.*

Layers of pecan, angel food cake, and butter pecan custard are wrapped in a tuile flavored with mint and raspberry; the dessert is topped with fried rice vermicelli. Raspberry, mint, mango, and black sesame sauces accent the flavors of the dessert. "I use Chinese black sesame," says Wayne Brachman. "It has a toasty flavor rather than the sharp flavor of Goma." When he employs sauces, Brachman always uses a variety. "It's like some schools of Indian cooking, where every bite is supposed to taste different."

YIELD: 8 SERVINGS

Special Equipment: Eight ring molds, 3" (7.5 cm) diameter x 1 3/4" (3.3 cm) high

ANGEL FOOD CAKE			
8.5 oz	*240 g*	*egg whites*
1 tsp	*2 g*	*cream of tartar*
1 tsp	*3 g*	*lemon juice*
7 oz	*198 g*	*granulated sugar, divided*
.25 tsp	*1 g*	*salt*
2.25 oz	*64 g*	*cake flour*
1 tsp	*4 g*	*vanilla extract*
1 oz	*28 g*	*toasted pecans, coarsely chopped*

1. Preheat the oven to 325°F (165°C). In a mixer combine the egg whites, cream of tartar, and lemon juice and whip to soft peaks. Add 3.5 oz (99 g) of the sugar in a slow steady stream and continue whipping to stiff peaks.

2. Sift together the salt, flour, and remaining 3.5 oz (99 g) of sugar. Fold the dry ingredients into the egg whites, followed by the vanilla and pecans. Divide the batter evenly into eight ring molds on a parchment-lined sheet pan. Bake for 25–30 minutes or until the cake springs back when gently pressed with a finger. Cool and unmold.

CUSTARD			
24 liq oz	*710 ml*	*heavy cream*
6.3 oz	*179 g*	*brown sugar*
1.75 oz	*50 g*	*granulated sugar*
1 liq oz	*30 ml*	*Myers's rum*
1 tsp	*4 g*	*vanilla extract*
5.2 oz	*147 g*	*egg yolks*

1. Preheat oven to 325°F (165°C). In a saucepan bring the cream to a boil.

2. Whisk together the remaining ingredients and temper in the hot cream. Strain the mixture into a 9" baking pan and bake in a water bath for one hour or until the edges are set but the center is still somewhat jiggly. Let cool to room temperature, then refrigerate until chilled.

MINT SAUCE			
	7 oz	198 g	granulated sugar
	4 liq oz	118 ml	water
	1 oz	28 g	fresh mint leaves, blanched and shocked

1. In a saucepan combine the sugar and water. Bring to a boil for two minutes, then remove the pan from heat and let cool.

2. Place the sugar syrup and mint in a blender and process until smooth. Refrigerate until ready to use.

TUILES			
	4 oz	113 g	unsalted butter, softened
	5 oz	142 g	granulated sugar
	4.25 oz	120 g	egg whites
	5 oz	142 g	all-purpose flour
	2 Tbs	43 g	mint sauce
	2 Tbs	30 g	raspberry purée

1. In a mixer with the paddle attachment cream the butter and sugar until light. Slowly mix in the egg whites. Add the flour and mix just until combined. Evenly divide the mixture into two bowls. Mix the mint sauce into one bowl and the raspberry purée into the other. Refrigerate until the batter is firm enough to pipe.

2. Preheat oven to 375°F (190°C) and place a sheet pan in the oven to warm. Place the green batter in a pastry bag with a 1/4" (.6 cm) plain tip and the red batter in a pastry bag with a 1/2" (1.2 cm) plain tip. On a silicone baking mat, using light pressure, pipe a line of green batter 10" (25 cm) long and spread it thinly with an offset spatula so that it is about 3/4" wide. Lightly pipe a 10" (25 cm) long line of red batter alongside the green and spread it to 1 1/2" (3.7 cm) wide. Repeat with the green batter on the other side of the red. The three strips should be touching.

3. Transfer the baking mat onto the warm baking sheet and bake for 5 minutes or just until set.

4. Remove the pan from the oven and immediately shape the tuiles around a 3 1/2" (8.7 cm) diameter cylinder. Let cool until set.

BLACK SESAME SAUCE			
	2 liq oz	59 ml	water
	3.5 oz	99 g	granulated sugar
	1.75 oz	50 g	ground black sesame seeds (available in Asian grocery stores)
	1 liq oz	30 ml	hot water

1. Combine the water and sugar in a saucepan and boil for two minutes. Remove the pan from heat and let cool.

2. Dissolve the ground sesame in the hot water. Add the syrup and let cool.

| CELLOPHANE NOODLES | 6 oz | 170 g | *cellophane noodles* |
| | 3 oz | 85 g | *confectioners' sugar* |

1. Heat a deep fryer to 350°F (175°C). Fry the noodles very quickly until they just puff. Place them on paper towels to drain and cool.

2. Toss the noodles with confectioners' sugar.

ASSEMBLY	*Confectioners' sugar*
	Raspberry sauce
	Mango sauce
	Toasted pecans, coarsely chopped

1. Dust a dessert plate with confectioners' sugar. Drizzle the plate with black sesame, raspberry, and mango sauces.

2. Place an angel food cake in the center of the plate with a tuile around it. Top the cake with a scoop of custard and spread it so that it is flush with the top of the tuile. Sprinkle the custard with toasted pecans. Top the custard with cellophane noodles and drizzle the noodles with mint sauce.

CHAPTER **S**IX

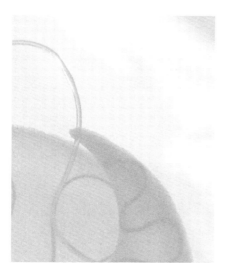

THE BUSINESS
OF MODERNISM

Purchasing, costing, budgeting, menu writing: "You hear from students, 'I don't want to know about it. I don't give a damn. I just want to cook or bake,'" says Markus Farbinger of The Culinary Institute of America. "My reply is, 'That's fine if you want to be a line cook all your life.'"

The fact is, the Modernist pastry chef must nurture experience in the management side of the business, if he or she ever dreams of running a kitchen. Readers who judge the desserts in this book as impractical will see that they can be quite profitable, if the kitchen that creates them is run efficiently.

In this chapter, three chefs from The Culinary Institute of America, Bo Friberg, Daniel Budd, and Markus Farbinger, have collaborated to create a dessert menu—it is menu-balanced to appeal to the largest number of potential customers; it is kitchen-balanced, to be feasible production-wise; and it is budget-balanced. The three CIA chefs then go on to explain the thinking behind this menu.

The skill we will focus on most closely here is costing. Other chefs will also put their two cents in, because all of the chefs in this book know the importance of management skills. Those of our chef-readers who are solidly in the weeds from the time they set foot in the kitchen until the time they schlep home will first want to know:

WHY SHOULD I LEARN COSTING PROCEDURES?

"Chefs must sometimes justify purchasing molds or ice cream machines or hiring new employees," says Markus Farbinger. "Without costing, you have no tool to show that you are profitable." The kind of thinking that costing inspires helps a young man or woman to think in terms of management. "With new equipment, you have to know what it will do for you; how much labor it will save; and how it can increase quantity, quality, and variety. How will it pay for itself? It's very important that you know these things, and that you can communicate them."

Even the most brilliant pastry kitchen can feel profitable, and not be. Stanton Ho of the Las Vegas Hilton checks and rechecks his costs—monthly, bi-monthly, weekly, sometimes daily. "It's not forced on me to do this," he says. "It's just something all chefs should do, rather than get carried away and think that they are free to do anything, then, at the end of the year, find that instead of making money, they are losing money."

Costing is just one skill among many that any ambitious chef should have. Markus Farbinger sings the praises of a bachelor's degree in pastry arts—or at the very least, for a chef to become interested in all phases of an operation. "Such a person will start out making the same base salary as the next guy, who had no training at all, but then you are able to understand the system beyond the stove, beyond the oven—sanitary, refrigeration, science of baking, interpersonal skills, design, understanding equipment. You should be able to take the hood off a malfunctioning Hobart and get some idea of how bad the situation is."

HOW DO I COST MY DESSERTS?

There are as many systems as there are styles of hotel and restaurant. Many large hotels have a system in place, with sheets providing a line-by-line template for how the institution wants its costs computed and displayed. Other restaurants may have no system at all, and management-ownership may feel it doesn't need one. "In smaller restaurants costing, figuring the labor costs down to the second, is not as important," admits Markus Farbinger. "The menu changes more often. You tend to go with the flow. In larger places, the menu doesn't change that often, and the chef tends to be there more."

At the Las Vegas Hilton, Stanton Ho and his kitchen staff must provide desserts and breads for more than eight restaurants, room service for a 3,000-room hotel, and banquet facilities that can seat 5,000 people at a clip. Not to scare the novice, but let's take a peek at Ho's costing procedure:

Like most chefs' systems, the costs will eventually be expressed as the cost per plate per dessert. The factors that go into this equation—in Stanton Ho's case, mind you—include ingredients (of course), the labor cost involved in mis en place, production (what an average person can do in a couple of seconds), and set up for service (down to the last berries on the plate, and the plates on the waiter trays); the cost of the plate itself (yes, the plate); timing and labor for every other procedure involved in getting the dessert from the kitchen to the customer and back again—from the waiters, busboys, and refrigeration staff who transport, maintain and serve the desserts to the stewards who clean the plates. Timing? "Yes, the timing," affirms Chef Ho. "Everything has to be timed here. By the time the dinner starts in a convention, everything must be plated. One hour and fifteen minutes before salad is served, you want all desserts finished and in refrigeration. The more you deviate from that formula, the more it costs." Transportation? Yes. At the Las Vegas Hilton, Stanton Ho's desserts might travel from a quarter to a half-mile to holding refrigeration, until they are served to the customers. "It's logistics," says Ho. "It's like plotting out a war game. That's what draws me to Las Vegas, the challenges necessitated by the volume. I learned by observing other chefs. Some of the best chefs in the world find endless time to fuss over dishes or buy the most expensive ingredients in the world. But this can make the difference between success and failure."

At the Waldorf-Astoria Hotel in New York, another high-volume, high-pressure operation, "Costing procedures are amazingly tight," says Michael Hu, the executive pastry chef. "We have to run 8 to 9 percent labor cost and an overall food cost of 21 to 22 percent. In order to do that, you have to run banquet food cost to 17 to 18 percent. It's easy to get bogged down by production alone. You have to manage yourself."

A more informal approach is taken by Donald Wressell, pastry chef at the Four Seasons Beverly Hills: "I don't cost every chocolate dessert because I know that every plated chocolate dessert is going to have upwards of three ounces of chocolate, maybe four, so I know the high end cost is going to be the chocolate," he says. "There's only so much cream, butter, eggs, and sugar we can cram on the same plate, so we came up with a generic cost for what a chocolate dessert would go for." The same situation exists for fruit desserts, ice creams, and so on. "We know where we stand with the ingredients we're working with," says Wressell. "We know how much a portion is going to cost.

"In the pastry kitchen," Wressell continues, "there aren't any ingredients in particular that are that outlandish. So I can go for a costly ingredient now and then. In the scheme of things, everything will balance out."

"The raw ingredient for a dessert is much less expensive than the raw ingredient for the hot kitchen," Norman Love of the Ritz-Carlton Hotel Company says. "Chocolate is an inexpensive ingredient." For this reason, if chefs want to spend a little more for an exotic ingredient for a special or a new seasonal item, they do not cut costs elsewhere. Rather than cut back on the quality of ingredients, some chefs will simplify the garnish.

DAN BUDD

Pastry Instructor,
*The Culinary Institute of America,
Hyde Park, New York.*

BORN: September 1967,
West Rutland, Vermont.
TRAINING/EXPERIENCE: The
Culinary Institute of America;
River Café and Park Avenue
Cafe, New York.

"I think that we should occasionally reflect upon our general appreciation for food and desserts, because I find that over time there are many things that make you happy, that you really like, and then there comes a point where you forget them. If you reflect back, not just on what you make but what you eat, it's always there for you to use for your benefit. {Executive chef} David Burke's food, and the experience of working with him, built an energy level in me, and built on my palate. It's an ongoing education, the building of knowledge for a chef."

MARKUS FARBINGER

Team Leader for Curriculum
and Instruction,
*Baking and Pastry Arts, The
Culinary Institute of America,
Hyde Park, New York.*

BORN: August 1964,
Taxenbach, Austria.
TRAINING/EXPERIENCE:
apprenticeship, Austria; Sacher
Hotel, Vienna; Amway Grand
Plaza Hotel, Michigan; Le
Cirque, New York City.

*"One of the major reasons that I'm
at the Institute is that it's a place
where you can influence the industry. I don't feel that I work for the
Institute, but for the industry, to
ensure that our profession will continue. At the school, we have the
responsibility to try new things, to
explore. The industry itself is busy
making money. They don't always
have time to try out new ingredients
and new equipment. We as a school
have a great responsibility to support, not just students, but research
and development."*

Most chefs, however, run costing procedures somewhere in between the Wressel informal-
ity and the Stan Ho exactitude. Most chefs break down the cost of making a single serving—ingredients plus labor. The variable is volume. Most chefs will be thinking in terms
of 20 or 30 portions nightly, but chefs in hotels will also need to consider whether the
dessert will be made in volume—for, say, a banquet for 500 people. In general, the higher the volume the lower the labor cost.

The price of raw ingredients will fluctuate also, but chefs deal with that in different ways.
Some chefs recost their desserts every year, to take into account changing costs of ingredients and labor. Thomas Worhach updates his costs weekly, but most chefs are more relaxed
on this issue; profits on desserts are so high, they say, that price fluctuations can be
absorbed.

The exceptions and caveats to this formula are endless. Bread, for example. That's a "hidden twist in your side," says Dan Budd, because it's a give-away. On labor: "I don't factor in labor," says Thomas Worhach. "Management doesn't care if it takes me three minutes or three hours. It's my time. I just report the actual cost of products." Norman Love
has a similar perspective in terms of labor: "You establish a standard, you enforce the
standard," he says. "You do not deviate from the standard. The standard becomes the
norm. If you demand perfection and never deviate from your expectations, what seems
like a difficult accomplishment becomes routine. Never sacrifice presentation because of
labor issues. Every plate must be perfect in every way, and if that requires a lot of work,
well . . ."

HOW DO I PRICE MY DESSERTS?

The formula most often cited to price the dessert is a simple one: set the price you charge
a customer at approximately three times your cost (not overhead; just ingredients and
labor). But there are other factors to consider.

Some chefs think of the 300 percent number as a starting point only; a minimum. They
then factor in "perceived value." This takes into consideration the environment that a
dessert is being served in (fine dining versus diner); the price of the entrées; the "wow"
factor of the presentation; and even the expectations of the customer—some banquet
clients will say the magic words, price is no object; their anticipation of the dessert will
heighten its value. There are desserts that are inherently easy to price up. As Dan Budd
says, when you sell a soufflé you're mostly selling air, but the perceived value of a soufflé
is very high.

"Pittsburgh's cost of living is relatively low," says Thaddeus Dubois of the Duquesne Club
there. "They were getting 4 dollars for desserts such as you see here [in this book]. Now
it's up to 6,7,8 bucks. Entrées were 18 to 26. I believe that desserts should be a third of
the entrées. I base it on that. Sales have actually gone up since the prices have gone up."

Some chefs believe that all the desserts on a menu should be priced the same; others disagree. Markus Farbinger has observed that management and chefs in small restaurants tend
to price desserts in accordance with a dessert already on the menu, pricing chocolate
desserts in one category, fruit desserts in another, and so on. "This is not wise for an item
that may be on the menu for a long time," he says.

"If there is more work involved, a higher price is justified," says Bo Friberg, "but you don't
inflate a price just because it is a best seller. That's the wrong way to go about it."

HOW DO I BALANCE MY MENU?

First, some anthropology: "When it comes time to look at the dessert menu, people are no longer hungry. You have a human animal that is fed and satiated," says Donald Wressell. "They don't need any more food. So you're appealing to an emotional reflex or whimsy or maybe something looks so good they have to have it. That's the real trick for the pastry chef. You have to entice someone into buying your product. I play into the emotional side—things that look really warm and inviting, but with very nice execution and attention to detail."

"On any menu you should have at least one 'wow' item," says Bo Friberg. "Something people will talk about. To compete today you must have that. You have to have one or two items with chocolate—a lighter one and a decadent, heavy one. You must have something with fruit, fresh, in season. You need to have something cold, an ice cream or sorbet. You need to have something on the lighter side. It's also nice to have a special of the day. This is also a good way to get rid of some waste. We're not talking about serving garbage. For example, if I have a banquet and maybe 75 of the people don't show up, I'm stuck with it. If it will hold up overnight—and only if—I might freshen it up and put it on special the next day.

"It never hurts to offer free items," adds Chef Friberg. "A little mignardise with the coffee. If the waiter can say, 'Something from the chef,' it makes the customer feel special, and it doesn't cost much."

"You don't need a huge menu," says Dan Budd. "If you can concentrate on a variety of things, six or seven items can be enough, and it gives you time to do them perfectly."

In the course of introducing new desserts on the menu, some will be money-losers, but that can have an upside too, says Dan Budd. "Money losers can be attention-getters," he points out. "The money loser might get the media. You might realize, this is costing me, but it's getting customers to come in and order desserts. So you have a sales factor, and media attention. Still, if they don't sell, you take them off the menu." Money losers will normally be balanced by winners. "Sorbets, for example. If you use fruits that are in season, you'll be making sorbet at two or three cents a scoop, the highest being 18 cents a scoop. You can sell three of those scoops for seven bucks. There are simple things you can do with less labor, like a soufflé. If you learn how to produce them efficiently, you can get good money for them.

"Chocolate is something you have to look out for," adds Budd. "It is the number one seller, but I've seen menus with too much chocolate. My students write menus, and they often do that."

When balancing a menu, according to Budd, "You have to relate to your customers, offer them their memories, things they're comfortable with." "You want to give them something they recognize," agrees Martin Howard of Rainbow! in New York. "I find it sells better if you give it a name they can recognize—chocolate chip, pie, a pudding, even if it's only a small portion of the dessert."

"I also believe that a customer needs to be able to relate to something on the menu," says Norman Love. "When you walk into a Ritz-Carlton in Atlanta, for example, you see a peach cobbler, something that people from that area are very familiar with. You want items that people from that area can relate to, and that visitors come to expect. You should have ingredients that are indigenous to the area. But it can be creative, totally dif-

BO FRIBERG

Chef Instructor, *The Culinary Institute of America at Greystone, St. Helena, California.*

TRAINING/EXPERIENCE: apprenticeship, Sweden; pastry school, Sweden (earned European Master Chef certificate); Sweden House Bakery, Tiburan, California; various cruise ships. Author: *The Professional Pastry Chef* (Van Nostrand Reinhold, 1996).

"For me, respect, a love of what you're doing, determination to learn, experience—these are what make a succesful pastry chef. When you enjoy what you're doing, you do a better job, rather than doing it as just a job. You want respect from your peers, or your students if you are a teacher. Part of this is showing them also that, yes, I make mistakes. That makes them feel better, gives them confidence. There is much to be said for experience, and unfortunately experience comes with age. It's taken me forty years of cooking pastries to write that book. Oh, and one more thing helps to make a succesful chef—pure luck. Sometimes it's just being in the right place at the right time."

ferent from a traditional concept, as long as the traditional concept is implied in the printed menu."

The recipes in this chapter reflect what the CIA chefs consider to be a good, balanced menu. Balanced, in the sense of variety to offer every customer as well as varying degrees of difficulty for the kitchen, in terms of production.

The menu includes three desserts that feature fruit, one of which (Apple Pie Soufflé) is apple, which is always a best-selling item, and another which is emphatically calorie light (Thin Ice Fruit Soup), an option that every menu should offer. Two items, excluding the mignardise, contain chocolate, a must, it goes without saying. These items, Mount Peppermint and Chocolate Marquise, are in the "decadence" category, where many customers like to visit. Four of the menu items contain a prominent vertical component, which many chefs believe has customer appeal and will help sell dessert items. Two of the items are relatively easy (and inexpensive) to produce in an average pastry kitchen—Thin Ice Fruit Soup and Mount Peppermint—while the Chocolate Marquise and Blueberry Financier, with all their garnishes, would be more labor intensive and, therefore, more expensive. Apple Pie Soufflé is inexpensive to produce but, like all soufflés, is tricky to make and requires someone in the kitchen with experience. Also included is an ultramodern mignardise presentation, which is generally offered gratis to preferred customers. The good will such a presentation generates cannot be calculated, nor can it be measured in any bottom line way, but experienced restauranteurs will attest that such premiums are crucial to a long-term business strategy.

A closer look at some of the prominent features of these desserts:

Thin Ice Fruit Soup is not only the ultimate light experience, but Markus Farbinger designed it to be a digestif, with the careful blending of herbs that he prefers for that purpose. It's a good option for waiters to offer to diners who clearly have already had too much of a good thing.

A marquise is normally, but not always, prepared in a loaf pan, but Chef Friberg has given his Chocolate Marquise a vertical dimension by preparing it in a PVC pipe; when unmolding, he measures standard lengths and cuts in alternate 45 then 90 degree angles, to give it a distinctive look. His Blueberry Financier is a lighter, custard-ish experience, but its simplicty is enhanced with the attention-getting, sweeping, and interlocking crescent cookies. Dan Budd's Mount Peppermint, a frozen peppermint mousse, offers the menu a rich option, mint, chocolate, and a vertical presentation, with both crunchy and smooth components on the plate. Budd's Apple Pie Soufflé has a crunchy apple texture and an eye-catching appearance with the garnish of poached, julienned apples, which of course can be made in bulk well ahead of time.

The mignardise presentation is somewhat outlandish, but that adds to its appeal in many settings. It has a deco, very modern appearance. The spicy chocolate dipping sauce is a welcome, unique addition—much talked-about afterward. Good food, good business.

WHAT OTHER MANAGEMENT CONSIDERATIONS ARE THERE?

Plenty. Most of it you will not learn in books, only in the field. Here, however, is a field guide:

Consider Quality Shortcuts. The quality of frozen fruit purées, chocolate cups, mixes, and other products has risen over the past decade. Most chefs agree, you do whatever it takes to get the job done. "In the last few years, the quality of ready made products has increased a great deal," says Markus Farbinger. "The companies seem to listen now to chefs, not just present a product without testing it. The fruit purées are fruits picked at the peak of their flavor. What can be better than that?"

Bo Friberg agrees. "I can be totally pure, use only the fresh stuff and wind up in the poor house. To compete, you have to compromise now and then. You don't use bad products like canned fruits, but the fruit purées are good. Some puff pastry and halfway products like florentine mix, the customer cannot tell the difference. If it tastes just as good and cuts down the cost by more than half and it can be stored on the shelf, why shouldn't you? In an emergency, if you have to, you purchase from the outside. You should draw the line if convenience is the only factor. If it doesn't have the right consistency or flavor you don't use it."

Organization, Refrigeration, Sanitation. "Much of a successful kitchen is proper storage and planning," says Bo Friberg. "'Freezer' used to be a dirty word. But if you know how to use it correctly, with things that don't break down, you can save a lot of time." Knowledge of refrigeration and storage is a very important skill to have, adds Friberg. "Some things you can take out of the freezer, let thaw, divide it in half, and put the other half back," he says. "Other things you absolutely cannot do that with. You have to know the difference. Anyone who is running a department should have a sanitation degree, so he or she can know what can be done. Certain things are against the law: raw eggs, for example. You still see them in recipes. You need to pasteurize the egg whites."

Developing Relationships with Purveyors. Once chefs are satisfied with their purveyor network, they tend not to shop around. "Competitive pricing is an issue, but not the most important one," says Norman Love. "You want dependability too. You don't shop around and switch purveyors to save twenty cents on a block of chocolate. You build relationships, based on the quality of the product and the service level they provide. The only thing you shop around for are unusual products. Pop-ups and banquets occur, and put the pastry chef in a bind, and the purveyor will bail them out sometimes. 'I need two more flats of strawberries. I need another case of chocolate cups.' These sorts of things are always occuring. It's the loyalty, the relationship, the level of surface, and the ingredients that are the most important thing."

People Skills. "The days of the screaming chefs are gone," says Michael Hu. "People are realizing that they can't do it alone. They're only as good as their staff. If you don't have those skills, people won't work for you."

In summary: "You have to be a hard worker," says Michael Hu. "If you're not, in this industry, you'll never survive. But it's not enough to be a hard worker. You have to be a smart worker. You have to know how to empower people and to pass the baton, give people the chance to prove themselves. They'll make mistakes, but you have to know to be there."

So many things to know, for the Modernist, the manager, the chef; the genius with flavor; the Rembrandt of color, composition, and surface texture; the simultaneous rule-breaker, and classicist; the people person, and the moody iconoclast.

The way of the Modernist is never easy. But the rewards are great. Not just the satisfaction of a job well done, a happy customer, a modest pay check, and the esteem of colleagues. No. Something more: immortality.

"In the future," Wayne Brachman predicts, "every dessert will be famous for fifteen minutes."

MOUNT PEPPERMINT

DAN BUDD

Pastry Instructor, *The Culinary Institute of America, Hyde Park, New York.*

The classic flavor combination of chocolate and mint is featured in a frozen peppermint mousse with chocolate chips and a peppermint chip brownie. The plate, by design, exhibits several shades of green, including sprayed white chocolate colored with green and a sugar mint leaf. "Like many people I over-did mint sprigs on desserts," admits Dan Budd. "In the modern age, I thought maybe I'd make a mint garnish myself."

YIELD: 15 SERVINGS

Special Equipment: Cone-shaped paper drinking cones

FROZEN PEPPERMINT MOUSSE			
3 oz	85 g	granulated sugar
3 liq oz	89 ml	water
4	4	mint tea bags
2.6 oz	74 g	egg yolks
1 liq oz	30 ml	crème de menthe
1/2 tsp	1 g	peppermint oil
12	12	mint leaves, finely chopped
28 liq oz	828 ml	heavy cream, whipped to soft peaks
1/4 tsp	.5 g	green liquid food coloring
8 oz	227 g	bittersweet chocolate, chopped into chips

1. In a saucepan, combine sugar and water; bring to a boil. Remove the pan from the heat, add the tea bags, and allow to steep.

2. In mixer fitted with a whisk attachment, beat yolks at high speed. Remove the tea bags from the sugar syrup, return the syrup to a boil, and then pour the hot syrup onto the whipping yolks. Continue beating until the yolks are fluffy and cool. In a bowl, combine the crème de menthe, peppermint oil, mint leaves, whipped cream, and food coloring. Gently fold the mixture into the yolks. Fold in the chocolate chips into the mixture and divide the mousse among fifteen paper drinking cones, filling them completely. Stand the cones upright in a sugar-filled hotel pan and freeze for at least 4 hours, but preferably overnight.

Dessert shown on page 218.

PEPPERMINT CHIP BROWNIES	10 oz	283 g	bittersweet chocolate, chopped
	10 oz	283 g	unsalted butter
	12 oz	340 g	cake flour
	.5 tsp	3.5 g	salt
	12 oz	340 g	light brown sugar
	12 oz	340 g	granulated sugar
	15	15	mint leaves, finely chopped
	10.5 oz	298 g	whole eggs, at room temperature
	.5 tsp	1 g	peppermint oil
	.5 oz	14 g	vanilla extract
	12 oz	340 g	bittersweet chocolate, chopped into chips

1. Preheat oven to 350°F (175°C). Line a half-sheet pan with buttered parchment paper. In a double boiler, melt together the 10 oz of chopped bittersweet chocolate with the butter; set aside.

2. In a bowl, sift together the cake flour and salt; set aside.

3. In mixer bowl, stir together the brown sugar, granulated sugar, and mint leaves. Add the eggs and whisk over simmering water until the mixture is just warm. Place the bowl in the mixer stand, and using the whisk attachment, beat at high speed until light and fluffy. Fold in the chocolate mixture, peppermint oil, and vanilla. Fold in the flour mixture and then the chips.

4. Pour the mixture into the prepared pan and bake until set but still soft, about 30 minutes Cool the brownies completely and then cut into rounds that are slightly larger than the bases of the paper cups.

CHOCOLATE SAUCE	12 oz	340 g	semisweet chocolate, finely chopped
	12 liq oz	355 ml	heavy cream
	4 oz	113 g	light corn syrup

1. Place the chocolate in a mixing bowl. In a saucepan, bring the cream and syrup to a boil and pour over the chocolate.

2. Stir until the chocolate is completely melted. Serve warm.

ASSEMBLY

Fresh mint sprigs
Peppermint-leaf sugar stems
Green leaves airbrushed onto plate

1. Place a brownie round in the center of a decorated dessert plate. Unmold a frozen peppermint mousse cone onto the brownie.

2. Pour chocolate sauce around the brownie just at the base of the cone. Stand a peppermint sugar stem into the frozen mousse.

> *"In a restaurant atmosphere it's sometimes difficult to make garnishes," admits Dan Budd. "This mint sprig is not difficult to make. You pull out long pieces of warm sugar and cut them into small pieces with scissors; that's the stems. You pull a lot of leaves—I flavor mine with peppermint extract—and store them away. Then, every day, you take out some stems and leaves, warm up the leaves and stick on a day's worth of stems."*

APPLE PIE SOUFFLÉ

DAN BUDD

Pastry Instructor, *The Culinary Institute of America, Hyde Park, New York.*

"I like to do things that relate to what people know about or already want," says Dan Budd. *"Apple pie is one of the best-selling desserts there is. So I tried to take the components of apple pie and do it in a more modern way. Then we added an element of another type of dessert that sells well, a soufflé. The best apple pie is a hot one, anyway. For service, the dessert works well. It's baked in the same dish, so it's sure to go out hot. Like a pie, the crust holds in the moisture."*

YIELD: 12 SERVINGS

Special Equipment:
Pinstripe-textured rolling pin
3" (7.6 cm) diameter x 2" (5 cm) high metal cake rings
3" (7.6 cm) diameter shallow pie dishes
3" (7.6 cm) dome molds or cut-off ladles

CRÈME FRÂICHE ICE CREAM			
1 qt	946 ml	milk
1 pt	473 ml	heavy cream
14 oz	397 g	granulated sugar, divided
2	2	vanilla beans, split and scraped
2 tsp	4 g	grated lemon zest
11.7 oz	332 g	egg yolks
1 lb	454 g	crème fraîche

1. In a saucepan, combine the milk, cream, half of the sugar, vanilla bean seeds, and lemon zest. Bring the mixture to a boil; remove from the heat.

2. In a bowl, whisk together the yolks and the remaining half of the sugar. Add some of the hot liquid to the yolks to temper them and pour the entire mixture into the saucepan. Cook over medium heat, stirring constantly, until the mixture coats the back of a spoon. Immediately strain the mixture into a bowl set over an ice bath. Stir until cold.

3. Fold in the crème fraîche. Process the mixture in an ice cream machine according to the manufacturer's instructions.

CRUST			
8 oz	227 g	granulated sugar
1 lb	454 g	unsalted butter, softened
1 tsp	2 g	finely grated lemon zest
3.5 oz	99 g	whole eggs
2 tsp	8 g	vanilla extract
1.5 lbs	680 g	all-purpose flour

1. In a mixer fitted with a paddle attachment, beat together at high speed the sugar, butter, and lemon zest until smooth and creamy. At medium speed, add the eggs and vanilla. At low speed, mix in the flour just until combined. Pat the dough into a round, wrap well, and chill for 2 hours.

2. Divide the dough into two parts. Roll each part into a 12" (30 cm) x 17" (43 cm) sheet, 1/4" (.6 cm) thick. Using the textured rolling pin, roll pinstripes into the dough lengthwise. Layer the sheets between parchment paper and chill thoroughly.

3. Using a pastry wheel, cut the textured dough into twelve 2" (5 cm) x 10" (25 cm) strips. Wrap the strips around the ring molds, pressing the dough together at the seams to seal. Chill the prepared rings well.

4. Preheat a convection oven to 350°F (175°C). Bake the rings until lightly golden, about 20 minutes.

APPLE CHIP GARNISH			
16 oz	454 g	granulated sugar
16 liq oz	473 ml	water
1 liq oz	30 ml	lemon juice
1	1	cinnamon stick
12	12	Granny Smith apples

1. In a saucepan, combine sugar, water, lemon juice, and cinnamon stick. Bring to a boil, stirring until the sugar is dissolved, and remove from heat.

2. Preheat oven to 180°F (82°C). Peel and core the apples and cut them into a julienne (2 x 1/8 x 1/8" / 5 x .3 x .3 cm). Add the apples to the syrup and gently stir until the apples become limp. Strain the apples and cool. Spread a thin lacy layer of apples into a circle on a Silpat mat. Bake until the chips are dry, about 2 hours. Remove the chips from the oven, and, before they are cool, mold them over a 3" (7.6 cm) diameter dome mold to create cage shapes. Store in an airtight container before serving.

Making the apple chip garnish.

APPLE FILLING			
8	8	Granny Smith apples
8 oz	227 g	granulated sugar
1 liq oz	30 ml	lemon juice
8 oz	227 g	unsalted butter
4 liq oz	118 ml	apple liquor

1. Peel and core apples and cut into a large dice (1/2 x 1/2"/1.3 x 1.3 cm).

2. In a small bowl, blend the sugar and lemon juice together. Heat a large sauté pan and add the sugar mixture. Cook to a golden caramel; add the butter and stir to combine. Add the apple dice and sauté until slightly soft and caramelized. Remove the pan from the heat. Add the apple liquor, return to the heat, and flambé. Cook the apples until the flame dies and the alcohol is burned off. Pour the filling into a container and cool.

3. Place 2 to 3 oz (56 to 85 g) of the filling into the bottom of each pie dish and place the prebaked rings over the filling.

APPLE SOUFFLÉ

27 oz	765 g	granulated sugar
8 liq oz	237 ml	water
1/4 tsp	.7 g	cream of tartar
.5 oz	14 g	ground cinnamon
20 oz	567 g	applesauce
15.75 oz	446 g	egg whites

1. Preheat the oven to 350°F (175°C). In a large heavy bottomed saucepan, combine the sugar, water, and cream of tartar. Cook to 240°F (115°C). Add the cinnamon and applesauce, and continue cooking.

2. At this point, in a mixer fitted with a whisk attachment, begin to whip the whites. When the applesauce mixture reaches 220°F (104°C), steadily pour it into the whites while continuing to whip to soft peaks, (do not overwhip). When the whites form soft peaks, and while the meringue is still warm, pipe the mixture into the rings of dough over the filling to the top of the ring. Bake the rings for 15 minutes, or until slightly risen and golden on top.

3. Sprinkle each soufflé with confectioners' sugar, top with an apple chip, and serve hot with crème fraîche ice cream on the side.

THIN ICE FRUIT SOUP

MARKUS FARBINGER

Team Leader for Curriculum and
Instruction, *Baking and Pastry Arts,*
The Culinary Institute of America,
Hyde Park, New York.

This dessert was inspired by a beautiful, familiar wintertime sight: when shallow ponds of water freeze, the unfrozen water, grass, and stones are visible just beneath the surface. From this Chef Farbinger has created a digestif— fresh fruit in a pool of half-frozen soup. The infusion can be anything that pleases your palate, but Chef Farbinger recommends herbs that aid digestion and freshen breath—lemongrass, fennel, pink pepper, coriander. This version includes lemonbalm, red peppercorns, vanilla beans, and sugar. Lemon and orange skin has been added to enhance the fruit flavors. The ratio of 20 percent sugar to water ensures that the soup will not freeze entirely.

YIELD: 24 SERVINGS

32 liq oz	946 ml	water
7 oz	198 g	granulated sugar
1 strip	1 strip	orange peel
1 strip	1 strip	lemon peel
1	1	vanilla bean, split
1 bunch	1 bunch	lemonbalm or mint
3	3	red peppercorns, crushed
1 liq oz	30 ml	lemon juice
2	2	oranges
2	2	nectarines
1	1	pineapple
2 oz	57 g	grapes
2	2	mangoes
4	4	kiwis

1. In a saucepan, combine water and sugar and bring them to a boil. Remove the pan from the heat and add the citrus peels, vanilla bean, lemonbalm, and peppercorns. Cover the pan and allow the mixture to infuse for 1 hour.

2. Transfer the mixture to a container and refrigerate for at least 8 hours; strain and stir in the lemon juice.

3. Peel the oranges and cut into segments. Cut the nectarines off the pits and slice thinly. Peel and core the pineapple and cut it into 1/8" (.3 cm) slices. Cut each slice into 1" (2.5 cm) wedges. Cut the grapes in half. Peel the mango and kiwis and cut into 1/8" (.3 cm) slices. Cut each slice into 1" (2.5 cm) wedges.

4. Place all the prepared fruit in a bowl. Pour over the chilled infusion. Refrigerate until ready to assemble.

ASSEMBLY   *Lavender*
Elderberry blossoms
Johnny Jump-ups

Pour about 8 liq oz (237 ml) of the fruit soup in each serving bowl. Sprinkle with the flowers. Freeze for about 1 hour before service. (The surface of the soup should be frozen.)

HOT CHOCOLATE WITH MIGNARDISES

MARKUS FARBINGER

Team Leader for Curriculum and
Instruction, *Baking and Pastry Arts,*
The Culinary Institute of America,
Hyde Park, New York.

This is a Modernist take on the old favorite, chocolate fondue, paired with mignardises. The chocolate dipping sauce is served warm, but the heat comes from the red jalapeño peppers and the spices. The mignardises are caramel grapes, with their bottoms dipped in chocolate, and honey-roasted peanuts; almond batter friandises with brandied cherries; sesame leaf croquant, which is folded into caramel; and orange and coffee flavored tuiles.

YIELD: 16 SERVINGS

Special Equipment:
Eighty-five 1" (2.5 cm) diameter x 3/4" (1.8 cm) high aluminum or paper cups
Binder clips

COFFEE-ORANGE TUILES			
(YIELD: 72 PIECES)	8.8 oz	250 g	*granulated sugar*
	8.8 oz	250 g	*sliced almonds, finely chopped*
	.8 oz	25 g	*coffee beans, coarsely ground*
	2.6 oz	75 g	*pastry flour*
	7 oz	198 g	*unsalted butter, melted*
	1	1	*orange, zested and juiced*

1. Preheat oven to 375°F (190°C). In a bowl, combine the sugar, almonds, coffee beans, and pastry flour. Stir in the melted butter, orange zest, and juice.

2. Spoon out .3 to .4 oz (10 to 12 g) balls of the batter onto a Teflon sheet pan. Flatten each ball with a fork to form a round disc. Bake until golden, about 10 minutes. Cool slightly and shape as desired. Store in an airtight container until serving.

LEAF KROKANT STICKS			
(YIELD: 75 PIECES)	5 oz	142 g	*almond flour, toasted*
	2 oz	57 g	*sesame seeds, lightly toasted*
	1	1	*vanilla bean, split and scraped*
	2 oz	57 g	*confectioners' sugar*
	10 oz	283 g	*granulated sugar*
	1 Tbs	15 ml	*lemon juice*

1. In a food processor, place the almond flour, sesame seeds, vanilla bean scrapings, and confectioners' sugar. Process until just slightly oily, about 30 seconds.

2. In a heavy saucepan, combine the granulated sugar and lemon juice; cook over medium-high heat until it becomes a medium-brown color. Immediately pour the hot sugar onto a silicone baking mat-lined sheet pan. Spread the caramel into an even rectangle. Sprinkle about one-third of the almond flour mixture over the rectangle. Carefully fold the puff pastry into a rectangle as you would for a letter, in thirds. Roll out to another rectangle and sprinkle with another third of the almond flour mixture. Fold in thirds again. Repeat with the remaining flour mixture. Roll out to 1/4" (.6 cm) thickness and, while still warm and using a caramel cutter or sharp French knife, cut into 3/8 x 2 1/2" (.9 x 6.3 cm) slices. Store in an airtight container until service.

SOUFFLÉS FRIANDISES		
GRIOTTINES (YIELD: 85)		

8.5 oz	241 g	almond flour
6 oz	170 g	granulated sugar
.25 tsp	1.6 g	salt
1 oz	28 g	cornstarch
1 tsp	2 g	grated lemon zest
6 oz	170 g	egg whites
2 oz	57 g	honey
5 oz	142 g	unsalted butter, melted and browned
42	42	brandied cherries, cut in half

1. Spray 85 aluminum or paper cups (1" / 2.5 cm diameter x 3/4" / 1.8 cm high) with nonstick cooking spray. Preheat oven to 350°F (175°C).

2. In a bowl, combine the almond flour, sugar, salt, and cornstarch. Whisk in the egg whites, honey, and browned butter until well-blended. Spoon about 1/4 oz (8 g) of batter into each of the prepared cups. Place half of a brandied cherry in each cup. Press down on each cherry lightly, submerging it slightly. Bake for 8 minutes, until puffed. Dust with confectioners' sugar and serve warm.*

Note. Batter-filled cups may be kept in the refrigerator or freezer and baked when needed.

CARAMELIZED GRAPES		

60	60	grapes, with stems
1 pt	.47 lt	water
3 lbs	1.36 kg	granulated sugar
4 oz	113 g	glucose
8 oz	227 g	bittersweet chocolate, tempered
8 oz	227 g	lightly salted peanuts, toasted

1. Trim the grape stems so that there is 1/2" (1.3 cm) of stem attached to each grape. Attach each grape stem to a binder clip. Place about 10 long skewers on the edge of a table, so that they extend beyond the edge of the table. Secure them by placing a heavy object on top of them on the table. Cover the floor area around the skewers with newspaper.

2. In a heavy saucepan, combine the water and sugar. Bring the mixture to a boil; stir in the glucose and cook the syrup to 300°F (149°C). Remove the pan from the heat.

3. Dip each grape halfway into the caramel. Hang each grape on the skewers, so that an "antenna" forms from the dripping caramel.

4. When cool, trim the antennae to 2" (5 cm) with scissors. Remove the clips and the stems from the grapes.

5. Dip the exposed end of each grape into the tempered chocolate. Immediately place the chocolate end of the grape in the chopped peanuts. Allow the grapes to set completely.

DIPPING SAUCE			
17 liq oz	503 ml	milk
1	1	vanilla bean, split
.7 oz	21 g	honey
pinch	pinch	salt
25 oz	700 g	El Rey Extra Amargo chocolate, melted
3.5 oz	100 g	unsalted butter, softened
1	1	ripe jalapeño (red), seeded and minced

1. In a saucepan, combine the milk, vanilla bean, honey, and salt. Bring the mixture to a boil. Remove the pan from the heat, cover, and allow to infuse for 10 minutes.

2. Remove the vanilla bean and pour the hot milk mixture over the melted chocolate. Whisk until combined. Whisk in the butter and minced jalapeño.

ASSEMBLY

Place the chocolate dipping sauce in a serving "bowl" set on a serving plate. Arrange a few of each of the mignardises on the plate surrounding the sauce. Serve one plate per table.

The "bowl" that contains the chocolate sauce is actually three interlocking sugar triangles. The triangles are exactly alike, though they don't need to be. To construct the "bowl," place the triangles one atop the other, exactly congruent. Then fan them out. Put the first two at an angle—the more severe the angle the more deep the bowl; you can submerge them in a bowl of granulated sugar to support them while you pour warm liquid sugar down the crease to join them. Add the third, and join it in a similar manner. The triangles meet roughly in the center of one long side.

BLUEBERRY FINANCIER WITH TOASTED LEMON VERBENA SABAYON AND MASCARPONE SHERBET

BO FRIBERG

Chef Instructor, *The Culinary Institute of America at Greystone, St. Helena, California.*

The sweeping, interlocking crescent cookies give this simple, classic dessert a dramatic, attention-getting appeal. A pleasantly tart hint of lemon permeates this dessert, as the custardy financier is accompanied by toasted lemon verbena sabayon and lemon-touched mascarpone sherbet.

YIELD: 16 SERVINGS

Special Equipment:
Sixteen 3 " (7.6 cm) diameter x 2 " (5 cm) high metal cake rings
One 4 to 4 1/2 " (10 to 11.4 cm) diameter tube or bain-marie insert or curved strip of aluminum

BLUEBERRY FINANCIER

1 lb	454 g	unsalted butter
1 pt	473 ml	fresh blueberries, cleaned
18 oz	510 g	confectioners' sugar
5.5 oz	156 g	all-purpose flour
5 oz	142 g	almond meal
14.7 oz	417 g	egg whites
2 Tbs	12 g	finely grated lemon zest
2 oz	57 g	lemon verbena, finely diced

1. Preheat oven to 325°F (165°C). Butter the interior of the ring molds and place on a parchment-lined sheet pan.

2. Place the butter in a skillet and cook over low heat until golden brown (buerre noisette stage), about 5 minutes.

3. Sift together the confectioners' sugar and flour. Blend in the almond meal. Place in a mixer fitted with a paddle attachment. While mixing on low speed, add the egg whites and blend until incorporated. Scrape down the side of the bowl and gradually mix in the buerre noisette. Beat at high speed until well combined. Mix in the lemon zest and verbena.

4. Remove the bowl from the mixer stand and gently fold in the blueberries by hand, being careful not to crush them. Divide the batter equally among the prepared cake rings and bake for about 25 minutes, or until the tops of the cakes feel firm. Allow to cool slightly before removing the cake rings. Invert the baked cakes, cover, and set aside.

> *Note.* Blueberry Financier should be served at room temperature, but may be prepared through step 4 up to two days in advance, if stored in the refrigerator.

LEMON VERBENA SABAYON			
24 liq oz	710 ml	champagne or dry white wine
2 oz	57 g	lemon verbena, finely diced
7.8 oz	221 g	egg yolks
12 oz	340 g	granulated sugar

1. In a medium saucepan, combine the champagne or wine with the lemon verbena and heat to about 180°F (82°C); do not boil. Remove from the heat and set aside to infuse for at least 30 minutes, but preferably longer.

2. In a stainless steel mixer bowl, using the whisk attachment, beat the egg yolks and sugar together at high speed until light and fluffy. Strain the wine mixture and then whisk it into the egg yolk mixture.

3. Place the mixer bowl over simmering water and continue to whisk constantly until the sabayon is hot and thick and reaches approximately 160°F (71°C).

> *Note.* If the sabayon must be prepared ahead of time, cook it to 180°F (82°C) to create a more stable mixture. Remove it from the heat and continue to whip until the sauce has cooled to the point where it no longer feels warm to the touch.

CRESCENT DECORATIONS			
6 oz	170 g	unsalted butter, softened
6 oz	170 g	confectioners' sugar, sifted
6.3 oz	179 g	egg whites, at room temperature
1 tsp	4 g	vanilla extract
6 oz	170 g	cake flour, sifted
1 tsp	2 g	unsweetend cocoa powder

1. Preheat oven to 400°F (205°C). In a mixer fitted with a paddle attachment, cream the butter and confectioners' sugar together. Incorporate the egg whites one at a time. Add the vanilla. Add the flour, and mix just until incorporated; do not overmix.

2. Store the paste covered in the refrigerator if not using right away. The paste will keep for several weeks. Allow it to soften slightly after removing it from the refrigerator and then stir it until it is smooth and of a spreadable consistency before using.

3. Cut out a crescent template (see photo on facing page).

4. Place 2 Tbs of the cookie paste in a small container. Add the cocoa powder and stir until completely smooth. Cover and reserve.

5. Place the template on top of a silicone mat. Spread a thin layer of the plain paste over the template and then lift it off. Repeat until you have about 40 cookies (two are used for each serving and some will inevitably break).

6. Place a portion of the reserved cocoa-colored paste into a parchment cone and cut a very small opening. Pipe a curved design on top of the cookies as shown in the drawing.

7. Bake one sheet at a time until halfway done, about 3 minutes. Remove from the oven and cut two holes in the center of each cookie on the top and bottom of the curve using a #2 plain piping tip. Return to the oven and continue baking until the cookie just begins to turn golden brown.

8. Working quickly, remove the cookies one at a time and place in the curved form right-side-up. You may have to remove the sheet pan from the oven while working to prevent the last cookies from getting too dark, depending on how many cookies are on the pan. Once the pan has been removed you may not be able to mold all of the remaining cookies in the form without breaking them. In this case, leave them flat and continue with the next sheet. You need an equal amount of curved and flat cookies for the presentation. Store the finished cookies in an airtight container at room temperature. They can be kept this way for up to one week.

MASCARPONE SHERBET

12 liq oz	355 ml	water
10 oz	283 g	granulated sugar
1 tsp	2 g	finely grated lemon zest
2 liq oz	60 ml	fresh lemon juice
21.25 oz	602 g	unflavored yogurt
12.75 oz	361 g	mascarpone cheese

1. In a medium saucepan, combine the water, sugar, lemon zest, and lemon juice. Cook over medium heat, stirring constantly, until the sugar is completely dissolved. Remove the pan from the heat and allow the mixture to cool.

2. Stir in the yogurt and mascarpone. Refrigerate until completely chilled.

3. Process the mixture in an ice cream maker according to the manufacturer's directions. Store the sherbet covered in the freezer.

SUGAR DECORATIONS

1 lb	454 g	granulated sugar
6 liq oz	177 ml	water
3.5 oz	99 g	light corn syrup
5 drops	5 drops	tartaric acid

1. In a heavy-bottom saucepan, combine the sugar and water. Cook over medium-high heat, stirring constantly until the mixture boils and the sugar is completely dissolved. Increase the heat to high, add the corn syrup, and cook the mixture until the temperature registers 260°F (127°C), brushing down the sides of the pan from time to time to prevent sugar crystals from forming. Add the tartaric acid and cook the syrup to 300°F (149°C).

2. Immediately plunge the bottom of the pan into a bowl of cold water to stop the cooking process. Leave the pan in the water for 10 seconds, then remove it, dry the bottom and sides, and set aside.

3. Have ready a silicone mat or lightly oiled sheet of baking paper, a pair of scissors, a dry towel, and a pastry bag made from a double thickness of baking paper.

4. When the sugar has cooled to a syrupy consistency, pour about 1 cup into the pastry bag, cover the top with a towel, cut a small opening; pipe as many straight lines as you can crosswise over the silicone mat or sheet of baking paper. They should be about 15" (38 cm) long.

Note. The sugar sticks can be used as a garnish straight or bent into any shape. However, you have to experiment with the cooking temperature and/or amount of tartaric acid used, depending on the climate where you live. In general, if the sugar gets too hot and/or if you do not use enough acid, you will not be able to bend the sticks. In this case, of course, they can still be used straight. Conversely, both not cooking to a high enough temperature and using too much acid will render the sticks useless. An alternate, and perhaps more reliable method under poor sugar-working conditions, is to omit the tartaric acid and cook the sugar to a light caramel. To soften the sticks and make them pliable enough to shape, warm them slightly by placing in an oven for a few seconds, or by very carefully using a torch.

BLUEBERRY SAUCE

3 oz	85 g	granulated sugar
6 liq oz	177 ml	cranberry juice
2 tsp	10 ml	lime juice
1 Tbs	7.5 g	cornstarch
1.5 Tbs	22.5 ml	rum
6 oz	170 g	small blueberries

1. In a saucepan, combine the sugar, cranberry juice, lime juice, cornstarch, and rum. Bring to a boil, reduce the heat to low, and cook for 1 minute longer. Stir in the blueberries and remove from the heat.

2. Let the sauce cool, then store covered in the refrigerator.

ASSEMBLY

1. Cover the base of a dessert plate with Lemon Verbena Sabayon, using about 4 liq oz (118 ml). Gratiné using an electric salamander or blowtorch. Cut a slit about 1/2" (1.3 cm) deep across the center of a blueberry financier and place it cut-side-up in the center of the plate. Carefully stand a flat crescent cookie, points down, in the slit.

2. Using a 1.5 oz (43 g) ice cream scoop, place a scoop of Mascarpone Sherbet on top of the financier toward the right side. Carefully push one of the points of a curved crescent cookie underneath the left side of a standing cookie, leaning it against the sherbet. Thread a sugar stick through one hole in each cookie at the right side. Bend the sugar into a soft curve above the cookies and then into the holes on the left side. Spoon blueberry sauce on top of the sabayon in three pools around the dessert. Place a sprig of lemon verbena on top of the sherbet and serve immediately.

Making the crescent decorations (see page 241).

CHOCOLATE MARQUISE WITH PASSION FRUIT PARFAIT AND LACE COOKIE BOUQUET

BO FRIBERG

Chef Instructor, *The Culinary Institute of America at Greystone, St. Helena, California.*

A chocolate marquise, normally prepared in a loaf pan, is given the Modernist, vertical treatment by Chef Friberg. Prepared in PVC-type pipe, this rich chocolate dessert can be (but does not have to be) frozen, so that it can be unmolded easily. As it is unmolded, it is shaped by alternating 45- and 90-degree cuts. It is served with passion fruit parfait and a lace cookie bouquet. "The trick is to make it look showy for the customer, to have them ask, 'How does he do it anyway?'" says Chef Friberg.

YIELD: 12 SERVINGS

Special Equipment:
Two clear plastic pipes that are 22" (55 cm) long and 1 1/2" (3.7 cm) in diameter
Cardboard egg carton
6 to 8" (15 to 20 cm) wide trowel (such as used to apply plaster)

CHOCOLATE MARQUISE
FILLING

1 pound, 5 oz	595 g	sweet dark chocolate
4.5 oz	128 g	unsweetened chocolate
30 liq oz	887 ml	heavy cream
3.9 oz	111 g	egg yolks
2 oz	57 g	granulated sugar
4 oz	113 g	honey
2 liq oz	59 ml	Frangelico liqueur

1. Chop the sweet and unsweetened chocolates into small chunks. Place in a bowl set over simmering water and melt together. Set aside, but keep warm.

2. Whip the heavy cream to soft peaks; set aside.

3. In mixer fitted with a whisk attachment, beat the egg yolks with the sugar at high speed for about 2 minutes, until light and fluffy. Meanwhile, in a small saucepan, bring the honey to a boil and gradually pour it into the yolks while whipping. Continue to beat the yolks until completely cooled.

4. Fold in the reserved chocolate and the Frangelico. Quickly stir in the whipped cream.

LACE COOKIE BOUQUETS	4 oz	113 g	unsalted butter, softened
	4 oz	113 g	confectioners' sugar, sifted
	4.2 oz	119 g	egg whites
	1/2 tsp	2 g	vanilla extract
	4 oz	113 g	cake flour, sifted
	12 oz	340 g	dark chocolate, tempered

1. Cover a cardboard egg carton loosely with plastic wrap, pushing the wrap way into the indentations. Set aside.

2. In a mixer with the paddle attachment, cream together the butter and confectioners' sugar. Gradually add the egg whites and the vanilla. Add the flour and mix until just incorporated; do not overmix.

3. Store the paste covered in the refrigerator if not using right away. The paste will keep for several weeks. Allow it to soften slightly after removing it from the refrigerator and then stir it into a smooth and spreadable consistency before using.

4. Preheat the oven to 400°F (204°C). Spread a small portion of the paste into a 5 to 6" (12.5 to 15 cm) round at one short side of a silicone mat. Fold the opposite (empty) side on top and press down lightly. Unfold. You should now have two thin, nonuniform rounds, one on each side of the mat. Bake the cookies for about 3 minutes or until the first sign of color appears on either of the cookies. Leaving the sheet pan in the oven with the door open, run a palette knife underneath one cookie and quickly pick it up, holding onto the center of the cookie and holding it upside-down, gather the center to form it into a bouquet shape. Set it right-side-up in the prepared egg carton. Form the second cookie in the same manner. Repeat until you have made at least 15 usable cookies, to allow for the possibility of breakage.

5. Pipe the tempered chocolate into four 1" (2.5 cm) ovals, spaced 4" (10 cm) apart, on a sheet of baking paper. Wait until the chocolate begins to set and then stand a cookie bouquet on top of each oval, placing it at a slight angle so that when it is placed on top of the angled cut of the marquise, it will appear to stand straight. Repeat to create bases for the remaining bouquets. Store the decorations in an airtight container until needed. The thin cookies will become soft very quickly if exposed to moist air.

RIBBON SPONGE	3 oz	85 g	cake flour, sifted
	1 oz	28 g	cocoa powder, sifted
	4 oz	113 g	unsalted butter, softened
	4 oz	113 g	confectioners' sugar, sifted
	6.3 oz	179 g	egg whites, divided
	1/2 tsp	4 g	vanilla extract
	5.25 oz	149 g	whole eggs
	1.3 oz	37 g	egg yolks
	3 oz	85 g	granulated sugar
	3 oz	85 g	finely ground blanched almonds (almond meal)
	1 oz	28 g	bread flour
	1 oz	28 g	unsalted butter

1. Combine the cake flour and cocoa powder; set aside. In a mixer fitted with a paddle attachment, cream together the butter and confectioners' sugar. Gradually add 4.2 oz (119 g) of the egg whites. Mix in the vanilla. Add the flour mixture and mix just until incorporated; do not overmix.

2. Spread the batter over a full-sheet pan-size silicone mat, spreading the paste in an even layer. Use a decorating comb or trowel with square notches to remove half of the paste in straight lines lengthwise, crosswise, or diagonally (or use a template of choice). Place the silicone mat on a sheet pan and freeze for approximately 30 minutes.

3. Preheat the oven to 500°F (260°C). While the paste is in the freezer, place the eggs, yolks, and half of the granulated sugar in a mixer bowl; using the whisk attachment, whip at high speed for 1 to 2 minutes.

4. In a bowl, combine the almonds and bread flour; set aside. Melt the butter and keep it warm.

5. In a mixer with a whisk attachment, whip the remaining 2.1 oz (60 g) egg whites with the remaining half of the granulated sugar until thick and foamy; do not overwhip. Stir the reserved almond mixture into the whipped whole egg mixture. Stir in the melted butter and the whipped whites.

6. Remove the silicone mat and sheet pan from the freezer and spread the sponge batter evenly over the chocolate design. Tap the sheet pan firmly against the table to remove any large air bubbles.

7. Bake the ribbons immediately for about 4 minutes or until the top begins to color lightly. Dust the top of the sponge sheet lightly with flour and invert onto a sheet of baking paper. Allow to cool for a few minutes and then carefully peel off the silicone mat.

PASSION FRUIT COULIS			
12	12	ripe passion fruit
2 Tbs	30 ml	water
2 Tbs	25 g	granulated sugar

1. Cut the passion fruit in half and scoop out the pulp and seeds, taking care not to include any of the reddish-white pith.

2. If necessary, sweeten to taste by heating the water and sugar together to dissolve the sugar, and then stir the syrup into the pulp. Cover and refrigerate until needed.

PASSION FRUIT PARFAIT			
3.25 oz	92 g	egg yolks
2 oz	57 g	light corn syrup
5.25 oz	149 g	egg whites
2 oz	57 g	granulated sugar
8 liq oz	237 ml	heavy cream
4 liq oz	118 ml	passion fruit pulp (about 6 passion fruit)
2 Tbs	30 ml	curaçao liqueur

1. In mixer with whisk attachment, beat the egg yolks until light, about 5 minutes. In a saucepan, heat the corn syrup until boiling. Pour the corn syrup into the egg yolks while whipping at medium speed. Increase the speed to high and whip until the mixture has cooled completely. Reserve.

2. Combine the egg whites and granulated sugar in a mixer bowl. Set the bowl over simmering water and heat, whipping constantly, to 140°F (60°C). Remove the bowl from the heat and continue whipping until the mixture has cooled and stiff peaks have formed. Reserve.

3. Whip the cream to soft peaks. Fold the cream into the yolk mixture together with the passion fruit pulp and the liqueur. Gently fold in the whipped egg whites. Pour into a container and place in the freezer until firm, at least 4 hours or, preferably, overnight.

CHOCOLATE CURLS   *8 oz*   *227 g*   *dark chocolate couverture*

1. Chop the chocolate into small pieces. Place the chocolate in a bowl set over hot water. Heat the water to approximately 150°F (65°C); it should never be allowed to reach boiling. Melt the chocolate, stirring frequently.

2. Remove the bowl from the water bath; wipe the bottom and side dry. Pour a small amount of chocolate onto a flat, cool work surface. Spread the chocolate into a 16" (40 cm) rectangle. Wait until the chocolate just begins to set up.

3. Hold a trowel at a 45° angle to the chocolate strip and test the consistency of the chocolate by first scraping along the edge. If the chocolate does not curl but instead sticks to the trowel, it needs to set further. If the chocolate forms curls that break right away, it has set too long. Chocolate that sticks to the trowel must be removed by scraping it off with another trowel or with a knife. Avoid touching the chocolate with your hands. Push the trowel against the work surface at the specified angle, making curls of the desired diameter.

4. Repeat steps 2 and 3 until you have made as many curls as needed. Store the finished curls between sheets of baking paper in an airtight container, placed in a cool location.

ASSEMBLY   1. Line the insides of the clear plastic pipes with baking paper. Cap one end of each pipe. Fill the pipes with the marquise filling. Tap lightly to remove air pockets and add more filling to reach the top if necessary. Cover the open ends and refrigerate until the filling is set, at least two hours. Reserve the remaining filling.

2. Cut the ribbon sponge into two pieces that are each 22" (56 cm) long and approximately 5 1/2" (14 cm) wide, or wide enough to cover the chocolate tubes. Invert the sponge pieces and spread a thin layer of the reserved filling over the sheets (soften the filling to a sticky consistency first, if needed).

3. Remove the chocolate tubes from the pipes by gently shaking the tubes until you can pull out the chocolate by holding onto the baking paper. Peel off the baking paper. Place each tube on top of one of the prepared sponge sheets. Roll one complete turn to cover the chocolate tubes with the sponge. Trim the edges of the sponge sheets if necessary.

4. Using a sharp, thin knife, trim the end of one tube and then cut it into six equal pieces alternating between a 45° cut and a 90° cut each time so that the finished pieces have one flat side and one angled side. Repeat with the second tube.

5. Place a marquise, standing upright on the flat end, in the center of a serving plate. Spread a small amount of reserved filling underneath the chocolate base of a lace cookie bouquet and carefully attach it to the angled top of the marquise. Sift powdered sugar

over the dessert and the base of the serving plate. Spoon some passion fruit coulis into three pools around the marquise. Place a small scoop of passion fruit parfait to the right of the marquise. Decorate the top of the marquise with the parfait scoop using two chocolate curls on each. Serve immediately.

S O U R C E   L I S T

ABC Emballuxe, Inc.
650 Crémanzie Est
Montréal, Qc. H2P 1E9
514-381-6978
individual pastry molds, demi-sphere molds, acetates and custom transfer sheets, silkscreens

Albert Uster
9211 Gaither Road
Gaithersburg, MD 20877
800-231-8154
fine Swiss baking and confectionery products, transfer sheets, professional tools

Assouline & Ting
314 Brown Street
Philadelphia, PA 19123
215-627-3000; 800-521-4491
chocolate, fruit purées, extracts, nut pastes, flours

The Baker's Catalogue
King Arthur Flour
P.O. Box 876
Norwich, VT 05055-0876
800-827-6836
specialty flours

Barry Callebaut
St. Albans Town Industrial Park
RD #2, Box 7
St. Albans, VT 05478-9126
800-556-8845
imported and domestic chocolate couvertures, praline paste, molds and more

Beryl's Cake Decorating Equipment
P.O. Box 1584
N. Springfield, VA 22151
703-256-6951; 800-488-2749
tools for wedding cakes, chocolate work, and confectionery work

Braun Brush Company
43 Albertson Avenue
Albertson, NY 11507
516-741-6000; 800-645-4111
extensive line of brushes for the baking industry; custom-made brushes

Bridge Kitchenware Corp.
214 E. 52nd Street
New York, NY 10022
212-838-6746; 800-274-3435
$3 for catalogue, refundable with first purchase
bakeware, pastry equipment, molds, cake rings

The Candy Factory
12530 Riverside Drive
N. Hollywood, CA 91607
818-766-8220
$5 for catalogue, refundable with first purchase
candy molds, custom molds, flavoring oils, colors

The Chef's Collection
10631 Southwest 146th Place
Miami, FL 33186
800-590-CHEF
brand-name professional cookware, cutlery, gourmet accessories

A Cook's Wares
211 37th Street
Beaver Falls, PA 15010
412-846-9490
chocolate, extracts, bakeware

Creative Culinary Tools
264 SE 46th Terrace
Cape Coral, FL 33904
813-549-7715; 800-340-7278
custom silkscreens, molds, grilles, mold-making compound

DeChoix Specialty Foods
58-25 52nd Avenue
Woodside, NY 11377
718-507-8080; 800-834-6881
chocolate, fruit purées and pastes, nuts and nut products

Demarle, Inc., USA
2666-B Rte 130 N
Cranbury, NJ 08512
609-395-0219
silpats, flexipan, custom flexipans, bread mats and forms

Gourmail
126A Pleasant Valley, #401
Methuen, MA 01844
800-366-5900 ext 96
chocolate

Gourmand
2869 Towerview Road
Herndon, VA 22071
703-708-0000; 800-627-7272
chocolate, flavorings, extracts, pastes

Harry Wils and Co., Inc.
182 Duane Street
New York, NY 10013
212-431-9731
no UPS-delivery within 75 miles of New York City
fruit purées, IQF fruit, chocolate, extracts, nuts and nut products

Holcraft Collection
P.O. Box 792
Davis, CA 95616
916-756-3023
chocolate molds, antique molds

Hygo
P.O. Box 267
Lyndhurst, NJ 07071
201-507-0447; 800-672-9727
disposable pastry bags for cold and hot fillings

Industrial Plastics Supply Co.
309 Canal Street
New York, NY 10013
212-226-2010
plastic demi-spheres, tubing, grilles

International School of Confectionery Arts
9290 Gaither Road
Gaithersburg, MD 20877
301-963-9077
sugar, candy and chocolate making equipment, Isomalt

J.B. Prince Company
36 E. 31st Street, 11th Floor
New York, NY 10016
212-683-3553
flexipans, cake rings, molds, stencil grilles, silpats, baking tools and equipment

Kerekes
7107 13th Avenue
Brooklyn, NY 11228
718-232-7044; 800-525-5556
molds, baking tools and equipment

La Cuisine
323 Cameron Street
Alexandria, VA 22314
800-521-1176
bakeware, molds, cake rings, silicon sheets, flexipans, chocolate, pastes, Triquel

Lamalle Kitchenware
36 W. 25th Street
New York, NY 10010
800-660-0750
bakeware, copper pots, molds, pastry tools

Metropolitan Cutlery, Inc.
649 Morris Turnpike
Springfield, NJ 07081
201-467-4222; 888-886-6083
professional bakeware, butane stoves

N.Y. Cake and Baking Distributors
56 W. 22nd Street
New York, NY 10010
212-675-CAKE; 800-94-CAKE-9
airbrushes, cake decorating supplies, gum paste supplies

Steven M. Palumbo
145 Ferncrest Avenue
Cranston, RI 02905-2620
401-461-8020
1322 10th NW
Washington, DC 20001-4216
202-232-2264
silicone for mold making

Patisfrance
161 East Union Avenue
E. Rutherford, NJ 07073
1-800-PASTRY-1
fruit purées, chocolate, transfer sheets, nut products, flavoring pastes, extracts and essences

Pearl Paint
308 Canal Street
New York, NY 10013
212-431-7932 x2297; 800-221-6845 x2297
acetate, custom silkscreens, airbrushes, art supplies

Rafal Spice Company
2521 Russell
Detroit MI 48207
313-259-6373; 800-228-4276
essential oils, extracts, flavorings

Sweet Celebrations (formerly Maid of Scandinavia)
7009 Washington Avenue S.
Edina, MN 55439
800-328-6722
chocolate, cake decorating and gumpaste supplies, chocolate and candy making supplies, molds, baking supplies and equipment

Swiss Chalet Fine Foods, Inc.
Miami (headquarters):305-592-0008
Houston: 713-868-9505
Los Angeles: 562-946-6816
marmalades, fruit compounds, chocolate, flavorings

White Toque, Inc.
536 Fayette Street
Perth Amboy, NJ 08861
800-237-6936
fruit purées, IQF wild berries, shelf-stable fruit, chocolate sauces

Williams-Sonoma
P.O. Box 7456
San Francisco, CA 94120-7456
800-541-2233
chocolate, flours, baking pans and equipment

Zabar's
2245 Broadway
New York, NY 10024
212-496-1234
specialty food products, kitchen equipment

INDEX